THE LOEB CLASSICAL LIBRARY

FOUNDED BY JAMES LOEB, LL.D.

PLOTINUS

II

PLOTINUS

WITH AN ENGLISH TRANSLATION BY
A. H. ARMSTRONG
PROFESSOR OF GREEK, UNIVERSITY OF LIVERPOOL

IN SIX VOLUMES

II

ENNEADS
II. 1–9

CAMBRIDGE MASSACHUSETTS
HARVARD UNIVERSITY PRESS
LONDON
WILLIAM HEINEMANN LTD
MCMLXVI

Printed in Great Britain

CONTENTS

SIGLA

A = Laurentianus 87, 3.
A′ = Codicis A primus corrector.
E = Parisinus Gr. 1976.
B = Laurentianus 85, 15.
R = Vaticanus Reginensis Gr. 97.
J = Parisinus Gr. 2082.
U = Vaticanus Urbinas Gr. 62.
S = Berolinensis Gr. 375.
N = Monacensis Gr. 215.
M = Marcianus Gr. 240.
C = Monacensis Gr. 449.
V = Vindobonensis philosophicus Gr. 226.
Q = Marcianus Gr. 242.
L = Ambrosianus Gr. 667.
D = Marcianus Gr. 209.

W = AE.
X = BRJ.
Y = USM.
Z = QL.

mg = in margine.
ac = ante correctionem.
pc = post correctionem.
γρ = γράφεται.

ORDO ENNEADVM COMPARATVR
CVM ORDINE CHRONOLOGICO

Enn.	chron.	Enn.	chron.	Enn.	chron.
I 1	53	II 1	40	III 1	3
I 2	19	II 2	14	III 2	47
I 3	20	II 3	52	III 3	48
I 4	46	II 4	12	III 4	15
I 5	36	II 5	25	III 5	50
I 6	1	II 6	17	III 6	26
I 7	54	II 7	37	III 7	45
I 8	51	II 8	35	III 8	30
I 9	16	II 9	33	III 9	13

Enn.	chron.	Enn.	chron.	Enn.	chron.
IV 1	21	V 1	10	VI 1	42
IV 2	4	V 2	11	VI 2	43
IV 3	27	V 3	49	VI 3	44
IV 4	28	V 4	7	VI 4	22
IV 5	29	V 5	32	VI 5	23
IV 6	41	V 6	24	VI 6	34
IV 7	2	V 7	18	VI 7	38
IV 8	6	V 8	31	VI 8	39
IV 9	8	V 9	5	VI 9	9

ORDO CHRONOLOGICVS COMPARATVR
CVM ORDINE ENNEADVM

chron.	Enn.	chron.	Enn.	chron.	Enn.
1	I 6	19	I 2	37	II 7
2	IV 7	20	I 3	38	VI 7
3	III 1	21	IV 1	39	VI 8
4	IV 2	22	VI 4	40	II 1
5	V 9	23	VI 5	41	IV 6
6	IV 8	24	V 6	42	VI 1
7	V 4	25	II 5	43	VI 2
8	IV 9	26	III 6	44	VI 3
9	VI 9	27	IV 3	45	III 7
10	V 1	28	IV 4	46	I 4
11	V 2	29	IV 5	47	III 2
12	II 4	30	III 8	48	III 3
13	III 9	31	V 8	49	V 3
14	II 2	32	V 5	50	III 5
15	III 4	33	II 9	51	I 8
16	I 9	34	VI 6	52	II 3
17	II 6	35	II 8	53	I 1
18	V 7	36	I 5	54	I 7

PLOTINUS
ENNEAD II

SVMMARIVM

Τάδε ἔνεστι Πλωτίνου φιλοσόφου ἐννεάδος δευτέρας·

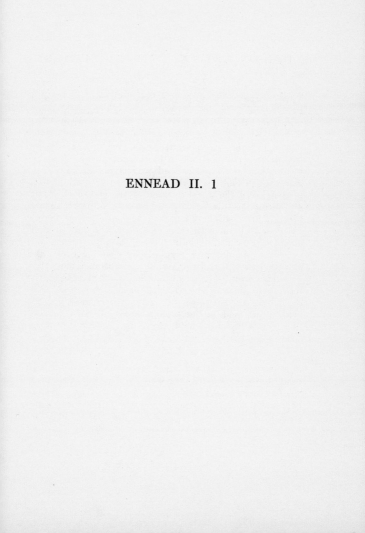

ENNEAD II. 1

II. 1. ON HEAVEN (ON THE UNIVERSE)

Introductory Note

THIS treatise is No. 40 in Porphyry's chronological order. Its purpose is to defend the doctrine, vigorously maintained by all pagan Neoplatonists, of the incorruptibility of the heavens and the heavenly bodies, the unchangingness and everlastingness of everything in the regions above the moon. This was one of the main points of disagreement between Christians and pagans in late antiquity. But, though Plotinus seems to have the Christian doctrine of the end of the world in mind at the end of ch. 4, his arguments in this treatise are mainly directed against Stoics and Stoicising Platonists who interpreted Plato's *Timaeus* to fit in with their own doctrines that the universe as a whole, including the heavenly regions, was subject to change in a regular, never-ending cycle, and that there was a real community of substance and interaction between the regions below and the regions above the moon. Plotinus is concerned to refute these errors without falling into the opposite, Aristotelian, heresy that the heavens are made of the " quintessence " or fifth element, and not, as Platonists held, of fire.

Synopsis

What is the reason why the visible heaven is everlasting in all its parts as well as the whole? The will of God and the fact that there is nothing outside it are not sufficient explanations (ch. 1). Plato's view that all bodies are in a state of flux, and our rejection of Aristotle's " fifth element " make the explanation more difficult, but none the

ON HEAVEN (ON THE UNIVERSE)

less, if we consider what the heavenly fire in its own proper region is like and how perfectly adapted it is to the control of the universal soul which contains it, we shall find in the action of universal soul (which it is quite unreasonable to suppose will ever bring the universe to an end) sufficient reason to be assured that the heaven is everlasting (ch. 2–4). It is everlasting in all its parts as well as the whole because it is made and ruled by a better soul than that which makes our bodies and other earthly things, as well as out of better material (ch. 5). The heavenly bodies do not contain any admixture of the elements of the sublunary world, and this is the true teaching of Plato if we interpret the *Timaeus* rightly. They need no nourishment, and are not nourished by exhalations from below; the elements of the lower world in no way affect the regions above the moon (chs. 6–8).

II. 1. (40) ΠΕΡΙ ΟΥΡΑΝΟΥ

1. Τὸν κόσμον ἀεὶ λέγοντες καὶ πρόσθεν εἶναι καὶ ἔσεσθαι σῶμα ἔχοντα εἰ μὲν ἐπὶ τὴν βούλησιν τοῦ θεοῦ ἀνάγοιμεν τὴν αἰτίαν, πρῶτον μὲν ἀληθὲς μὲν ἂν ἴσως λέγοιμεν, σαφήνειαν δὲ οὐδεμίαν ἂν
5 παρεχοίμεθα. Ἔπειτα τῶν στοιχείων ἡ μεταβολὴ καὶ τῶν ζῴων τῶν περὶ γῆν ἡ φθορὰ τὸ εἶδος σῴζουσα μήποτε οὕτω καὶ ἐπὶ τοῦ παντὸς ἀξιώσει γίγνεσθαι ὡς τῆς βουλήσεως τοῦτο δυναμένης ἀεὶ ὑπεκφεύγοντος καὶ ῥέοντος τοῦ σώματος ἐπιτιθέναι τὸ εἶδος τὸ αὐτὸ ἄλλοτε ἄλλῳ, ὡς μὴ σῴζεσθαι τὸ
10 ἐν ἀριθμῷ εἰς τὸ ἀεί, ἀλλὰ τὸ ἓν τῷ εἴδει· ἐπεὶ διὰ τί τὰ μὲν οὕτω κατὰ τὸ εἶδος μόνον τὸ ἀεὶ ἕξει. τὰ δ' ἐν οὐρανῷ καὶ αὐτὸς ὁ οὐρανὸς κατὰ τὸ τόδε ἕξει τὸ ἀεί; Εἰ δὲ τῷ πάντα συνειληφέναι καὶ μὴ εἶναι εἰς ὃ τὴν μεταβολὴν ποιήσεται μηδὲ τὸ ἔξωθεν ἂν προσπεσὸν φθεῖραι δύνασθαι τούτῳ
15 δώσομεν τὴν αἰτίαν τῆς οὐ φθορᾶς, τῷ μὲν ὅλῳ καὶ παντὶ δώσομεν ἐκ τοῦ λόγου τὸ μὴ ἂν φθαρῆναι, ὁ δὲ ἥλιος ἡμῖν καὶ τῶν ἄλλων ἄστρων ἡ οὐσία τῷ

---

[1] This is a reference to Plato, *Timaeus* 41B4 (the address of the Demiurge to the gods whom he has made, of whom

8

II. 1. ON HEAVEN [ON THE UNIVERSE]

1. When we say that the universe has always existed before and will always exist, although it has a body, if we refer the cause of its everlasting existence to the will of God [1], then, first of all, we may quite likely be speaking the truth, but we are not giving any sort of a clear explanation. Next, the preservation of the form in the changing of the elements and the passing away of the living beings on earth may perhaps make us think that the same happens with the All, that God's will is able as the body continually fleets and flows to impose the same form now on one thing and now on another, so that it is not the single individual thing which lasts for ever but the unity of form; for why should the things of earth have only an everlasting duration of form, while the things in heaven and the heaven itself have an everlasting duration of particular individuals? But if we say that the cause why the heaven does not pass away is that it contains everything and there is nothing it can change into or anything outside which could fall upon it and destroy it, then by this argument we shall grant indestructibility to the Whole and the All, but since our sun and the substance of the other stars

the " visible gods," the heavenly bodies, are the most important group).

μέρη καὶ μὴ ὅλον ἕκαστον εἶναι καὶ πᾶν, οὐχ ἕξει
τὴν πίστιν παρὰ τοῦ λόγου, ὅτι εἰς ἅπαντα μένει
20 τὸν χρόνον, τὸ δὲ κατ᾽ εἶδος τὴν μονὴν αὐτοῖς
εἶναι, ὥσπερ καὶ πυρὶ καὶ τοῖς τοιούτοις μόνον ἂν
δόξειε παρεῖναι καὶ αὐτῷ δὲ παντὶ τῷ κόσμῳ.
Οὐδὲν γὰρ κωλύει ὑπ᾽ ἄλλου ἔξωθεν μὴ φθειρόμενον, ὑπ᾽ αὐτοῦ, τῶν μερῶν ἄλληλα φθειρόντων,
τὴν φθορὰν ἀεὶ ἔχοντα, τῷ εἴδει μόνον μένειν, καὶ
25 ῥεούσης ἀεὶ τῆς φύσεως τοῦ ὑποκειμένου, τὸ εἶδος
ἄλλου διδόντος, γίγνεσθαι τὸ αὐτὸ ἐπὶ τοῦ παντὸς
ζῴου, ὅπερ καὶ ἐπὶ ἀνθρώπου καὶ ἵππου καὶ τῶν
ἄλλων· ἀεὶ γὰρ ἄνθρωπος καὶ ἵππος, ἀλλ᾽ οὐχ ὁ
αὐτός. Οὐ τοίνυν ἔσται τὸ μὲν μένον αὐτοῦ ἀεί,
ὥσπερ ὁ οὐρανός, τὰ δὲ περὶ γῆν φθειρόμενα, ἀλλ᾽
30 ὁμοίως ἅπαντα, τὴν διαφορὰν ἔχοντα μόνον τῷ
χρόνῳ· ἔστω γὰρ πολυχρονιώτερα τὰ ἐν οὐρανῷ.
Εἰ μὲν οὖν οὕτω συγχωρησόμεθα τὸ ἀεὶ ἐπὶ τοῦ
παντὸς καὶ ἐπὶ τῶν μερῶν εἶναι, ἧττον ἂν τὸ
ἄπορον τῇ δόξῃ προσείη· μᾶλλον δὲ παντάπασιν
ἔξω ἀπορίας ἂν γιγνοίμεθα, εἰ τὸ τῆς βουλήσεως
35 τοῦ θεοῦ ἱκανὸν εἶναι δεικνύοιτο κἂν οὕτω καὶ
τοῦτον τὸν τρόπον συνέχειν τὸ πᾶν. Εἰ δὲ καὶ τὸ
τόδε τι αὐτοῦ ὁποσονοῦν λέγοιμεν ἔχειν τὸ ἀεί, ἥ
τε βούλησις δεικτέα εἰ ἱκανὴ ποιεῖν τοῦτο, τό τε
ἄπορον μένει διὰ τί τὰ μὲν οὕτω, τὰ δὲ οὐχ οὕτως,
ἀλλὰ τῷ εἴδει μόνον, τά τε μέρη τὰ ἐν οὐρανῷ πῶς
40 καὶ αὐτά· ἐπειδὴ οὕτω καὶ αὐτὰ τὰ πάντα εἶναι.

2. Εἰ οὖν ταύτην παραδεχόμεθα τὴν δόξαν καὶ
φαμεν τὸν μὲν οὐρανὸν καὶ πάντα τὰ ἐν αὐτῷ κατὰ

are parts, and not each of them a whole and all, the argument will give no assurance that they will last for ever; they will have only permanence of form, and the same will apply to fire and such-like things, and even to the whole universe itself. For there is nothing to prevent it, even if it is not being destroyed by something from outside, from having its own continual destruction as its parts destroy each other, and so being permanent only in form; as its substratum is in continual flux and its form comes from elsewhere it will be in the same state as every living thing, man and horse and the rest; man and horse always exist, but not the same man and horse. So there will not be one permanent part of the universe, like the heaven, while the things on earth pass away, but all will be alike, differing only in the time they last; for we can grant that the things in heaven last longer. If then we admit that both the whole and the parts are permanent in this way, our doctrine will be less difficult: or rather we shall have got completely out of our difficulty, if it can be shown that the will of God is adequate to hold the All together in this way and manner. But if we say that any individual constituent of the All, whatever its size, is permanent, we must show that the divine will is adequate to make it so; and the difficulty remains why some things are permanent in this way and others are not, but have only permanence of form, and also why the parts in heaven are permanent as well as the whole; since on the supposition that they are it would seem that all the parts of the universe were permanent.

2. If, then, we accept this view and maintain that the heaven and everything in it last for ever as

τὸ τόδε ἔχειν τὸ ἀεί, τὰ δὲ ὑπὸ τῇ τῆς σελήνης
σφαίρᾳ τὸ κατ' εἶδος, δεικτέον πῶς σῶμα ἔχων
5 ἕξει τὸ τόδε ἐπὶ τοῦ αὐτοῦ κυρίως, ὡς τὸ καθ'
ἕκαστον καὶ τὸ ὡσαύτως, τῆς φύσεως τοῦ σώματος
ῥεούσης ἀεί. Τοῦτο γὰρ δοκεῖ τοῖς τε ἄλλοις τοῖς
περὶ φύσεως εἰρηκόσι καὶ αὐτῷ τῷ Πλάτωνι οὐ
μόνον περὶ τῶν ἄλλων σωμάτων, ἀλλὰ καὶ περὶ
τῶν οὐρανίων αὐτῶν. Πῶς γὰρ ἄν, φησι, σ ώ μ α τ α
10 ἔ χ ο ν τ α κ α ὶ ὁ ρ ώ μ ε ν α τὸ ἀ π α ρ α λ λ ά κ τ ω ς ἕξει
κ α ὶ τὸ ὡ σ α ύ τ ω ς; Συγχωρῶν καὶ ἐπὶ τούτων
δηλονότι τῷ Ἡρακλείτῳ, ὃς ἔφη ἀεὶ καὶ τὸν
ἥλιον γίνεσθαι. Ἀριστοτέλει μὲν γὰρ οὐδὲν ἂν
πρᾶγμα εἴη, εἴ τις αὐτοῦ τὰς ὑποθέσεις τοῦ
πέμπτου παραδέξαιτο σώματος. Τοῖς δὲ μὴ τοῦτο
15 τιθεμένοις, τοῦ σώματος δὲ ἐκ τούτων ὄντος τοῦ
οὐρανοῦ, ἐξ ὧνπερ καὶ τὰ τῇδε ζῷα, πῶς τὸ τόδε
ἂν ἔχοι; Ἔτι δὲ μᾶλλον πῶς ἥλιος καὶ τὰ ἄλλα
τὰ ἐν τῷ οὐρανῷ μόρια ὄντα; Συγκειμένου δὴ
παντὸς ζῴου ἐκ ψυχῆς καὶ τῆς σώματος φύσεως
ἀνάγκη τὸν οὐρανόν, εἴπερ ἀεὶ κατ' ἀριθμὸν ἔσται,
20 ἢ δι' ἄμφω ἔσεσθαι, ἢ διὰ θάτερον τῶν ἐνόντων,
οἷον ψυχὴν ἢ σῶμα. Ὁ μὲν δὴ τῷ σώματι διδοὺς
τὸ ἄφθαρτον οὐδὲν ἂν εἰς τοῦτο τῆς ψυχῆς δέοιτο,

---

[1] *Republic* VII. 530B2–3 (slightly adapted). Plato is
here arguing that the true, philosophical astronomer should
not seriously study the motions of the visible heavenly bodies,
which, being material, are imperfect and changeable, but de-
vote his attention to the laws of motion perceived by the
intellect alone.

individuals, but the things below the sphere of the moon are only everlasting in form, we must show how heaven, which has a body, can have proper individual identity, in the sense that each particular detail remains unchanged, when the nature of body is in continual flux. This is the view held by Plato himself, as well as by all other natural philosophers, not only about other bodies but about the heavenly bodies themselves. For " how," he says, " when they have bodies and are visible can they be unchangeable and always the same? " [1]—agreeing, obviously, in this, too, with Heraclitus, who said that the sun kept on coming into being.[2] There would be no difficulty for Aristotle, if one accepted his assumption of the fifth body.[3] But for those who do not postulate this fifth element but hold that the body of the heaven is composed of the same elements of which the living creatures down here are made, the question does arise how there can be individual identity. And still more, how can the sun and the other things in heaven be individually everlasting when they are parts? Now every living thing is composed of soul and the nature of body; so it follows necessarily that the heaven, if it exists for ever as one and the same individual, must owe its immortality either to both of its component parts or to one or other of them, i.e. soul or body. Anyone, then, who attributes indestructibility to the body will have no need of the soul for this purpose, except that it will always have

[2] Cp. Diels–Kranz, B6 (quoted by Aristotle, *Meteorologica* B. 2. 355a13–15, from where Plotinus probably takes it).

[3] For Aristotle's conception of the " fifth body," cp. *De Caelo* A. 3. 270b1 ff.

ἢ τοῦ ὁμοῦ ἀεὶ εἶναι πρὸς ζῴου σύστασιν· τῷ δὲ
τὸ σῶμα παρ' αὑτοῦ φθαρτὸν εἶναι λέγοντι καὶ τῇ
ψυχῇ διδόντι τὴν αἰτίαν πειρατέον καὶ τὴν τοῦ
25 σώματος ἕξιν μηδ' αὐτὴν ἐναντιουμένην τῇ
συστάσει καὶ τῇ διαμονῇ δεικνύναι, ὅτι μηδὲν
ἀσύμφωνον ἐν τοῖς συνεστηκόσιν ἐστὶ κατὰ φύσιν,
ἀλλὰ πρόσφορον καὶ τὴν ὕλην πρὸς τὸ βούλημα
τοῦ ἀποτελέσαντος [1] ὑπάρχειν προσήκει.

3. Πῶς οὖν ἡ ὕλη καὶ τὸ σῶμα τοῦ παντὸς
συνεργὸν ἂν εἴη πρὸς τὴν τοῦ κόσμου ἀθανασίαν
ἀεὶ ῥέον; Ἢ ὅτι, φαῖμεν ἄν, ⟨ῥεῖ ἐν αὑτῷ·⟩ ῥεῖ
γὰρ οὐκ ἔξω. Εἰ οὖν ἐν αὑτῷ καὶ οὐκ ἀπ' αὑτοῦ,
5 μένον τὸ αὐτὸ οὔτ' ἂν αὔξοιτο οὔτε φθίνοι· οὐ
τοίνυν οὐδὲ γηράσκει. Ὁρᾶν δὲ δεῖ καὶ γῆν
μένουσαν ἀεὶ ἐν σχήματι τῷ αὐτῷ ἐξ ἀιδίου καὶ
ὄγκῳ, καὶ ἀὴρ οὐ μήποτε ἐπιλείπῃ οὐδὲ ἡ ὕδατος
φύσις· καὶ τοίνυν ὅσον μεταβάλλει αὐτῶν οὐκ
ἠλλοίωσε τὴν τοῦ ὅλου ζῴου φύσιν. Καὶ γὰρ
10 ἡμῖν ἀεὶ μεταβαλλόντων μορίων καὶ εἰς τὸ ἔξω
ἀπιόντων μένει ἕκαστος εἰς πολύ· ᾧ δὲ ἔξω
μηδέν, οὐκ ἀσύμφωνος ἂν τούτων ἡ σώματος
φύσις πρὸς ψυχὴν πρὸς τὸ τὸ αὐτὸ εἶναι ζῷον καὶ
ἀεὶ μένον. Πῦρ δὲ ὀξὺ μὲν καὶ ταχὺ τῷ μὴ ὧδε
15 μένειν, ὥσπερ καὶ γῆ τῷ μὴ ἄνω· γενόμενον δὲ
ἐκεῖ, οὗ στῆναι δεῖ, οὗτοι δεῖν νομίζειν οὕτως
ἔχειν ἐν τῷ οἰκείῳ ἱδρυμένον, ὡς μὴ καὶ αὐτὸ
ὥσπερ καὶ τὰ ἄλλα στάσιν ἐπ' ἄμφω ζητεῖν.
Ἀνωτέρω μὲν γὰρ οὐκ ἂν φέροιτο· οὐδὲν γὰρ ἔτι·
κάτω δ' οὐ πέφυκε. Λείπεται δὲ αὐτῷ εὐαγώγῳ

---

[1] ἀποτελέσαντος H-S², ἀποτελέσματος codd.

to be with the body to make up the living creature. But anyone who says that the body is in itself destructible and makes the soul the cause of immortality will have to try and show that the character of body is not essentially opposed to permanent association with soul, that there is no natural discord between the components, but that even the matter of body must be favourably disposed to assist the purpose of the accomplishing power.

3. How, then, can the matter and body of the All, when it is always in a state of flux, co-operate towards the immortality of the universe? It is, we should say, because it flows in itself; it does not flow out. If, then, it flows *in* itself and not away from itself, it remains the same and does not increase or decrease; so it does not grow old either. One must observe that the earth, too, remains always from eternity in the same shape and bulk and the air never fails, nor does the nature of water; and all that changes of them does not alter the nature of the total living thing. With us too, though parts of us change and go away outside us, each individual lasts a long time; and when something has no outside, the nature of body is not so discordant with the soul as to prevent it being one and the same everlasting living thing. Fire is keen and swift by not staying here below (just as earth will not stay above); when it comes there where it has to stop one must not think of it as being so firmly established in its own place that it does not, like the other elements, seek a position for itself in both directions. Now it cannot go any higher, for there is nothing beyond; and it is not its nature to go down. It remains for it to be tractable

τε εἶναι καὶ κατὰ φυσικὴν ὁλκὴν ἑλκομένῳ ὑπὸ
20 ψυχῆς πρὸς τὸ ζῆν εὖ μάλα ἐν καλῷ τόπῳ
κινεῖσθαι ἐν τῇ ψυχῇ. Καὶ γάρ, εἴ τῳ φόβος μὴ
πέσῃ, θαρρεῖν δεῖ· φθάνει γὰρ ἡ τῆς ψυχῆς
περιαγωγὴ πᾶσαν νεῦσιν, ὡς κρατοῦσαν ἀνέχειν.
Εἰ δὲ μηδὲ ῥοπὴν πρὸς τὸ κάτω ἔχει παρ' αὐτοῦ,
οὐκ ἀντιτεῖνον μένει. Τὰ μὲν οὖν ἡμέτερα μέρη
25 ἐν μορφῇ γενόμενα οὐ στέγοντα αὐτῶν τὴν
σύστασιν ἀπαιτεῖ ἀπ' ἄλλων μόρια, ἵνα μένοι· εἰ
δ' ἐκεῖθεν μὴ ἀπορρέοι, οὐδὲν δεῖ τρέφεσθαι. Εἰ
δὲ ἀπορρέοι ἀποσβεννύμενον ἐκεῖθεν, πῦρ δεῖ
ἕτερον ἐξάπτεσθαι καί, εἰ ἄλλου τινὸς ἔχοι καὶ
ἐκεῖθεν ἀπορρέοι, δεῖ καὶ ἀντ' ἐκείνου ἄλλου.
30 Ἀλλὰ διὰ τοῦτο οὐ μένοι ἂν τὸ πᾶν ζῷον τὸ αὐτό,
εἰ καὶ οὕτως.

4. Ἀλλ' αὐτό γε ἐφ' ἑαυτοῦ, οὐχ ὡς πρὸς τὸ
ζητούμενον, σκεπτέον εἴτε τι ἀπορρεῖ ἐκεῖθεν,
ὥστε δεῖσθαι κἀκεῖνα τῆς λεγομένης οὐ κυρίως
τροφῆς, ἢ ἅπαξ τὰ ἐκεῖ ταχθέντα κατὰ φύσιν
5 μένοντα οὐδεμίαν πάσχει ἀπορροήν· καὶ πότερον
πῦρ μόνον ἢ πλέον τὸ πῦρ καὶ ἔστι τοῖς ἄλλοις
αἰωρεῖσθαι καὶ μετεωρίζεσθαι ὑπὸ τοῦ κρατοῦντος.
Εἰ γάρ τις προσθείη καὶ τὴν κυριωτάτην αἰτίαν,
τὴν ψυχήν, μετὰ τῶν οὕτω σωμάτων καθαρῶν
καὶ πάντως ἀμεινόνων—ἐπεὶ καὶ ἐν τοῖς ἄλλοις
10 ζῴοις ἐν τοῖς κυρίοις αὐτῶν τὰ ἀμείνω ἐκλέγεται

and, drawn by soul to an excellent life in a way according with its nature, to move in soul in a noble place. If anyone is afraid it will fall, he should feel reassured; the soul's guidance on its circular path anticipates any tendency to decline, mastering it and holding it up: and if fire has no spontaneous inclination downward, it stays in place without resistance. Our own members, which come to be in a definite shape, cannot maintain their own structure and demand portions from other things to make them last: but if there is no loss by flux in heaven there is no need for nourishment. If anything was lost there through fire being extinguished, other fire would have to be kindled; and if it had this other fire from something else and that something else lost it by flux, that again would have to replaced by other fire. But as a result of this the universal living creature would not remain the same thing, even if it remained the same sort of thing.

4. But we ought to consider this question in itself, and not in relation to our main investigation, whether anything in heaven is lost by flux so that the heavenly bodies do need nutrition (not in the strict and proper sense of the word), or whether the beings there, once established, remain naturally and endure no loss by flux; and also whether there is only fire or whether fire predominates and it is possible for the other elements to be carried up and held on high by the dominant fire. If one takes into account the sovereign cause, the soul, along with bodies of the kind which exist in heaven, pure and altogether better than those of earth (for in other living things, too, nature selects and places in their most important

ἡ φύσις—πάγιον ἂν τὴν δόξαν περὶ τοῦ οὐρανοῦ
τῆς ἀθανασίας λάβοι. Ὀρθῶς γὰρ καὶ Ἀριστοτέλης
τὴν φλόγα ζέσιν τινὰ καὶ πῦρ οἷον διὰ κόρον
ὑβρίζον· τὸ δὲ ἐκεῖ ὁμαλὸν καὶ ἠρεμαῖον καὶ τῇ
τῶν ἄστρων πρόσφορον φύσει. Τὸ δὲ δὴ μέγιστον,
15 τὴν ψυχὴν ἐφεξῆς τοῖς ἀρίστοις κινουμένην δυνάμει
θαυμαστῇ κειμένην, πῶς ἐκφεύξεταί τι αὐτὴν εἰς
τὸ μὴ εἶναι τῶν ἅπαξ ἐν αὐτῇ τεθέντων; Μὴ
παντὸς δὲ δεσμοῦ οἴεσθαι κρείττονα εἶναι ἐκ θεοῦ
ὡρμημένην, ἀνθρώπων ἀπείρων ἐστὶν αἰτίας τῆς
συνεχούσης τὰ πάντα. Ἄτοπον γὰρ τὴν καὶ
20 ὁποσονοῦν χρόνον δυνηθεῖσαν συνέχειν μὴ καὶ ἀεὶ
ποιεῖν τοῦτο, ὥσπερ βίᾳ τοῦ συνέχειν γεγονότος
καὶ τοῦ κατὰ φύσιν ἄλλου ἢ τούτου ὄντος, ὃ ἐν τῇ
τοῦ παντός ἐστι φύσει καὶ ἐν τοῖς καλῶς τεθεῖσιν,
ἢ ὄντος τινὸς τοῦ βιασομένου καὶ διαλύσοντος τὴν
σύστασιν καὶ οἷον βασιλείας τινὸς καὶ ἀρχῆς
25 καταλύσοντος τὴν ψυχῆς φύσιν. Τό τε μήποτε
ἄρξασθαι—ἄτοπον γὰρ καὶ ἤδη εἴρηται—πίστιν
καὶ περὶ τοῦ μέλλοντος ἔχει. Διὰ τί γὰρ ἔσται,
ὅτε καὶ οὐκ ἤδη; Οὐ γὰρ ἐκτέτριπται τὰ στοιχεῖα,
ὥσπερ ξύλα καὶ τὰ τοιαῦτα· μενόντων δ' ἀεὶ καὶ
τὸ πᾶν μένει. Καὶ εἰ μεταβάλλει ἀεί, τὸ πᾶν
30 μένει· μένει γὰρ καὶ ἡ τῆς μεταβολῆς αἰτία. Ἡ
δὲ μετάνοια τῆς ψυχῆς ὅτι κενόν ἐστι δέδεικται,

---

[1] Cp. Aristotle, *Meteorologica* A. 3. 340b23 and 4. 341b22.

[2] Plotinus particularly disliked the idea that the divine
power which made the universe might change its mind and

ON HEAVEN (ON THE UNIVERSE)

parts the bodies of better quality), one will have a solid conviction about the immortality of the heaven. Aristotle, certainly, is right in calling flame a " boiling-over," [1] fire rioting because it is full fed; but fire in heaven is equable and placid, adapted to the nature of the stars. But the greatest argument of all is: when soul, moved with a marvellous power, is situated next after the best of realities, how can anything which was once set in it escape from it into non-being? Only those who have no understanding of the cause which holds all things together would not think soul, sprung from God, stronger than any bond. For it would be absurd for soul, if it is able to hold the universe together for any length of time, however short, not to do so for ever, as if it held it together by force and the natural state of affairs was other than this existing one which is in the nature of the universe and the noble disposition of things, or as if there was someone who was going to dissolve the universal structure by violence and depose the nature of soul as if from some sort of kingship or magistracy. The fact, too, that it had no beginning—we have already said that that would be absurd—gives us assurance for the future. For why should there come a time when it exists no more? The elements do not wear out like pieces of wood and things of that kind; and if they last the All lasts. And even if they are continually changing, the All lasts; for the cause of change endures. And we have shown that it is empty to suppose that soul might change its mind,[2] for its direction of the

destroy it. He had already attacked it in his treatise *Against the Gnostics* (II9. 4).

19

ὅτι ἄπονος καὶ ἀβλαβὴς ἡ διοίκησις· καὶ εἰ πᾶν
οἷόν τε σῶμα ἀπολέσθαι, οὐδὲν ἂν ἀλλοιότερον
αὐτῇ γίγνοιτο.

5. Πῶς οὖν τὰ ἐκεῖ μέρη μένει, τὰ δ' ἐνταῦθα
στοιχεῖα τε καὶ ζῷα οὐ μένει; Ἤ, φησὶν ὁ
Πλάτων, τὰ μὲν παρὰ θεοῦ γεγένηται, τὰ δ'
ἐνταῦθα ζῷα παρὰ τῶν γενομένων παρ' αὐτοῦ
θεῶν· γενόμενα δὲ παρ' ἐκείνου οὐ θεμιτὸν φθεί-
5 ρεσθαι. Τοῦτο δὲ ταὐτὸν τῷ ἐφεξῆς μὲν τῷ
δημιουργῷ εἶναι τὴν ψυχὴν τὴν οὐρανίαν, καὶ τὰς
ἡμετέρας δέ· ἀπὸ δὲ τῆς οὐρανίας ἴνδαλμα αὐτῆς
ἰὸν καὶ οἷον ἀπορρέον ἀπὸ τῶν ἄνω τὰ ἐπὶ γῆς ζῷα
ποιεῖν. Ψυχῆς οὖν μιμουμένης τοιαύτης τὴν ἐκεῖ,
ἀδυνατούσης δὲ τῷ καὶ χείροσι σώμασι χρῆσθαι
10 πρὸς τὴν ποίησιν καὶ ἐν τόπῳ χείρονι καὶ τῶν εἰς
τὴν σύστασιν ληφθέντων οὐκ ἐθελόντων μένειν, τά
τε ζῷα ἐνταῦθα οὐκ ἀεὶ δύναται μένειν, τά τε
σώματα οὐχ ὁμοίως κρατοῖτο ἄν, ὡς ἂν ἄλλης
ψυχῆς αὐτῶν προσεχῶς ἀρχούσης. Τὸν δὲ ὅλον
15 οὐρανὸν εἴπερ ἔδει μένειν, καὶ τὰ μόρια αὐτοῦ, τὰ
ἄστρα τὰ ἐν αὐτῷ, ἔδει· ἢ πῶς ἂν ἔμεινε μὴ
ὁμοίως καὶ τούτων μενόντων; Τὰ γὰρ ὑπὸ τὸν
οὐρανὸν οὐκέτι οὐρανοῦ μέρη· ἢ οὐ μέχρι σελήνης
ὁ οὐρανός. Ἡμεῖς δὲ πλασθέντες ὑπὸ τῆς διδο-
μένης παρὰ τῶν ἐν οὐρανῷ θεῶν ψυχῆς καὶ
20 αὐτοῦ τοῦ οὐρανοῦ κατ' ἐκείνην καὶ σύνεσμεν τοῖς
σώμασιν· ἡ γὰρ ἄλλη ψυχή, καθ' ἣν ἡμεῖς, τοῦ εὖ

universe is without trouble or harm to it; and even if it were possible for all body to perish, nothing unpleasant would happen to soul.

5. How then do the parts in heaven last, but down here the elements and living things do not last? Because, Plato says, the heavenly things derive their being from God, but the living things down here from the gods derived from him;[1] and it is not lawful for the things which derive their being from him to perish.[2] This amounts to saying that the heavenly soul (and our souls too) comes next in order after the maker of the universe; from the heavenly soul comes out an image of it and so to speak flows down from above and makes the living things on earth. Since, then, this kind of soul tries to imitate the soul up there but is unable to because it is using worse bodies for its making and is working in a worse place, and since the ingredients which it takes for its composition are unwilling to endure, the living things here cannot last for ever and the bodies are not as effectively mastered by soul as if the other (heavenly) soul ruled them directly. But if the heaven must last as a whole, then its parts, the stars in it, must last too; how could it last if they do not last as well? (The things under heaven are no longer part of heaven; if we assumed that they were, then heaven would not stop at the moon.) We, however, are formed by the soul given from the gods in heaven and heaven itself, and this soul governs our association with our bodies. The other soul, by which we are ourselves, is cause of our well-being, not of our

[1] *Timaeus* 69C3–5.
[2] Cp. *Timaeus* 41A7–B5.

εἶναι, οὐ τοῦ εἶναι αἰτία. Ἤδη γοῦν τοῦ σώματος
ἔρχεται γενομένου μικρὰ ἐκ λογισμοῦ πρὸς τὸ εἶναι
συνεκλαμβανομένη.

6. Ἀλλὰ πότερον πῦρ μόνον καὶ εἰ ἀπορρεῖ
ἐκεῖθεν καὶ δεῖται τροφῆς νῦν σκεπτέον. Τῷ μὲν
οὖν Τιμαίῳ τὸ τοῦ παντὸς σῶμα πεποιηκότι
πρῶτον ἐκ γῆς καὶ πυρός, ἵνα ὁρατόν τε ᾖ διὰ τὸ
5 πῦρ, στερρὸν δὲ διὰ τὴν γῆν, ἀκολουθεῖν ἔδοξε καὶ
τὰ ἄστρα ποιεῖν οὐ πᾶν, ἀλλὰ τὸ πλεῖστον πυρὸς
ἔχειν, ἐπειδὴ τὰ ἄστρα τὸ στερεὸν φαίνεται ἔχοντα.
Καὶ ἴσως ὀρθῶς ἂν ἔχοι συνεπικρίναντος καὶ
Πλάτωνος τῷ εἰκότι τὴν γνώμην ταύτην. Παρὰ
10 μὲν γὰρ τῆς αἰσθήσεως κατά τε τὴν ὄψιν κατά τε
τὴν τῆς ἁφῆς ἀντίληψιν πυρὸς ἔχειν τὸ πλεῖστον ἢ
τὸ πᾶν φαίνεται, διὰ δὲ τοῦ λόγου ἐπισκοποῦσιν,
εἰ τὸ στερεὸν ἄνευ γῆς οὐκ ἂν γένοιτο, καὶ γῆς ἂν
ἔχοι. Ὕδατος δὲ καὶ ἀέρος τί ἂν δέοιτο; Ἄτοπόν
τε γὰρ δόξει ὕδατος εἶναι ἐν τοσούτῳ πυρί, ὅ τε
ἀὴρ εἰ ἐνείη μεταβάλλοι ἂν εἰς πυρὸς φύσιν.
15 Ἀλλ' εἰ δύο στερεὰ ἄκρων λόγον ἔχοντα δύο
μέσων δεῖται, ἀπορήσειεν ἄν τις, εἰ καὶ ἐν φυσικοῖς
οὕτως· ἐπεὶ καὶ γῆν ἄν τις ὕδατι μίξειεν οὐδενὸς
δεηθεὶς μέσου. Εἰ δὲ λέγοιμεν· ἐνυπάρχει γὰρ
ἤδη ἐν τῇ γῇ καὶ τῷ ὕδατι καὶ τὰ ἄλλα, δόξομεν
ἴσως τι λέγειν· εἴποι δ' ἄν τις· ἀλλ' οὐ πρὸς τὸ

---

[1] *Timaeus* 31B4–8.
[2] *Timaeus* 40A2–3.
[3] This is, perhaps, a reference to what Plato makes Timaeus

being. It comes when our body is already in existence, making only minor contributions from reasoning to our being.

6. But now we must consider whether the heavenly
bodies are made of fire only, and whether anything
flows away from them and so they need nourishment.
To Timaeus, who formed the body of the All primarily
from earth and fire, so that it might be visible by
means of the fire and solid by means of the earth,[1]
it seemed consistent to make the stars contain, not
all fire but mostly fire, since the stars obviously have
solidity.[2] And he is probably right, since Plato
agrees that this view is probable.[3] From our sense-
perception, by sight and the apprehension of contact
[with their rays], they seem to contain all fire or
mostly fire; but when we consider them rationally,
we see that, if there is no solidity without earth, they
must contain earth. But what need would they have
of water and air? It will seem absurd to suppose
that there is any water in so much fire, and if there
was any air in it, it would change into the nature of
fire. But even if two solids standing in the relationship of extremes need two middle terms,[4] one might
find it difficult to suppose that this logical relationship
held good for natural bodies; for one can mix earth
and water without needing any middle term. But
if we say " The other elements are already present in
earth and water " there will, perhaps, appear to be
some sense in this argument, though one might
object " These other elements will not serve to bind

say at 29B3–D3, that his account of the formation of the
universe is a probable but not a certain one.
[4] *Timaeus* 32B2–3.

20 συνδῆσαι συνιόντα τὰ δύο. Ἀλλ' ὅμως ἐροῦμεν
ἤδη συνδεῖσθαι τῷ ἔχειν ἑκάτερον πάντα. Ἀλλ'
ἐπισκεπτέον, εἰ ἄνευ πυρὸς οὐχ ὁρατὸν γῆ, καὶ
ἄνευ γῆς οὐ στερεὸν πῦρ· εἰ γὰρ τοῦτο, τάχ' ἂν
οὐδὲν ἔχοι ἐφ' ἑαυτοῦ τὴν αὐτοῦ οὐσίαν, ἀλλὰ
πάντα μὲν μέμικται, λέγεται δὲ κατὰ τὸ ἐπικρατοῦν
25 ἕκαστον. Ἐπεὶ οὐδὲ τὴν γῆν ἄνευ ὑγροῦ φασι
συστῆναι δύνασθαι· κόλλαν γὰρ εἶναι τῇ γῇ τὴν
ὕδατος ὑγρότητα. Ἀλλ' εἰ καὶ δώσομεν οὕτως,
ἀλλὰ ἕκαστόν γε ἄτοπον λέγοντα εἶναί τι ἐφ'
ἑαυτοῦ μὲν μὴ διδόναι σύστασιν αὑτῷ, μετὰ δὲ
τῶν ἄλλων ὁμοῦ, οὐδενὸς ἑκάστου ὄντος. Πῶς
30 γὰρ ἂν εἴη γῆς φύσις καὶ τὸ τί ἦν εἶναι γῆ μηδενὸς
ὄντος μορίου γῆς ὃ γῆ ἐστιν, εἰ μὴ καὶ ὕδωρ ἐνείη
εἰς κόλλησιν; Τί δ' ἂν κολλήσειε μὴ ὄντος ὅλως
μεγέθους, ὃ πρὸς ἄλλο μόριον συνεχὲς συνάψει;
Εἰ γὰρ καὶ ὁτιοῦν μέγεθος γῆς αὐτῆς ἔσται, ἔσται
γῆν φύσει καὶ ἄνευ ὕδατος εἶναι· ἤ, εἰ μὴ τοῦτο,
35 οὐδὲν ἔσται, ὃ κολλήσεται ὑπὸ τοῦ ὕδατος. Ἀέρος
δὲ τί ἂν δέοιτο γῆς ὄγκος πρὸς τὸ εἶναι ἔτι ἀέρος
μένοντος πρὶν μεταβάλλειν; Περὶ δὲ πυρὸς εἰς
μὲν τὸ γῆ εἶναι οὐκ εἴρηται, εἰς δὲ τὸ ὁρατὴ εἶναι
καὶ αὐτὴ καὶ τὰ ἄλλα· εὔλογον μὲν γὰρ συγχωρεῖν
παρὰ φωτὸς τὸ ὁρᾶσθαι γίνεσθαι. Οὐ γὰρ δὴ τὸ

---

[1] This is the doctrine of *Epinomis* 981D–E, where all living
beings are composed of all the elements, but in the earthly
group (men, animals, plants) the earthly and solid element

the two when they come together." But all the
same we shall say [for the sake of argument] that
they are joined because each of them contains all
things. But we must consider whether it is true that
earth is not visible without fire and fire is not solid
without earth. If this is so, it looks as if no element
would ever have its own essential nature by itself,
but all are mixed and take their names from the
dominant element in each.[1] They say that earth
cannot have concrete existence without moisture;
the moisture of water is earth's adhesive. But even
if we grant that this is so, it is absurd to say that each
element is a separate something and not give it any
concrete existence but only an existence along with
the others, without anything being separate. How
could there be a nature and substantial reality of
earth if there is no particle of earth which is earth
unless water is present in it to stick it together?
What could the water stick if there was no bulk of
earth at all which it could join to another contiguous
particle? And if there is any bulk of absolute earth
at all, then earth can exist by nature without water;
and if it is not so, there will be nothing to be stuck
together by the water. And how could the mass of
earth require air for its existence, air that was still
air, before it changed? As for fire, it was not maintained that it was needed for earth to exist, but for
it and the other elements to be visible,[2] and it is
certainly reasonable to agree that visibility comes
from light. For we should not say that darkness is

predominates, in the heavenly group (the heavenly bodies)
the element of fire.

[2] *Timaeus* 31B5.

40 σκότος ὁρᾶσθαι, ἀλλὰ μὴ ὁρᾶσθαι φατέον, ὥσπερ
τὴν ἀψοφίαν μὴ ἀκούεσθαι. Ἀλλὰ πῦρ γε ἐν
αὐτῇ οὐκ ἀνάγκη παρεῖναι· φῶς γὰρ ἀρκεῖ. Χιὼν
γοῦν καὶ τὰ ψυχρότατα πολλὰ λαμπρὰ πυρὸς ἄνευ.
Ἀλλ' ἐνεγένετο, φήσει τις, καὶ ἔχρωσε πρὶν
45 ἀπελθεῖν. Καὶ περὶ ὕδατος δὲ ἀπορητέον, εἰ μὴ
ἔστιν ὕδωρ, εἰ μὴ γῆς λάβοι. Ἀὴρ δὲ πῶς ἂν
λέγοιτο μετέχειν γῆς εὔθρυπτος ὤν; Περὶ δὲ
πυρός, εἰ γῆς δεῖ αὐτῷ τὸ συνεχὲς παρ' αὐτοῦ οὐκ
ἔχοντι οὐδὲ τὸ διάστατον τριχῇ. Ἡ δὲ στερεότης
50 αὐτῷ, οὐ κατὰ τὴν διάστασιν τὴν τριχῇ, ἀλλὰ
κατὰ τὴν ἀντέρεισιν δηλονότι, διὰ τί οὐκ ἔσται ἢ
φυσικὸν σῶμα; Σκληρότης δὲ γῇ μόνῃ. Ἐπεὶ
καὶ τὸ πυκνὸν τῷ χρυσῷ ὕδατι ὄντι προσγίνεται
οὐ γῆς προσγενομένης, ἀλλὰ πυκνότητος ἢ πήξεως.
Καὶ πῦρ δὲ ἐφ' αὑτοῦ διὰ τί ψυχῆς παρούσης οὐ
55 συστήσεται πρὸς τὴν δύναμιν αὐτῆς; Καὶ ζῷα δὲ
πύρινά ἐστι δαιμόνων. Ἀλλὰ κινήσομεν τὸ πᾶν
ζῷον ἐκ πάντων τὴν σύστασιν ἔχειν. Ἢ τὰ ἐπὶ
γῆς τις ἐρεῖ, γῆν δὲ εἰς τὸν οὐρανὸν αἴρειν παρὰ
φύσιν εἶναι καὶ ἐναντίον τοῖς ὑπ' αὐτῆς τεταγμένοις·
συμπεριάγειν δὲ τὴν ταχίστην φορὰν γεηρὰ σώματα
οὐ πιθανὸν εἶναι ἐμπόδιόν τε καὶ πρὸς τὸ φανὸν
60 καὶ λευκὸν τοῦ ἐκεῖ πυρός.

7. Ἴσως οὖν βέλτιον χρὴ ἀκούειν τοῦ Πλάτωνος
λέγοντος ἐν μὲν τῷ παντὶ κόσμῳ δεῖν εἶναι τὸ
τοιοῦτον στερεόν, τὸ ἀντίτυπον ὄν, ἵνα τε ἡ γῆ ἐν
μέσῳ ἱδρυμένη ἐπιβάθρα καὶ τοῖς ἐπ' αὐτῆς

visible but that it is invisible, just as noiselessness is inaudible. But there is no need for fire to be present in earth: light is enough. Snow, anyhow, and many very cold things are bright without fire—but there *was* fire in them, someone will say, and it coloured them before it went away. And there is a difficulty about water, too; is it not water unless it contains some earth? And how could one say that air has earth in it when it is so unstable? As for fire, one must ask if it needs earth because it has neither continuity nor three-dimensionality of itself. But why has it not solidity (in the sense not of three-dimensionality but of resistance) simply from being a natural body? Hardness is the property of earth alone. For gold, for example, which is water, acquires density not by the accession of earth but of denseness or coagulation.[1] And why, then, should not fire, since soul is present to it, attain existence by itself through soul's power? There are, in fact, fiery living beings among the spirits. We shall question the assumption that every living thing is constituted of all the elements. One can agree that this is true of the things on earth, but to lift up earth into heaven is against nature and opposed to her laws; it is not probable that the swiftest of all movements carries round earthly bodies; it would impede the brightness and clearness of the heavenly fire.

7. So perhaps we should listen more carefully to Plato; this is what he says: there must in the universal order be a solidity, that is a resistance, of such a kind that the earth set in the middle may be a founda-

---

[1] *Timaeus* 59B1–4.

5 βεβηκόσιν ἑδραία ᾖ, τά τε ζῷα τὰ ἐπ᾿ αὐτῆς ἐξ
ἀνάγκης τὸ τοιοῦτον στερεὸν ἔχῃ, ἡ δὲ γῆ τὸ μὲν
εἶναι συνεχὴς καὶ παρ᾿ αὐτῆς ἔχοι, ἐπιλάμποιτο δὲ
ὑπὸ πυρός· μετέχειν δὲ ὕδατος πρὸς τὸ μὴ
αὐχμηρόν—ἔχειν δέ—καὶ μερῶν πρὸς μέρη μὴ
κωλύεσθαι συναγωγήν· ἀέρα δὲ κουφίζειν γῆς
10 ὄγκους· μεμῖχθαι δὲ τῷ ἄνω πυρὶ οὐκ ἐν τῇ
συστάσει τῶν ἄστρων τὴν γῆν, ἀλλ᾿ ἐν κόσμῳ
γενομένου ἑκάστου καὶ τὸ πῦρ ἀπολαῦσαί τι τῆς
γῆς, ὥσπερ καὶ τὴν γῆν τοῦ πυρὸς καὶ ἕκαστον
ἑκάστων, οὐχ ὡς τὸ ἀπολαῦσαν γενέσθαι ἐξ ἀμφοῖν,
ἑαυτοῦ τε καὶ οὗ μετέσχεν, ἀλλὰ κατὰ τὴν ἐν
15 κόσμῳ κοινωνίαν ὂν ὅ ἐστι λαβεῖν οὐκ αὐτὸ ἀλλά
τι αὐτοῦ, οἷον οὐκ ἀέρα, ἀλλ᾿ ἀέρος τὴν ἀπαλότητα
καὶ τὴν γῆν πυρὸς τὴν λαμπρότητα· τὴν δὲ μῖξιν
πάντα διδόναι καὶ τὸ συναμφότερον τότε ποιεῖν,
οὐ γῆν μόνον καὶ τὴν πυρὸς φύσιν, τὴν στερεότητα
20 ταύτην καὶ τὴν πυκνότητα. Μαρτυρεῖ δὲ καὶ
αὐτὸς τούτοις εἰπών· φῶς ἀνῆψεν ὁ θεὸς περὶ
τὴν δευτέραν ἀπὸ γῆς περιφοράν, τὸν ἥλιον
λέγων, καὶ λαμπρότατόν που λέγει ἀλλαχοῦ
τὸν ἥλιον, τὸν αὐτὸν δὲ λευκότατον, ἀπάγων ἡμᾶς
τοῦ ἄλλο τι νομίζειν ἢ πυρὸς εἶναι, πυρὸς δὲ
25 οὐδετέρων τῶν εἰδῶν αὐτοῦ τῶν ἄλλων, ἀλλὰ τὸ
φῶς ὅ φησιν ἕτερον φλογὸς εἶναι, θερμὸν δὲ

---

[1] Cp. *Timaeus* 55E1–3 and 59D6. This is not exactly what
Plato says but what Plotinus thinks he means. Here, as

28

tion and firm support for those who stand upon it,
and the living beings upon it may necessarily have a
solidity of this kind;[1] the earth will possess continuity from itself and will be illuminated by fire;
it has a share of water to prevent dryness (as, in fact,
it has) and so as not to hinder the cohesion of its
particles; and air gives lightness to the bulk of earth;
but earth is mingled with the upper fire, not in the
constitution of the stars but because, since they are
both in the universal order, fire gains something from
earth as earth does from fire and each element from
each of the others; not in the sense that the element
which gains something is composed of both, itself
and that of which it has a share; but, through the
community of the universe, while remaining itself
it takes, not the actual other element but something
which belongs to it, not air, for instance, but the
yielding softness of air, and earth the brightness of
fire: the mixture gives all qualities and consequently
produces the compound thing, not supplying earth
only and the nature of fire but this solidity and density
of earth. Plato himself supports this view when he
says " God kindled a light in the second circuit from
the earth," meaning the sun;[2] and elsewhere he
calls the sun " the brightest,"[3] and also says it is
the clearest; so he prevents us from thinking that
it is made of anything but fire, but by fire he does
not mean either of the other kinds of fire but the

always in his Platonic exegesis, Plotinus shows himself determined to extract some meaning from Plato which will fit in
with his own ideas of what is reasonable and true.

[2] *Timaeus* 39B4–5.

[3] *Theaetetus* 208D2: *Republic* 616E9.

προσηνῶς μόνον· τοῦτο δὲ τὸ φῶς σῶμα εἶναι,
ἀποστίλβειν δὲ ἀπ' αὐτοῦ τὸ ὁμώνυμον αὐτῷ
φῶς, ὃ δή φαμεν καὶ ἀσώματον εἶναι· τοῦτο δὲ
ἀπ' ἐκείνου τοῦ φωτὸς παρέχεσθαι, ἐκλάμπον ἐξ
30 ἐκείνου ὥσπερ ἄνθος ἐκείνου καὶ στιλπνότητα, ὃ
δὴ καὶ εἶναι τὸ ὄντως λευκὸν σῶμα. Ἡμεῖς δὲ
τὸ γεηρὸν πρὸς τὸ χεῖρον λαμβάνοντες, τοῦ
Πλάτωνος κατὰ τὴν στερεότητα λαβόντος τὴν γῆν,
ἔν τι γοῦν δὴ ὀνομάζομεν ἡμεῖς διαφορὰς γῆς
ἐκείνου τιθεμένου. Τοῦ δὴ τοιούτου πυρὸς τοῦ
35 φῶς παρέχοντος τὸ καθαρώτατον ἐν τῷ ἄνω τόπῳ
κειμένου καὶ κατὰ φύσιν ἐκεῖ ἱδρυμένου, ταύτην
τὴν φλόγα οὐκ ἐπιμίγνυσθαι τοῖς ἐκεῖ ὑποληπτέον,
ἀλλὰ φθάνουσαν μέχρι τινὸς ἀποσβέννυσθαι ἐντυχοῦ-
σαν πλείονι ἀέρι ἀνελθοῦσάν τε μετὰ γῆς ῥίπτεσθαι
κάτω οὐ δυναμένην ὑπερβαίνειν πρὸς τὸ ἄνω,
40 κάτω δὲ τῆς σελήνης ἵστασθαι, ὥστε καὶ λεπτότε-
ρον ποιεῖν τὸν ἐκεῖ ἀέρα καὶ φλόγα, εἰ μένοι,
μαραινομένην εἰς τὸ πραότερον γίνεσθαι καὶ τὸ
λαμπρὸν μὴ ἔχειν ὅσον εἰς τὴν ζέσιν, ἀλλ' ἢ ὅσον
παρὰ τοῦ φωτὸς τοῦ ἄνω ἐναυγάζεσθαι· τὸ δὲ
φῶς ἐκεῖ, τὸ μὲν ποικιλθὲν ἐν λόγοις, τοῖς ἄστροις,
45 ὥσπερ ἐν τοῖς μεγέθεσιν, οὕτω καὶ ἐν ταῖς χρόαις
τὴν διαφορὰν ἐργάσασθαι, τὸν δ' ἄλλον οὐρανὸν
εἶναι καὶ αὐτὸν τοιούτου φωτός, μὴ ὁρᾶσθαι δὲ
λεπτότητι τοῦ σώματος καὶ διαφανείᾳ οὐκ ἀν-

---

[1] Cp. *Timaeus* 58C5–7.
[2] Light for Plotinus is the incorporeal ἐνέργεια of the

light which he says is other than flame, and only
gently warm.[1] This light is a body, but another light
shines from it which has the same name, which we
teach is incorporeal. [2] This is given from that first
light, shining out from it as its flower and splendour;
that first light is the truly bright and clear body.
We take " earthly " in the lower sense, but Plato
understands " earth " in the sense of " solidity ";[3]
we apply the name " earth " in one and the same
sense, but Plato distinguishes different kinds of
" earth ".[4] Now since fire of this kind, which gives
the purest light, rests in the upper region and is
established there by nature, we must not suppose that
the flame down here mingles with the fires of heaven;
it reaches a certain way and then is extinguished
when it encounters a greater quantity of air, and as it
takes earth with it on its ascent it falls back and is
not able to get up to the upper fire but comes to a
standstill below the moon, so as to make the air finer
there; the flame, if it lasts, fades into softness and has
not enough brightness to blaze out but only enough
to be illuminated by the upper light; the light in
the heavens, being varied in different proportions,
brings about the distinction of the stars both in size
and colour; the rest of the heaven is also made of
light of this kind, but is not seen because of the

luminous body, closely parallel to life, the ἐνέργεια of the
soul. Cp. IV. 5. 6–7. I have discussed this doctrine and the
important place which it holds in the thought of Plotinus in
my *Architecture of the Intelligible Universe in Plotinus*, pp.
54–58.

[3] *Timaeus* 31B6.

[4] Plotinus may be thinking of *Timaeus* 60B6, but the passage is really quite irrelevant to his argument here.

τιτύπῳ, ὥσπερ καὶ τὸν καθαρὸν ἀέρα· πρόσεστι
δὲ τούτοις καὶ τὸ πόρρω.

8. Τούτου δὴ μείναντος ἄνω τοῦ τοιούτου φωτὸς
ἐν ᾧ τέτακται καθαροῦ ἐν καθαρωτάτῳ, τίς ἂν
τρόπος ἀπορροῆς ἀπ' αὐτοῦ ἂν γένοιτο; Οὐ γὰρ
δὴ πρὸς τὸ κάτω πέφυκεν ἀπορρεῖν ἡ τοιαύτη
5 φύσις, οὐδ' αὖ τί ἐστιν ἐκεῖ τῶν βιαζομένων
ὠθεῖν πρὸς τὸ κάτω. Πᾶν δὲ σῶμα μετὰ ψυχῆς
ἄλλο καὶ οὐ ταυτόν, οἷον μόνον ἦν· τοιοῦτον δὲ τὸ
ἐκεῖ, οὐχ οἷον τὸ μόνον. Τό τε γειτονοῦν εἴτε ἀὴρ
εἴτε πῦρ εἴη, ἀὴρ μὲν τί ἂν ποιήσειε; Πυρὸς δὲ
οὐδ' ἂν ἓν ἁρμόσειε πρὸς τὸ ποιῆσαι, οὐδ' ἂν
10 ἐφάψαιτο εἰς τὸ δρᾶσαι· τῇ ῥύμῃ τε γὰρ παραλ-
λάξειεν ἂν πρὶν παθεῖν ἐκεῖνο, ἔλαττόν τε τοῦτο
ἰσχῦόν τε οὐκ ἴσα τοῖς ἐνθάδε. Εἶτα καὶ τὸ
ποιῆσαι θερμῆναί ἐστι· δεῖ τε τὸ θερμανθησόμενον
μὴ θερμὸν παρ' αὐτοῦ εἶναι. Εἰ δέ τι φθαρήσεται
παρὰ πυρός, θερμανθῆναι δεῖ πρότερον αὐτὸ καὶ
15 παρὰ φύσιν αὐτὸ ἐν τῷ θερμαίνεσθαι γίνεσθαι.
Οὐδὲν δεῖ τοίνυν ἄλλου σώματος τῷ οὐρανῷ, ἵνα
μένῃ, οὐδ' αὖ, ἵνα κατὰ φύσιν ἡ περιφορά· οὐ
γάρ πω δέδεικται οὐδὲ ἐπ' εὐθείας οὖσα ἡ κατὰ
φύσιν αὐτῷ φορά· ἢ γὰρ μένειν ἢ περιφέρεσθαι
κατὰ φύσιν αὐτοῖς· αἱ δ' ἄλλαι βιασθέντων. Οὐ
20 τοίνυν οὐδὲ τροφῆς δεῖσθαι φατέον τὰ ἐκεῖ, οὐδὲ
ἀπὸ τῶν τῇδε περὶ ἐκείνων ἀποφαντέον οὔτε ψυχὴν

fineness and non-reflecting transparency of its body (just like pure air); and besides this it is far away.

8. Now when light of this kind stays on high in the place in which it is set, pure in the purest region, what kind of outflow could there possibly be from it? A nature of this kind is certainly not naturally adapted to flow downwards; and there is nothing of a violent sort up there to push it down. Every body is different when it is combined with soul, and not the same as it is when it is left to itself; and body in the heavens is with soul, and not as it would be by itself. And that which borders on it would be either air or fire, and what could air do? And there is no single kind of fire which would be fitted for acting on the heavenly fire, nor could it make contact to do anything; the heavenly fire would be carried on by its momentum to another place before anything could happen to it; and the fire in the upper air is less in strength, not equal to the fires here on earth. Then, too, it would act by heating; and that which is going to be heated must not be hot of itself. And if anything is going to be destroyed by fire, it must be heated first, and be brought in the heating into an unnatural state. So, then, the heaven needs no other body for it to last or for its revolution to take its natural course; for it has never been demonstrated that its natural movement is in a straight line: it is natural to the heavenly bodies either to stay still or to go round in a circle; other movements belong to beings which are subject to force. We must assert, then, too, that the heavenly beings have no need of nourishment, nor must we base our statements about them on the things here on earth, since they have not the

33

τὴν αὐτὴν τὴν συνέχουσαν ἐχόντων οὔτε τὸν αὐτὸν
τόπον οὔτε αἰτίας οὔσης ἐκεῖ, δι' ἣν τὰ τῇδε
τρέφεται συγκρίματα ἀεὶ ῥέοντα, τήν τε μεταβολὴν
τῶν τῇδε σωμάτων ἀφ' αὐτῶν μεταβάλλειν ἄλλης
25 ἐπιστατούσης φύσεως αὐτοῖς, ἢ ὑπ' ἀσθενείας οὐκ
οἶδε κατέχειν ἐν τῷ εἶναι, μιμεῖται δὲ ἐν τῷ
γίνεσθαι ἢ γεννᾶν τὴν πρὸ αὐτῆς φύσιν. Τὸ δὲ μὴ
ὡσαύτως πάντη, ὥσπερ τὰ νοητά, εἴρηται.

same soul holding them together and do not inhabit the same region; and the reason why the compound things on earth are nourished does not apply in heaven; the bodies here are always in a state of flux, and their change is a change away from their true selves, for they are under the direction of another nature, which because of its weakness has no way of keeping them in being, but imitates the nature before it in becoming and generating.—But we have already explained that the heavenly bodies are not in every way unchanging like the beings of the realm of Intellect.

ENNEAD II. 2

II. 2. ON THE MOVEMENT OF HEAVEN

Introductory Note

THIS short treatise (No. 14 in Porphyry's chronological order), has an alternative title, *On the Circular Motion*, in the *Life* (ch. 4. 49 and 24. 42), which is used in some modern editions and translations. It is a defence of the Platonic doctrine (the movement of heaven is the bodily expression of the spiritual movement of the soul of the universe) against the Aristotelian conception of movement by an unmoved mover and the materialist explanation given by the Stoics. Heinemann denied the authenticity of the treatise: but its opening words are quoted as being by Plotinus by Proclus, Damascius, Simplicius and Philoponus (references in the Henry–Schwyzer edition and Cilento's commentary): and Heinemann's arguments drawn from the contents of the treatise are adequately refuted by Bréhier in his introduction to it (Vol. II, pp. 17–19).

Synopsis

What makes the heaven move in a circle? Its movement cannot be the result of any local or spatial movement of soul, for soul is not moved spatially. The movement of heaven is only local accidentally; it is a movement of awareness and life, the movement of an ensouled living thing. It cannot be the natural movement of fire; fire, like all other bodies, moves naturally in a straight line; circular motion is the result of providence, the action of universal soul—it is not of course unnatural, for " nature " is just what universal soul ordains. Argument against the idea of an unmoved mover (ch. 1). Why do we not move in circles? Our souls, our real selves, which are " private wholes," do so move, circling lovingly round God; but our bodies are only parts, and parts whose nature is to move in straight lines (ch. 2). Explanation of *Timaeus* 36E in terms of Plotinus's own psychology (ch. 3).

II. 2. (14) ΠΕΡΙ ΚΙΝΗΣΕΩΣ ΟΥΡΑΝΟΥ

1. Διὰ τί κύκλῳ κινεῖται; Ὅτι νοῦν μιμεῖται.
Καὶ τίνος ἡ κίνησις, ψυχῆς ἢ σώματος; Τί οὖν
ὅτι ψυχὴ ἐν αὐτῇ ἐστι καὶ πρὸς αὐτήν; Ἢ
σπεύδει ἰέναι; ἢ ἔστιν ἐν αὐτῇ οὐ συνεχεῖ οὖσα;
5 ἢ φερομένη συμφέρει; Ἀλλ' ἔδει συμφέρουσαν
μηκέτι φέρειν, ἀλλ' ἐνηνοχέναι, τουτέστι στῆναι
μᾶλλον ποιῆσαι καὶ μὴ ἀεὶ κύκλῳ. Ἢ καὶ αὐτὴ
στήσεται ἤ, εἰ κινεῖται, οὔτι γε τοπικῶς. Πῶς
οὖν τοπικῶς κινεῖ αὐτὴ ἄλλον τρόπον κινουμένη;
Ἢ ἴσως οὐδὲ τοπικὴ ἡ κύκλῳ, ἀλλ' εἰ ἄρα, κατὰ
10 συμβεβηκός. Ποία οὖν τις; Εἰς αὑτὴν συναισθη-
τικὴ καὶ συννοητικὴ καὶ ζωτικὴ καὶ οὐδαμοῦ ἔξω
οὐδ' ἄλλοθι· καὶ τὸ πάντα δεῖν περιλαμβάνειν·
τοῦ γὰρ ζῴου τὸ κύριον περιληπτικὸν καὶ ποιοῦν
ἕν. Οὐ περιλήψεται δὲ ζωτικῶς, εἰ μένοι, οὐδὲ
σώσει τὰ ἔνδον σῶμα ἔχον· καὶ γὰρ σώματος ζωὴ
15 κίνησις. Εἰ οὖν καὶ τοπική, ὡς δυνήσεται κινήσεται

---

[1] Cp. *Timaeus* 34A4. Throughout this chapter Plotinus
seems to have in mind Aristotle's criticism of the *Timaeus*
in *De Anima* A. 3. 407a6–407b12, and to be answering Aristotle's arguments there.

II. 2. ON THE MOVEMENT OF HEAVEN

1. Why does it move in a circle?[1] Because it imitates intellect. And what does the movement belong to, soul or body? Is it that soul is in the movement and directed towards it? Or [does it move] because soul is eager to go? Or does soul exist in a state of discontinuity? Or is soul carried along itself and carries heaven with it? But if that was so, it would be no longer carrying it round; it would have finished its conveyance; that is, it would rather make it stand still, and not always go round in a circle. Surely soul will stand still, or if it is moved is certainly not moved spatially. How, then, does it move heaven spatially when it is moved in another way itself? Perhaps the circular movement is not spatial, or if it is, only accidentally. What sort of movement, then, is it? A movement of self-concentrated awareness and intellection and of life, and at no point outside or elsewhere. And [what about] the necessity of encompassing everything? It does so in the sense that the dominant part of the living being is that which encompasses it and makes it one. If it stayed still, it would not encompass it in a living way, nor would it, since it has a body, preserve what is within it; for the life of the body is movement. If, then, there is local movement

καὶ οὐχ ὡς ψυχὴ μόνον, ἀλλ' ὡς σῶμα ἔμψυχον καὶ
ὡς ζῷον· ὥστε εἶναι μικτὴν ἐκ σωματικῆς καὶ
ψυχικῆς, τοῦ μὲν σώματος εὐθὺ φερομένου φύσει,
τῆς δὲ ψυχῆς κατεχούσης, ἐκ δ' ἀμφοῖν γενομένου
φερομένου τε καὶ μένοντος. Εἰ δὲ σώματος ἡ
20 κύκλῳ λέγοιτο, πῶς παντὸς εὐθυποροῦντος καὶ τοῦ
πυρός; Ἢ εὐθυπορεῖ, ἕως ἂν ἥκῃ εἰς τὸ οὗ
τέτακται· ὡς γὰρ ἂν ταχθῇ, οὕτω δοκεῖ καὶ
ἑστάναι κατὰ φύσιν καὶ φέρεσθαι εἰς ὃ ἐτάχθη.
Διὰ τί οὖν οὐ μένει ἐλθόν; Ἆρα, ὅτι ἡ φύσις τῷ
πυρὶ ἐν κινήσει; Εἰ οὖν μὴ κύκλῳ, σκεδασθήσεται
25 ἐπ' εὐθύ· δεῖ ἄρα κύκλῳ. Ἀλλὰ τοῦτο προνοίας·
ἀλλ' ἐν αὐτῷ παρὰ τῆς προνοίας· ὥστε, εἰ ἐκεῖ
γένοιτο, κύκλῳ κινεῖσθαι ἐξ αὐτοῦ. Ἢ ἐφιέμενον
τοῦ εὐθέος οὐκ ἔχον οὐκέτι τόπον ὥσπερ περιολισθά-
νον ἀνακάμπτει ἐν οἷς τόποις δύναται· οὐ γὰρ
ἔχει τόπον μεθ' ἑαυτό· οὗτος γὰρ ἔσχατος. Θεῖ
30 οὖν ἐν ᾧ ἔχει καὶ αὐτὸς αὐτοῦ τόπος, οὐχ ἵνα
μένῃ γεγενημένος, ἀλλ' ἵνα φέροιτο. Καὶ κύκλου
δὲ τὸ μὲν κέντρον μένει κατὰ φύσιν, ἡ δὲ ἔξωθεν
περιφέρεια εἰ μένοι, κέντρον ἔσται μέγα. Μᾶλλον
οὖν ἔσται περὶ τὸ κέντρον καὶ ζῶντι καὶ κατὰ
35 φύσιν δὲ ἔχοντι σώματι. Οὕτω γὰρ συννεύσει
πρὸς τὸ κέντρον, οὐ τῇ συνιζήσει—ἀπολεῖ γὰρ τὸν
κύκλον—ἀλλ' ἐπεὶ τοῦτο οὐ δύναται, τῇ περι-

---

[1] This is Aristotelian doctrine. Cp. *De Caelo* A. 9. 279a17–18.

too, then it will move as it can, and not as soul alone but as an ensouled body and a living thing; so its movement will be a mixture of body-movement and soul-movement; body is naturally transported in a straight line and soul's natural tendency is to contain, and from both of them together there comes to be something which is both carried along and at rest. If circular motion is to be attributed to body, how can it be when all body, including fire, moves in a straight line? It moves in a straight line till it comes to its ordained place; for as it is ordained, so it appears both to rest naturally and to be conveyed to the place where it was ordained to be. Why, then, does it not stay still when it has come to heaven? It is, is it not, because the nature of fire is to be in motion. So if it does not move in a circle, going on in a straight line will dissipate it; so it must move in a circle. But this is the doing of providence; rather, it is something in it which comes from providence, so that if it comes to heaven it moves in a circle of its own accord. It seeks to go on in a straight line, but has no longer any place to go to, so it glides round, we may say, and curves back in the regions where it can; for it has no place beyond itself; this is the last.[1] So it runs in the space it occupies and is its own place; it came to be there not in order to stay still but to move. The centre of a circle naturally stays still, but if the outside circumference stayed still, it would be a big centre. So it can rather be expected, in the case of a living body in its natural state, to go round the centre. In this way, then, it will direct itself towards the centre, not by coinciding with it— that would abolish the circle—but, since it cannot

δινήσει· οὕτω γὰρ μόνως ἀποπληρώσει τὴν ἔφεσιν.
Εἰ ψυχὴ δὲ περιάγοι, οὐ καμεῖται· οὐ γὰρ ἕλκει,
οὐδὲ παρὰ φύσιν· ἡ γὰρ φύσις τὸ ὑπὸ ψυχῆς τῆς
40 πάσης ταχθέν. Ἔτι πανταχοῦ οὖσα ἡ ψυχὴ ὅλη
καὶ οὐ διειλημμένη ἡ τοῦ παντὸς κατὰ μέρος δίδωσι
καὶ τῷ οὐρανῷ, ὡς δύναται, πανταχοῦ εἶναι·
δύναται δὲ τῷ πάντα μετιέναι καὶ ἐπιπορεύεσθαι.
Ἔστη μὲν γάρ, εἴ που ἑστῶσα ἦν ἡ ψυχή, ἐλθὸν
ἐκεῖ· νῦν δέ, ἐπειδὴ πᾶσά ἐστιν, αὐτῆς πάντη [1]
45 ἐφίεται. Τί οὖν; Οὐδέποτε τεύξεται; Ἢ οὕτως
ἀεὶ τυγχάνει, μᾶλλον δὲ αὐτὴ πρὸς αὑτὴν ἄγουσα
ἀεὶ ἐν τῷ ἀεὶ ἄγειν ἀεὶ κινεῖ, καὶ οὐκ ἀλλαχοῦ
κινοῦσα ἀλλὰ πρὸς αὑτὴν ἐν τῷ αὐτῷ, οὐκ ἐπ᾽
εὐθὺ ἀλλὰ κύκλῳ ἄγουσα δίδωσιν αὐτῷ οὗ ἐὰν
ἥκῃ ἐκεῖ ἔχειν αὐτήν. Εἰ δὲ μένοι, ὡς ἐκεῖ οὔσης
50 μόνον, οὗ ἕκαστον μένει, στήσεται. Εἰ οὖν μὴ
ἐκεῖ μόνον ὁπουοῦν, πανταχοῦ οἰσθήσεται καὶ οὐκ
ἔξω· κύκλῳ ἄρα.
  2. Τὰ οὖν ἄλλα πῶς; Ἢ οὐχ ὅλον ἕκαστον,
μέρος δὲ καὶ κατεχόμενον μερικῷ τόπῳ. Ἐκεῖνο
δὲ ὅλον καὶ οἷον τόπος καὶ οὐδὲν κωλύει· αὐτὸ
γὰρ τὸ πᾶν. Πῶς οὖν ἄνθρωποι; Ἢ, ὅσον παρὰ

---

[1] ἐστιν, αὐτῆς πάντη nunc proponunt Henry et Schwyzer:
ἐστιν αὐτῆς, παντὸς codd: H-S: ἐστιν πάντη, παντὸς Sleeman.

---

[1] This answers Aristotle, *De Anima* 407b2. Cp. *De Caelo*
B1. 284a27–35.
[2] I print and translate the reading which Schwyzer now
proposes, with Henry's agreement. The MSS πᾶσά ἐστιν

do that, by whirling round it; for in this way alone can it satisfy its impulse. But if soul does carry it round, it will not get tired; for it does not drag it, nor is the movement against nature.[1] " Nature " is just what has been ordained by universal soul. Then again, since the whole soul is everywhere and, being the soul of the All, is not divided part to part, it gives omnipresence to the heaven too, as far as it is capable of it; and it is capable of it by pursuing and reaching all things. If soul stood still anywhere, the heavenly fire would stand when it came to that point; but as it is, since soul is universal,[2] the heavenly fire seeks it in every direction. Will it never, then, attain it? In this way it always attains it; or rather, soul itself, drawing heaven to itself, moves it continually in drawing it continually, not moving it to some other place but towards itself in the same place; it does not draw it on in a straight line but in a circle, and so gives it possession of soul at every stage in its progress. If soul stayed still, being only at that point where each individual thing was at rest, then the heaven would stand still too. If, then, soul is not just there at any particular point, the heaven will move everywhere, and not outside soul; in a circle, therefore.

2. Then what about other things? Each of them is not a whole but a part, and contained in a partial place. But that other [that is heaven] is a whole; it *is* space, in a way, and there is nothing to hinder it, because it is the All. What about men, then? In

αὐτῆς, παντός, retained in the Oxford text, would give the sense, " soul all belongs to itself," which is a good Plotinian expression but not relevant to the context.

5 τοῦ παντός, μέρος, ὅσον δ' αὐτοί, οἰκεῖον ὅλον.
Εἰ οὖν πανταχοῦ οὗ ἂν ᾖ ἔχει αὐτήν, τί δεῖ
περιιέναι; Ἢ ὅτι μὴ μόνον ἐκεῖ. Εἰ δὲ ἡ δύναμις
αὐτῆς περὶ τὸ μέσον, καὶ ταύτῃ ἂν κύκλῳ· μέσον
δὲ οὐχ ὡσαύτως σώματος καὶ φύσεως ψυχῆς
ληπτέον, ἀλλ' ἐκεῖ μὲν μέσον, ἀφ' οὗ ἡ ἄλλη,
10 τοπικῶς δὲ σώματος. Ἀνάλογον οὖν δεῖ τὸ μέσον·
ὡς γὰρ ἐκεῖ, οὕτω καὶ ἐνταῦθα μέσον δεῖ εἶναι, ὃ
μόνως ἐστὶ μέσον σώματος καὶ σφαιρικοῦ· ὡς
γὰρ ἐκεῖνο περὶ αὐτό, οὕτω καὶ τοῦτο. Εἰ δὴ
ψυχῆς ἐστι, περιθέουσα τὸν θεὸν ἀμφαγαπάζεται
καὶ περὶ αὐτὸν ὡς οἷόν τε αὐτὴ ἔχει· ἐξήρτηται
15 γὰρ αὐτοῦ πάντα. Ἐπεὶ οὖν οὐκ ἔστι πρὸς αὐτόν,
περὶ αὐτόν. Πῶς οὖν οὐ πᾶσαι οὕτως; Ἢ
ἑκάστη ὅπου ἐστὶν οὕτως. Διὰ τί οὖν οὐ καὶ τὰ
σώματα ἡμῶν οὕτως; Ὅτι τὸ εὐθύπορον προσήρ-
τηται καὶ πρὸς ἄλλα αἱ ὁρμαὶ καὶ τὸ σφαιροειδὲς
ἡμῶν οὐκ εὔτροχον· γεηρὸν γάρ· ἐκεῖ δὲ συνέπεται
20 λεπτὸν καὶ εὐκίνητον· διὰ τί γὰρ ἂν καὶ σταίη
ἡντινοῦν κίνησιν τῆς ψυχῆς κινουμένης; Ἴσως
δὲ καὶ παρ' ἡμῖν τὸ πνεῦμα τὸ περὶ τὴν ψυχὴν
τοῦτο ποιεῖ. Εἰ γὰρ ἔστιν ὁ θεὸς ἐν πᾶσι, τὴν
συνεῖναι βουλομένην ψυχὴν περὶ αὐτὸν δεῖ γίγνεσθαι·

---

[1] " Our spherical part " is the head, which according to the
Timaeus (44D) is mounted on the body as its vehicle so that it
shall not have to roll about.

[2] This is a reference to the description of respiration as a
circular process, like a turning wheel, in *Timaeus* 79A5–E9.

so far as he derives from the All, man is a part, in so far as men are themselves, each is a private universe. If, then, heaven, wherever it is, possesses soul everywhere, why does it have to go round? Because it does not possess it only in that particular place. And if the soul's power is movement round its centre, in this way, too, it would make heaven move in a circle: though " centre " is not to be understood in the same way when one is speaking of the nature of soul as it is when one is speaking of a body: with soul the centre is the source from which the other nature derives, with body " centre " has a spatial meaning. So one must use " centre " analogically; there must be a centre for soul as there is for body (though " centre " in the literal sense means the middle point of a body, a spherical one), because just as a body is round its centre, so is soul. If it is the centre of soul that is in question, soul runs round God and embraces him lovingly and keeps round him as far as it can; for all things depend on him: since it cannot go to him, it goes round him. Then why do not all souls do this? Each individual soul does, in its own place. Why, then, do our bodies not go round too? Because there is an additional constituent in them which moves in straight lines, and the impulses of body are directed elsewhere, and our spherical part does not run easily, being earthy.[1] But there the body of heaven follows along with soul, being light and easy to move; why ever should it stop when it goes on moving, whatever its motion? And in us, too, it seems that the breath which is around the soul moves in a circle.[2] If God is in all things, the soul which desires to be with him must

47

οὐ γάρ πῃ. Καὶ Πλάτων δὲ τοῖς ἄστροις οὐ
25 μόνον τὴν μετὰ τοῦ ὅλου σφαιρικὴν κίνησιν, ἀλλὰ
καὶ ἑκάστῳ δίδωσι τὴν περὶ τὸ κέντρον αὐτῶν·
ἕκαστον γάρ, οὗ ἐστι, περιειληφὸς τὸν θεὸν
ἀγάλλεται οὐ λογισμῷ ἀλλὰ φυσικαῖς ἀνάγκαις.

3. Ἔστω δὲ καὶ ὧδε· τῆς ψυχῆς ἡ μέν τις
δύναμις ἡ ἐσχάτη ἀπὸ γῆς ἀρξαμένη καὶ δι᾽ ὅλου
διαπλεκεῖσά ἐστιν, ἡ δὲ αἰσθάνεσθαι πεφυκυῖα
καὶ ἡ λόγον δοξαστικὸν δεχομένη πρὸς τὸ ἄνω ἐν
5 ταῖς σφαίραις ἑαυτὴν ἔχει ἐποχουμένη καὶ τῇ
προτέρᾳ καὶ δύναμιν διδοῦσα παρ᾽ αὐτῆς εἰς τὸ
ποιεῖν ζωτικωτέραν. Κινεῖται οὖν ὑπ᾽ αὐτῆς
κύκλῳ περιεχούσης καὶ ἐφιδρυμένης παντὶ ὅσον
αὐτῆς εἰς τὰς σφαίρας ἀνέδραμε. Κύκλῳ οὖν
ἐκείνης περιεχούσης συννεύουσα ἐπιστρέφεται πρὸς
10 αὐτήν, ἡ δὲ ἐπιστροφὴ αὐτῆς περιάγει τὸ σῶμα,
ἐν ᾧ ἐμπέπλεκται. Ἑκάστου γὰρ μορίου κἂν
ὁπωσοῦν κινηθέντος ἐν σφαίρᾳ, εἰ μόνον[1] κινοῖτο,
ἔσεισεν ἐν ᾧ ἐστι καὶ τῇ σφαίρᾳ κίνησις γίνεται.
Καὶ γὰρ ἐπὶ τῶν σωμάτων τῶν ἡμετέρων τῆς
ψυχῆς ἄλλως κινουμένης, οἷον ἐν χαραῖς καὶ τῷ
15 φανέντι ἀγαθῷ, τοῦ σώματος ἡ κίνησις καὶ τοπικὴ
γίνεται. Ἐκεῖ δὴ ἐν ἀγαθῷ γινομένη ψυχὴ καὶ
αἰσθητικωτέρα γενομένη κινεῖται πρὸς τὸ ἀγαθὸν
καὶ σείει ὡς πέφυκεν ἐκεῖ τοπικῶς τὸ σῶμα. Ἥ
τε αἰσθητικὴ ἀπὸ τοῦ ἄνω αὖ καὶ αὐτὴ τὸ ἀγαθὸν

[1] μόνον H-S²: μένον codd.

48

move around him; for he is not in any place. And
Plato gives the stars not only their spherical motion
with the whole universe but also individual motions,
each around its own centre:[1] for each in its place
encompasses God and rejoices, not by rational
planning but by natural necessity.

3. This, too, is another way of putting it; there is
the ultimate power of soul which begins at the earth
and is interwoven through the whole universe,[2] and
there is the power of soul which is naturally perceptive and receives the opinionative kind of reasoning;
this keeps itself above in the heavenly spheres and is
in contact with the other from above and gives it
power from itself to make it more alive. The lower
soul, therefore, is moved by the higher which encompasses it in a circle and bears upon all of it that has
risen to the spheres. So the lower soul, as the higher
encircles it, inclines and tends towards it, and its
tendency carries round the body with which it is
interwoven. For if any particular part of a sphere
is moved even in the slightest degree, then, if it
only is moved, it stirs that in which it is and the
sphere is set in motion. In our bodies too, when
our soul is moved in a different way from the body
—by joy, for instance, and by something which
appears good to it—then there is a spatial movement of the body as well. And in heaven, where
the soul is in good and more vividly perceptive, it
moves to the good and sets its body moving in space
in the manner natural to it there. The perceptive
power in its turn receives the good from that which

---

[1] Cp. *Timaeus* 40A8–B2.
[2] *Timaeus* 36E2.

λαβοῦσα καὶ τὰ αὐτῆς ἡσθεῖσα διώκουσα αὐτὸ ὂν
20 πανταχοῦ πρὸς τὸ πανταχοῦ συμφέρεται. Ὁ δὲ
νοῦς οὕτω κινεῖται· ἔστηκε γὰρ καὶ κινεῖται· περὶ
αὐτὸν γάρ. Οὕτως οὖν καὶ τὸ πᾶν τῷ κύκλῳ
κινεῖται ἅμα καὶ ἔστηκεν.

is above and in delight pursues its own and is
carried everywhere to the good which is everywhere.
This is how intellect is moved; it is both at rest and
in motion; for it moves around Him [the Good]. So,
then, the universe, too, both moves in its circle and is
at rest.

ENNEAD II. 3

II. 3. ON WHETHER THE STARS ARE CAUSES

Introductory Note

THIS very late treatise (No. 52 in Porphyry's chronological order) takes up again and develops the objections to the ideas of the astrologers about the stars which Plotinus had already put forward in the early work *On Destiny* (III. 1: No. 3 in the chronological order). Plotinus does not deny that the stars foretell, or even that influences coming from them may make a limited contribution to our fortunes and physical make-up. He finds the astrologers objectionable because: (1) they make stars evil and causes of evil to us; (2) they make them changeable, varying in mood and activity according to their aspect and position, a view which Plotinus shows is unscientific, incompatible with the findings of the astronomers, as well as unorthodox from the point of view of Platonic astral theology; (3) they reduce the universe to a disorderly chaos by making the stars act independently and capriciously, instead of seeing it as a living organic whole in which star-movements and influences as well as everything else form part of the pattern of its rational direction by Universal Soul; (4) they very much exaggerate the degree to which the stars are responsible for our physical constitution and fortunes; star-influences are only one kind of cause among many, and not the most important. Further, Plotinus maintains in this as in other treatises (notably that which he wrote next, I. 1) that our true, higher self transcends the physical universe and is beyond the reach of its necessity.

A curious little problem is presented by the section

printed in square brackets in ch. 12 (if it really belongs to this treatise it would fit in better where the translation of Ficino and the *editio princeps* of Perna place it, immediately before the last sentence of ch. 5). This seems to be more favourable to the views of the astrologers than the rest of the treatise, and even to be trying to answer the scientific objections brought against them in ch. 5, though it expresses the view of the universe as an organic whole which is found elsewhere in the treatise and is always taken by Plotinus. It looks almost as if it was a fragment of an essay written by a member of the school in defence of astrology, rather like the papers written by Porphyry in defence of the doctrine of Longinus and answered by Amelius which are mentioned in ch. 18 of the *Life*. But, if this were really what it was, it would be very difficult to explain how it got into the text of this treatise—there is no parallel anywhere else in the *Enneads*.

Synopsis

Detailed refutation of astrological doctrines by scientific and common-sense arguments (chs. 1–6). Explanation of why the stars give signs of things to come from the organic unity of the universe (chs. 7–8). Our higher and lower self (ch. 9). The real nature and limitations of astral influences and the modest part they play in determining our constitution and fortunes (chs. 10–15). How soul directs the All, and reasons for the existence of evils in this world (chs. 16–18).

II. 3. (52) ΠΕΡΙ ΤΟΥ ΕΙ ΠΟΙΕΙ ΤΑ ΑΣΤΡΑ

1. Ὅτι ἡ τῶν ἄστρων φορὰ σημαίνει περὶ
ἕκαστον τὰ ἐσόμενα, ἀλλ' οὐκ αὐτὴ πάντα ποιεῖ,
ὡς τοῖς πολλοῖς δοξάζεται, εἴρηται μὲν πρότερον
ἐν ἄλλοις,[1] καὶ πίστεις τινὰς παρείχετο ὁ λόγος,
5 λεκτέον δὲ καὶ νῦν ἀκριβέστερον διὰ πλειόνων·
οὐ γὰρ μικρὸν τὸ ἢ ὧδε ἢ ὧδε ἔχειν δοξάζειν.
Τοὺς δὴ πλανήτας φερομένους ποιεῖν λέγουσιν οὐ
μόνον τὰ ἄλλα, πενίας καὶ πλούτους καὶ ὑγιείας
καὶ νόσους, ἀλλὰ καὶ αἴσχη καὶ κάλλη αὖ, καὶ δὴ
τὸ μέγιστον, καὶ κακίας καὶ ἀρετὰς καὶ δὴ καὶ τὰς
10 ἀπὸ τούτων πράξεις καθ' ἕκαστα ἐπὶ καιρῶν
ἑκάστων, ὥσπερ θυμουμένους εἰς ἀνθρώπους, ἐφ'
οἷς μηδὲν αὐτοὶ οἱ ἄνθρωποι ἀδικοῦσιν οὕτω παρ'
αὐτῶν κατεσκευασμένοι, ὡς ἔχουσι· καὶ τὰ λεγό-
μενα ἀγαθὰ διδόναι οὐκ ἀγασθέντας τῶν λαμβανόντων, ἀλλ' αὐτοὺς ἢ κακουμένους κατὰ τόπους
15 τῆς φορᾶς ἢ αὖ εὐπαθοῦντας καὶ αὖ ἄλλους αὐτοὺς
ταῖς διανοίαις γιγνομένους ὅταν τε ἐπὶ κέντρων
ὧσι καὶ ἀποκλίνοντας ἄλλους· τὸ δὲ μέγιστον,

---

[1] III.1. 5. 33 ff.
[2] For a full explanation of the astrological doctrines criticised in these first six chapters see A. Bouché-Leclercq,
L'Astrologie Grecque; there is an excellent short account

II. 3. ON WHETHER THE STARS
ARE CAUSES

1. That the course of the stars indicates what is
going to happen in particular cases, but does not
itself cause everything, as most people think, has
been said before elsewhere [1] (and the argument of-
fered some proofs); but now we need a more precise
and detailed discussion, for to take one view rather
than the other is of no small importance. They say
that the planets in their courses do not only cause
everything else, poverty and riches, sickness and
health, but also ugliness and beauty and, what is
most important of all, virtue and vice, and even the
actions which result from them in each particular
case on each particular occasion; just as if they were
angry with men over things in which men have done
them no wrong, since it was the planets which made
the men what they are; and that they give benefits
(so-called), not because they feel kindly towards those
who receive them but because they themselves are
either pleasantly or unpleasantly affected according
to the point they have reached on their course, and
again are in a different state of mind when they are
at their zeniths and when they are declining; [2] and

of the basic absurdities of this pseudo-science in A. J. Festugière, *La Révélation d'Hermès Trismégiste* I. ch. V, pp. 89–
101.

τοὺς μὲν κακοὺς αὐτῶν λέγοντες, τοὺς δὲ ἀγαθοὺς
εἶναι, ὅμως καὶ τοὺς κακοὺς αὐτῶν λεγομένους
ἀγαθὰ διδόναι, τοὺς δ' ἀγαθοὺς φαύλους γίγνεσθαι·
20 ἔτι δὲ ἀλλήλους ἰδόντας ποιεῖν ἕτερα, μὴ ἰδόντας
δὲ ἄλλα, ὥσπερ οὐχ αὑτῶν ὄντας ἀλλὰ ἰδόντας μὲν
ἄλλους, μὴ ἰδόντας δὲ ἑτέρους· καὶ τόνδε μὲν
ἰδόντα ἀγαθὸν εἶναι, εἰ δ' ἄλλον ἴδοι, ἀλλοιοῦσθαι·
καὶ ἄλλως μὲν ὁρᾶν, εἰ κατὰ σχῆμα τόδε ἡ ὄψις,
ἄλλως δέ, εἰ κατὰ τόδε· ὁμοῦ τε πάντων τὴν
25 κρᾶσιν ἑτέραν γίγνεσθαι, ὥσπερ ἐξ ὑγρῶν διαφόρων
τὸ κρᾶμα ἕτερον παρὰ τὰ μεμιγμένα. Ταῦτα οὖν
καὶ τὰ τοιαῦτα δοξαζόντων περὶ ἑκάστου λέγειν
ἐπισκοπουμένους προσήκει. Ἀρχὴ δ' ἂν εἴη
προσήκουσα αὕτη.

2. Πότερα ἔμψυχα νομιστέον ἢ ἄψυχα ταῦτα τὰ
φερόμενα; Εἰ μὲν γὰρ ἄψυχα, οὐδὲν ἀλλ' ἢ θερμὰ
καὶ ψυχρὰ παρεχόμενα, εἰ δὴ καὶ ψυχρὰ ἄττα τῶν
ἄστρων φήσομεν, ἀλλ' οὖν ἐν τῇ τῶν σωμάτων
5 ἡμῶν φύσει στήσουσι τὴν δόσιν φορᾶς δηλονότι
σωματικῆς εἰς ἡμᾶς γινομένης, ὡς μηδὲ πολλὴν
τὴν παραλλαγὴν τῶν σωμάτων γίνεσθαι τῆς τε
ἀπορροῆς ἑκάστων τῆς αὐτῆς οὔσης καὶ δὴ ὁμοῦ
εἰς ἓν ἐπὶ γῆς μιγνυμένων, ὡς μόνον κατὰ τοὺς
τόπους τὰς διαφορὰς γίγνεσθαι ἐκ τοῦ ἐγγύθεν καὶ
10 πόρρωθεν, πρὸς τὴν διαφορὰν διδόντος καὶ τοῦ
ψυχροῦ ὡσαύτως. Σοφοὺς δὲ καὶ ἀμαθεῖς καὶ
γραμματικοὺς ἄλλους, τοὺς δὲ ῥήτορας, τοὺς δὲ

the most important point is, they say that some of the planets are bad and others good, but that the ones which are called bad give good gifts, and the good ones become wicked; and again that when they see each other they cause one kind of thing, when they do not see, another, as if they were not really in control of themselves but varied according to whether they saw or not; and that a planet is good when it sees this particular other planet, but changes if it sees another one; and that it sees differently according to whether its seeing is in this figure or in that; and that the mixture of all the planets together is different again, just as the mixture of distinct liquids is something unlike any of the ingredients. These, and others of the same kind, are their opinions: now we ought to examine and discuss each individual point. This would be a good starting-point.

2. Should we think that these things which go round in their courses have souls or not? If they have no souls, they will have nothing to offer but heat or cold—if we assume that some of the stars are cold; however that may be, they will determine our given destiny only in our bodily nature, since there is a corporeal transference from them to us, and one of such a kind that the alteration it produces in our bodies is not great, since the outflow from each individual star is the same, and they are all mixed together into one on earth, so that the only differences are local differences, according to how near or far we are from the stars—and the cold kind of star will give an influence differentiated in the same way. But, then, how will they make some men wise and some foolish, some teachers of letters and others of rhetoric,

κιθαριστὰς καὶ τὰς ἄλλας τέχνας, ἔτι δὲ πλουσίους
καὶ πένητας, πῶς; Καὶ τὰ ἄλλα, ὅσα μὴ ἐκ
σωμάτων κράσεως τὴν αἰτίαν ἔχει τοῦ γίγνεσθαι;
15 Οἷον καὶ ἀδελφὸν τοιόνδε καὶ πατέρα καὶ υἱὸν
γυναῖκά τε καὶ τὸ νῦν εὐτυχῆσαι καὶ στρατηγὸν
καὶ βασιλέα γενέσθαι. Εἰ δ' ἔμψυχα ὄντα προαιρέ-
σει ποιεῖ, τί παρ' ἡμῶν παθόντα κακὰ ἡμᾶς ποιεῖ
ἑκόντα, καὶ ταῦτα ἐν θείῳ τόπῳ ἱδρυμένα καὶ
αὐτὰ θεῖα ὄντα; Οὐδὲ γάρ, δι' ἃ ἄνθρωποι
20 γίγνονται κακοί, ταῦτα ἐκείνοις ὑπάρχει, οὐδέ γε
ὅλως γίνεται ἢ ἀγαθὸν ἢ κακὸν αὐτοῖς ἡμῶν ἢ
εὐπαθούντων ἢ κακὰ πασχόντων.

3. Ἀλλ' οὐχ ἑκόντες ταῦτα, ἀλλ' ἠναγκασμένοι
τοῖς τόποις καὶ τοῖς σχήμασιν. Ἀλλ' εἰ ἠναγκασμένοι, τὰ αὐτὰ δήπουθεν ἐχρῆν ἅπαντας ποιεῖν
ἐπὶ τῶν αὐτῶν τόπων καὶ σχημάτων γινομένους.
5 Νῦν δὲ τί διάφορον πέπονθεν ὅδε τόδε τὸ τμῆμα
τοῦ τῶν ζῳδίων κύκλου παριὼν καὶ αὖ τόδε;
Οὐ γὰρ δὴ οὐδ' ἐν αὐτῷ τῷ ζῳδίῳ γίνεται, ἀλλ'
ὑπ' αὐτὸ πλεῖστον ἀπέχων, καὶ καθ' ὁποῖον ἂν
γίγνηται κατὰ τὸν οὐρανὸν ὤν. Γελοῖον γὰρ καθ'
ἕκαστον ὧν τις παρέρχεται ἄλλον καὶ ἄλλον
10 γίγνεσθαι καὶ διδόναι ἄλλα καὶ ἄλλα· ἀνατέλλων
δὲ καὶ ἐπὶ κέντρου γεγονὼς καὶ ἀποκλίνας ἄλλος.
Οὐ γὰρ δὴ τοτὲ μὲν ἥδεται ἐπὶ τοῦ κέντρου ὤν,
τοτὲ δὲ λυπεῖται ἀποκλίνας ἢ ἀργὸς γίνεται, οὐδ'

and others lyre-players and practitioners of the other arts, or again rich and poor? How will they produce the other effects which do not have their cause of origin in bodily mixture? For instance, how will they give a man a brother or a father, a son or a wife of a particular kind, or make him prosper for the moment and become a general or a king? But if they have souls and act with conscious purpose, what have we done to them to make them deliberately injure us, these beings which are set in a divine region and are divine themselves? They do not have what makes men evil, nor does any good or evil to them result from our happiness or suffering.

3. But the planets do not do these things willingly, but under the compulsion of their positions and figures! But if they are under compulsion, they ought, surely, all to do the same things when they are in the same positions and figures. And really, what difference can it make to a particular planet that it is passing through, now this and now that section of the zodiac? It is not even in the zodiac itself but far below it, and at whatever point it is, it is in heaven. It is ridiculous for a planet to become different and to give different gifts according to the sign it is passing; and to be different when it is rising and when it stands at the centre and when it is declining. It is certainly not pleased when it is at the centre, nor is it distressed and enfeebled when it is declining, nor does a planet grow angry when it is rising and gentle when it is declining—and another of them is even better when it is declining. For each particular planet is at the centre for some when it is declining in relation to others, and when it is declining for one group it is at

61

αὖ θυμοῦται ἀνατείλας ἄλλος, πραΰνεται δὲ ἀποκλίνας, εἷς δέ τις αὐτῶν καὶ ἀποκλίνας ἀμείνων.
15 Ἔστι γὰρ ἀεὶ ἕκαστος καὶ ἐπίκεντρος ἄλλοις
ἀποκλίνας ἄλλοις καὶ ἀποκλίνας ἑτέροις ἐπίκεντρος
ἄλλοις· καὶ οὐ δήπου κατὰ τὸν αὐτὸν χρόνον
χαίρει τε καὶ λυπεῖται καὶ θυμοῦται καὶ πρᾶός
ἐστι. Τὸ δὲ τοὺς μὲν αὐτῶν χαίρειν λέγειν
δύνοντας, τοὺς δὲ ἐν ἀνατολαῖς ὄντας, πῶς οὐκ
20 ἄλογον; Καὶ γὰρ οὕτω συμβαίνει ἅμα λυπεῖσθαί
τε καὶ χαίρειν. Εἶτα διὰ τί ἡ ἐκείνων λύπη ἡμᾶς
κακώσει; Ὅλως δὲ οὐδὲ λυπεῖσθαι οὐδ' ἐπὶ
καιροῦ χαίρειν αὐτοῖς δοτέον, ἀλλ' ἀεὶ τὸ ἵλεων
ἔχειν χαίροντας ἐφ' οἷς ἀγαθοῖς ἔχουσι καὶ ἐφ' οἷς
ὁρῶσι. Βίος γὰρ ἑκάστῳ ἐφ' αὑτοῦ, ἑκάστῳ καὶ
25 ἐν τῇ ἐνεργείᾳ τὸ εὖ· τὸ δὲ οὐ πρὸς ἡμᾶς. Καὶ
μάλιστα τοῖς οὐ κοινωνοῦσιν ἡμῖν ζῴοις κατὰ
συμβεβηκός, οὐ προηγούμενον· οὐδὲ ὅλως τὸ
ἔργον πρὸς ἡμᾶς, εἰ ὥσπερ ὄρνισι κατὰ συμβεβηκὸς
τὸ σημαίνειν.

4. Κἀκεῖνο δὲ ἄλογον, τόνδε μὲν τόνδε ὁρῶντα
χαίρειν, τόνδε δὲ τόνδε τοὐναντίον· τίς γὰρ
αὐτοῖς ἔχθρα ἢ περὶ τίνων; Διὰ τί δὲ τρίγωνος
μὲν ὁρῶν ἄλλως, ἐξ ἐναντίας δὲ ἢ τετράγωνος
5 ἄλλως; Διὰ τί δὲ ὡδὶ μὲν ἐσχηματισμένος ὁρᾷ,
κατὰ δὲ τὸ ἑξῆς ζῴδιον ἐγγυτέρω ὢν μᾶλλον οὐχ
ὁρᾷ; Ὅλως δὲ τίς καὶ ὁ τρόπος ἔσται τοῦ ποιεῖν
ἃ λέγονται ποιεῖν; Πῶς τε χωρὶς ἕκαστος καὶ ἔτι
πῶς ὁμοῦ πάντες ἄλλο ἐκ πάντων; Οὐ γὰρ δὴ
συνθέμενοι πρὸς ἀλλήλους οὕτω ποιοῦσιν εἰς ἡμᾶς

the centre for another; and it cannot, presumably, be glad and sad and angry and gentle all at the same time. And surely it is quite irrational to say that some planets are glad when they are setting and others when they are rising; this would again have the consequence that they are glad and sad at the same time. And then, why should their grief harm us? But one cannot admit at all that they are glad on one occasion and sad on another. They are always serene and rejoice in the goods they have and in what they see. For each has its own life to itself, and each one's good is in its own act, and has nothing to do with us. The action on us of living beings that have no part with us is always something incidental, not their dominant activity. If, as with birds, their acting as signs is incidental, their work is not directed to us at all.

4. It is irrational, too, to say that one planet is glad when it sees a particular other planet, but another is in the opposite state when it sees another: for what enmity is there between them, and about what? And why should it make a difference whether one planet sees another triangularly or in opposition or quadrilaterally?[1] And why should one see another in one particular figure, but not see it when it is in the next sign of the zodiac, and so nearer? And altogether, how ever do they manage to do what they are supposed to do? How does each act separately, and again how do they all together produce an effect different from all their separate effects? They certainly do not hold meetings and then execute the

[1] On the doctrine of " aspects " see Bouché-Leclercq, p. 165 (summarised in Festugière, p. 100).

10 τὰ δόξαντα ὑφεὶς ἕκαστός τι τῶν ἀφ' αὑτοῦ, οὐδ'
αὖ ἄλλος ἐκώλυσε τὴν τοῦ ἑτέρου δόσιν γενέσθαι
βιασάμενος, οὐδ' αὖ ὁ ἕτερος παρεχώρησε τῷ
ἑτέρῳ πεισθεὶς αὐτῷ πράττειν. Τὸ δὲ τόνδε μὲν
χαίρειν ἐν τοῖς τοῦδε γενόμενον, ἀνάπαλιν δὲ τὸν
ἕτερον ἐν τοῖς τοῦ ἑτέρου γενόμενον. πῶς οὐχ
15 ὅμοιον, ὥσπερ ἂν εἴ τις ὑποθέμενος δύο φιλοῦντας
ἀλλήλους ἔπειτα λέγοι τὸν μὲν ἕτερον φιλεῖν τὸν
ἕτερον, ἀνάπαλιν δὲ θάτερον μισεῖν θάτερον;

5. Λέγοντες δὲ ψυχρόν τινα αὐτῶν εἶναι, ἔτι
πόρρω γινόμενον ἀφ' ἡμῶν μᾶλλον ἡμῖν ἀγαθὸν
εἶναι, ἐν τῷ ψυχρῷ τὸ κακὸν αὐτοῦ εἰς ἡμᾶς
τιθέμενοι· καίτοι ἔδει ἐν τοῖς ἀντικειμένοις ζῳδίοις
5 ἀγαθὸν ἡμῖν εἶναι· καὶ ἐναντίους γινομένους τὸν
ψυχρὸν τῷ θερμῷ δεινοὺς ἀμφοτέρους γίνεσθαι·
καίτοι ἔδει κρᾶσιν εἶναι· καὶ τόνδε μὲν χαίρειν τῇ
ἡμέρᾳ καὶ ἀγαθὸν γίνεσθαι θερμαινόμενον, τόνδε
δὲ τῇ νυκτὶ χαίρειν πυρώδη ὄντα, ὥσπερ οὐκ ἀεὶ
ἡμέρας αὐτοῖς οὔσης, λέγω δὲ φωτός, ἢ τοῦ ἑτέρου
10 καταλαμβανομένου ὑπὸ νυκτὸς πολὺ ὑπεράνω τῆς
σκιᾶς τῆς γῆς ὄντος. Τὸ δὲ τὴν σελήνην πλησίφω-
τον μὲν οὖσαν ἀγαθὴν εἶναι τῷδε συνερχομένην,
λείπουσαν δὲ κακήν, ἀνάπαλιν, εἴπερ δοτέον.
Πλήρης γὰρ οὖσα πρὸς ἡμᾶς ἐκείνῳ ὑπεράνω ὄντι
ἀφώτιστος ἂν εἴη τῷ ἑτέρῳ ἡμισφαιρίῳ, λείπουσα
15 δὲ ἡμῖν ἐκείνῳ πλησίφως· ὥστε τὰ ἐναντία ποιεῖν
ἔδει λείπουσαν, ἐκεῖνον[1] μετὰ φωτὸς ὁρῶσαν. Αὐτῇ

[1] ἐκεῖνον Müller, H-S²: ἐκείνῳ codd.

decision of the meeting on us, each surrendering something of his own influence, nor does one hinder by force the giving of another from coming to pass, nor does one yield under persuasion a free field of action to another. And to suppose that one is glad when it is in the region of another, but the other, when it is in the region of the first, feels the reverse, is like saying that two people love each other, and then going on to add that one loves the other but the other hates the first!

5. Then they say that one of the planets is cold, and further, that when it is far away from us it is better for us, assuming that its harmfulness for us consists in its coldness; but it ought, when it is in the opposed signs of the zodiac, to be good for us: and they say that when the cold planet is in opposition to the hot both are dangerous: but there ought to be a blend of temperaments. They allege that one planet delights in the day and becomes good when it is warmed, but another, a fiery one, enjoys the night—as if it was not always day (that is, light) for the planets, and as if the second one was ever overtaken by night, though it is far above the shadow of the earth. And as for their statement that the moon when she is full is good in conjunction with a particular planet, but bad when she is waning, the reverse would be true, if this sort of thing is to be admitted as possible at all. For when she is full in relation to us she would be dark in the other hemisphere to the planet which stands above her, and when she is waning for us she is full for that planet: so she ought to do the opposite when she is waning [for us] since she is looking at that planet with her full light. It will make no difference

65

μὲν οὖν ὅπως ἐχούσῃ οὐδὲν διαφέροι ἂν τὸ ἥμισυ
ἀεὶ φωτιζομένῃ· τῷ δ' ἴσως διαφέροι ἂν θερμαινο-
μένῳ, ὡς λέγουσιν. Ἀλλὰ θερμαίνοιτο ἄν, εἰ
ἀφώτιστος πρὸς ἡμᾶς ἡ σελήνη εἴη· πρὸς δὲ τὸν
20 ἕτερον ἀγαθὴ οὖσα ἐν τῷ ἀφωτίστῳ πλήρης ἐστὶ
πρὸς αὐτόν. Ταῦτ' οὖν πῶς οὐ σημεῖα ἐξ ἀναλογίας
εἴη ἄν;

6. Ἄρεα δὲ τόνδε ἢ Ἀφροδίτην θεμένους
μοιχείας ποιεῖν, εἰ ὡδὶ εἶεν, ὥσπερ ἐκ τῆς τῶν
ἀνθρώπων ἀκολασίας αὐτοὺς ἐμπιπλάντας ὧν πρὸς
ἀλλήλους δέονται, πῶς οὐ πολλὴν ἀλογίαν ἔχει;
5 Καὶ τὴν μὲν θέαν αὐτοῖς τὴν πρὸς ἀλλήλους, εἰ
οὑτωσὶ θεῶντο, ἡδεῖαν εἶναι, πέρας δὲ αὐτοῖς
μηδὲν εἶναι, πῶς ἄν τις παραδέξαιτο; Μυριάδων
δὲ ζῴων ἀναριθμήτων γινομένων καὶ οὐσῶν ἑκάστῳ
τελεῖν ἀεὶ τὸ τοι⟨όν⟩δε, δόξαν αὐτοῖς διδόναι,
πλουτεῖν ποιεῖν, πένητας, ἀκολάστους, καὶ τὰς
10 ἐνεργείας ἑκάστων αὐτοὺς τελεῖν, τίς αὐτοῖς ἐστι
βίος; Ἢ πῶς δυνατὸν τοσαῦτα ποιεῖν; Τὸ δὲ
ἀναφορὰς ζῳδίων ἀναμένειν καὶ τότε τελεῖν, καὶ
ὅσαις μοίραις ἀνατέλλει ἕκαστον, ἐνιαυτοὺς εἶναι
τοσούτους τῆς ἀναφορᾶς, καὶ οἷον ἐπὶ δακτύλων
τίθεσθαι, ὅτε ποιήσουσι, μὴ ἐξεῖναι δ' αὐτοῖς πρὸ

---

[1] At this point the *editio princeps* and Ficino's translation
insert the puzzling passage printed in square brackets in ch.
12 (on which see *Introductory Note*) which would certainly be
more in place here.

[2] This sentence, which does not seem to belong to the argument here, may possibly have strayed from the beginning of
ch. 7.

whatever to the moon herself what phase she is in since half of her is always illuminated; it might, however, on their assumption, make some difference to the planet when it is warmed. But it would be warmed when the moon is dark in relation to us: when it is good in relation to the other planet in the dark phase it is, in relation to it, full.[1] Surely, then, these things are signs from the correspondence of different spheres . . .[2]

6. But it is surely absolute nonsense for the astrologers, having called one planet Ares and another Aphrodite, to say they cause adulteries when they are in a certain relationship, as if they satisfied their desires for each other from men's abandoned wickedness. And how could anyone accept that the sight of each other, in a particular aspect, gives them pleasure, but they have no limit[3]? And what sort of a life is it for the planets if, when innumerable living beings have been born and continue to exist, they are always effecting something for each one of them, giving them reputation, making them rich or poor or wicked, being themselves responsible for bringing the activities of all the separate individuals to completion. How could they do so much? And as for thinking that they wait for the ascendancy of the signs of the zodiac and then act, and that according to the number of degrees it has risen are the number of years of its ascendancy, and that they reckon on their fingers the time when they will act, and may not act before these periods are reached, and altogether to refuse

---

[3] πέρας here seems to make very little sense. L. A. Post suggests πεῖρας in the sexual sense, "intercourse".

15 τούτων τῶν χρόνων, ὅλως δὲ μηδενὶ ἑνὶ τὸ κύριον
τῆς διοικήσεως διδόναι, τούτοις δὲ τὰ πάντα
διδόναι, ὥσπερ οὐκ ἐπιστατοῦντος ἑνός, ἀφ᾽ οὗ
διηρτῆσθαι τὸ πᾶν, ἑκάστῳ διδόντος κατὰ φύσιν
τὸ αὑτοῦ περαίνειν καὶ ἐνεργεῖν τὰ αὑτοῦ συντεταγ-
μένον αὖ μετ᾽ αὐτοῦ, λύοντός ἐστι καὶ ἀγνοοῦντος
20 κόσμου φύσιν ἀρχὴν ἔχοντος καὶ αἰτίαν πρώτην
ἐπὶ πάντα ἰοῦσαν.

7. Ἀλλ᾽ εἰ σημαίνουσιν οὗτοι τὰ ἐσόμενα, ὥσπερ
φαμὲν πολλὰ καὶ ἄλλα σημαντικὰ εἶναι τῶν
ἐσομένων, τί ἂν τὸ ποιοῦν εἴη; Καὶ ἡ τάξις πῶς;
Οὐ γὰρ ἂν ἐσημαίνετο τεταγμένως μὴ ἑκάστων
5 γιγνομένων. Ἔστω τοίνυν ὥσπερ γράμματα ἐν
οὐρανῷ γραφόμενα ἀεὶ ἢ γεγραμμένα καὶ κινούμενα,
ποιοῦντα μέν τι ἔργον καὶ ἄλλο· ἐπακολουθείτω δὲ
τῷδε ἡ παρ᾽ αὐτῶν σημασία, ὡς ἀπὸ μιᾶς ἀρχῆς
ἐν ἑνὶ ζῴῳ παρ᾽ ἄλλου μέρους ἄλλο ἄν τις μάθοι.
Καὶ γὰρ καὶ ἦθος ἄν τις γνοίη εἰς ὀφθαλμούς
10 τινος ἰδὼν ἤ τι ἄλλο μέρος τοῦ σώματος καὶ
κινδύνους καὶ σωτηρίας. Καὶ οὖν μέρη μὲν ἐκεῖνα,
μέρη δὲ καὶ ἡμεῖς· ἄλλα οὖν ἄλλοις. Μεστὰ δὲ
πάντα σημείων καὶ σοφός τις ὁ μαθὼν ἐξ ἄλλου
ἄλλο. Πολλὰ δὲ ἤδη ἐν συνηθείᾳ γιγνόμενα
γινώσκεται πᾶσι. Τίς οὖν ἡ σύνταξις ἡ μία;
15 Οὕτω γὰρ καὶ τὸ κατὰ τοὺς ὄρνεις εὔλογον καὶ τὰ

---

[1] The thought here is Stoic. Cp., e.g., Seneca, *Naturales Quaestiones* II. 32.

to grant to any one principle authority over the direction of the universe, but to give everything to the planets, as if there was not one ruler, from whom the universe has separated out, and who gives to each according to its nature to fulfil its own function and do its own work, in union with the ruling principle— this is the opinion of someone who wants to dissolve the unity of the universe and knows nothing about its nature; the universe which has a principle and first cause which reaches to everything.

7. But if these planets give signs of things to come —as we maintain that many other things do—what might the cause be? How does the order work? There would be no signifying if particular things did not happen according to some order. Let us suppose that the stars are like characters always being written on the heavens, or written once for all and moving as they perform their task, a different one: and let us assume that their significance results from this, just as because of the one principle in a single living being, by studying one member we can learn something else about a different one. For instance, we can come to conclusions about someone's character, and also about the dangers that beset him and the precautions to be taken, by looking at his eyes or some other part of his body. Yes, they are members and so are we; so we can learn about one from the other. All things are filled full of signs,[1] and it is a wise man who can learn about one thing from another. Yet, all the same, many processes of learning in this way are customary and known to all. Then what is the single-linked order? If there is one, our auguries from birds and other living creatures, by which we

ἄλλα ζῷα, ἀφ' ὧν σημαινόμεθα ἕκαστα. Συνη-
ρτῆσθαι δὴ δεῖ ἀλλήλοις τὰ πάντα—καὶ μὴ μόνον ἐν
ἑνὶ τῶν καθ' ἕκαστα—τοῦ εὖ εἰρημένου—σύμπνοια
μία, ἀλλὰ πολὺ μᾶλλον καὶ πρότερον ἐν τῷ παντί—
καὶ μίαν ἀρχὴν ἓν πολὺ ζῷον ποιῆσαι καὶ ἐκ
20 πάντων ἕν, καὶ ὡς ἑνὶ ἑκάστῳ τὰ μέρη ἕν τι ἔργον
ἕκαστον εἴληφεν, οὕτω καὶ τὰ ἐν τῷ παντὶ ἕκαστα
ἔργα ἕκαστον ἔχειν καὶ μᾶλλον ἢ ταῦτα, ὅσον μὴ
μόνον μέρη, ἀλλὰ καὶ ὅλα καὶ μείζω. Πρόεισι
μὲν δὴ ἕκαστον ἀπὸ μιᾶς τὸ αὐτοῦ πρᾶττον,
συμβάλλει δὲ ἄλλο ἄλλῳ· οὐ γὰρ ἀπήλλακται τοῦ
25 ὅλου· καὶ δὴ καὶ ποιεῖ καὶ πάσχει ὑπ' ἄλλων καὶ
ἄλλο αὖ προσῆλθε καὶ ἐλύπησεν ἢ ἦσε. Πρόεισι
δὲ οὐκ εἰκῇ οὐδὲ κατ' ἐπιτυχίαν· καὶ γὰρ ἄλλο τι
καὶ ἐκ τούτων καὶ ἐφεξῆς κατὰ φύσιν ἄλλο.

8. Καὶ δὴ καὶ ψυχὴ τὸ αὑτῆς ἔργον ποιεῖν
ὡρμημένη—ψυχὴ γὰρ πάντα ποιεῖ ἀρχῆς ἔχουσα
λόγον—κἂν εὐθυποροῖ καὶ παράγοιτο αὖ, καὶ
ἕπεται τοῖς δρωμένοις ἐν τῷ παντὶ δίκη, εἴπερ μὴ
5 λυθήσεται. Μένει δ' ἀεὶ ὀρθουμένου τοῦ ὅλου
τάξει καὶ δυνάμει τοῦ κρατοῦντος· συνεργοῦντα

---

[1] The σύμπνοια of the universe is also Stoic (Posidonius and
others), cp. Diogenes Laertius VII. 140.
[2] This Platonic conception (*Timaeus* 30D–31A) developed
by the Stoics of the universe as a single living being is of great
importance in the thought of Plotinus cp. e.g., IV. 4. 32 ff.
[3] Bouillet is probably right in supposing that Plotinus here
had in mind the great passage about Soul, divine and human,

predict particular events, are reasonable. All things must be joined to one another; not only must there be in each individual part what is well called a single united breath of life [1] but before them, and still more, in the All. One principle must make the universe a single complex living creature, one from all; [2] and just as in individual organisms each member undertakes its own particular task, so the members of the All, each individual one of them, have their individual work to do; this applies even more to the All than to particular organisms, in so far as the members of it are not merely members but wholes, and more important than the members of particular things. Each one goes forth from one single principle and does its own work, but they also co-operate one with another; for they are not cut off from the whole. They act on and are affected by others; one comes up to another, bringing it pain or pleasure. Their going out has nothing random or casual about it. Something else proceeds again from these; and something else in succession from that, according to the order of nature.

8. Soul, then, is set upon doing its own work—for soul, since it has the status of a principle, does everything—and it may keep to the straight path [3] and it may also be led astray; and just payment follows upon what is done in the All; otherwise it will be dissolved.[4] But the All remains for ever, since the whole is directed by the ordering and the power of its ruler. And the stars co-operate towards the whole,

---

in Plato, *Phaedrus* 245C ff.: so εὐθυποροῖ here may be a reminiscence of μετεωροπορεῖ 246C1.

[4] A reminiscence of *Timaeus* 41A8.

δὲ καὶ τὰ ἄστρα ὡς ἂν μόρια οὐ σμικρὰ ὄντα τοῦ
οὐρανοῦ πρὸς τὸ ὅλον ἀριπρεπῆ καὶ πρὸς τὸ
σημαίνειν ἐστί. Σημαίνει μὲν οὖν πάντα, ὅσα ἐν
αἰσθητῷ, ποιεῖ δὲ ἄλλα, ὅσα φανερῶς ποιεῖ.
10 Ἡμεῖς δὲ ψυχῆς ἔργα κατὰ φύσιν ποιοῦμεν, ἕως
μὴ ἐσφάλημεν ἐν τῷ πλήθει τοῦ παντός· σφαλέντες
δὲ ἔχομεν δίκην καὶ τὸ σφάλμα αὐτὸ καὶ τὸ ἐν
χείρονι μοίρᾳ εἰς ὕστερον. Πλοῦτοι μὲν οὖν καὶ
πενίαι συντυχίᾳ τῶν ἔξω· ἀρεταὶ δὲ καὶ κακίαι;
Ἀρεταὶ μὲν διὰ τὸ ἀρχαῖον τῆς ψυχῆς, κακίαι δὲ
15 συντυχίᾳ ψυχῆς πρὸς τὰ ἔξω. Ἀλλὰ περὶ μὲν
τούτων ἐν ἄλλοις εἴρηται.

9. Νῦν δὲ ἀναμνησθέντες τοῦ ἀτράκτου, ὃν
τοῖς μὲν πρόπαλαι αἱ Μοῖραι ἐπικλώθουσι, Πλάτωνι
δὲ ὁ ἄτρακτός ἐστι τό τε πλανώμενον καὶ τὸ
ἀπλανὲς τῆς περιφορᾶς, καὶ αἱ Μοῖραι δὲ καὶ ἡ
5 Ἀνάγκη μήτηρ οὖσα στρέφουσι καὶ ἐν τῇ γενέσει
ἑκάστου ἐπικλώθουσι καὶ δι' αὐτῆς εἰσιν εἰς
γένεσιν τὰ γεννώμενα. Ἔν τε Τιμαίῳ θεὸς μὲν ὁ
ποιήσας τὴν ἀρχὴν τῆς ψυχῆς δίδωσιν, οἱ δὲ
φερόμενοι θεοὶ τὰ δεινὰ καὶ ἀναγκαῖα πάθη,
θυμοὺς καὶ ἐπιθυμίας καὶ ἡδονὰς καὶ λύπας αὖ,
10 καὶ ψυχῆς ἄλλο εἶδος, ἀφ' οὗ τὰ παθήματα
ταυτί. Οὗτοι γὰρ οἱ λόγοι συνδέουσιν ἡμᾶς τοῖς
ἄστροις παρ' αὐτῶν ψυχὴν κομιζομένους καὶ
ὑποτάττουσι τῇ ἀνάγκῃ ἐνταῦθα ἰόντας· καὶ ἤθη
τοίνυν παρ' αὐτῶν καὶ κατὰ τὰ ἤθη πράξεις καὶ

---

[1] The reference back is probably to I. 8 (51), cp. ch. 12. 5–7.

since they are no small part of the heaven; this is
why they are so bright and well adapted for signs.
So they signify everything that happens in the sense-
world, but do other things, the things which they
are seen to do. We, however, do the works of soul
according to nature, as long as we do not fail in the
multiplicity of the All; if we fail we have as just
penalty both the failure itself and the being in a worse
position afterwards. Wealth, then, and poverty are
due to chance encounters with things outside. But
what about virtues and vices? Virtues are due to
the ancient state of our soul, vices to its chance encounter with things outside it. But this has been
discussed elsewhere.[1]

9. But now we should call to mind the Spindle,
which according to the ancients the Fates spin; but
for Plato the Spindle is the wandering and the fixed
parts of the heavenly circuit,[2] and the Fates and
Necessity, who is their mother, turn the spindle and
spin a thread at the birth of each one of us, and
what is born comes to birth through Necessity.
And in the *Timaeus*[3] the God who makes the
world gives the " first principle of the soul," but
the gods who are borne through the heavens "the
terrible and inevitable passions," " angers " and
desires and " pleasures and pains," and the " other
kind of soul," from which come passions of this kind.
These statements bind us to the stars, from which
we get our souls, and subject us to necessity when
we come down here; from them we get our moral
characters, our characteristic actions, and our

[2] *Republic* X. 616C4 ff.
[3] 69C5–D3.

73

πάθη ἀπὸ ἕξεως παθητικῆς οὔσης· ὥστε τί λοιπὸν
15 ἡμεῖς; Ἢ ὅπερ ἐσμὲν κατ᾽ ἀλήθειαν ἡμεῖς, οἷς
καὶ κρατεῖν τῶν παθῶν ἔδωκεν ἡ φύσις. Καὶ γὰρ
ὅμως ἐν τούτοις τοῖς κακοῖς διὰ τοῦ σώματος
ἀπειλημμένοις ἀδέσποτον ἀρετὴν θεὸς ἔδωκεν.
Οὐ γὰρ ἐν ἡσύχῳ οὖσιν ἀρετῆς δεῖ ἡμῖν, ἀλλ᾽ ὅταν
κίνδυνος ἐν κακοῖς εἶναι ἀρετῆς οὐ παρούσης.
20 Διὸ καὶ φεύγειν ἐντεῦθεν δεῖ καὶ χωρίζειν
αὐτοὺς ἀπὸ τῶν προσγεγενημένων καὶ μὴ τὸ
σύνθετον εἶναι σῶμα ἐψυχωμένον ἐν ᾧ κρατεῖ
μᾶλλον ἡ σώματος φύσις ψυχῆς τι ἴχνος λαβοῦσα,
ὡς τὴν ζωὴν τὴν κοινὴν μᾶλλον τοῦ σώματος εἶναι·
πάντα γὰρ σωματικά, ὅσα ταύτης. Τῆς δὲ ἑτέρας
25 τῆς ἔξω ἡ πρὸς τὸ ἄνω φορὰ καὶ τὸ καλὸν καὶ τὸ
θεῖον ὧν οὐδεὶς κρατεῖ, ἀλλ᾽ ἢ προσχρῆται, ἵν᾽ ᾖ
ἐκεῖνο καὶ κατὰ τοῦτο ζῇ ἀναχωρήσας· ἢ ἔρημος
ταύτης τῆς ψυχῆς γενόμενος ζῇ ἐν εἱμαρμένῃ, καὶ
ἐνταῦθα τὰ ἄστρα αὐτῷ οὐ μόνον σημαίνει, ἀλλὰ
30 γίνεται αὐτὸς οἷον μέρος καὶ τῷ ὅλῳ συνέπεται,
οὗ μέρος. Διττὸς γὰρ ἕκαστος, ὁ μὲν τὸ συναμφό-
τερόν τι, ὁ δὲ αὐτός· καὶ πᾶς ὁ κόσμος δὲ ὁ μὲν
τὸ ἐκ σώματος καὶ ψυχῆς τινος δεθείσης σώματι,
ὁ δὲ ἡ τοῦ παντὸς ψυχὴ ἡ μὴ ἐν σώματι, ἐλλάμπουσα δὲ ἴχνη τῇ ἐν σώματι· καὶ ἥλιος δὴ καὶ
35 τἆλλα διττὰ οὕτω· καὶ τῇ μὲν ἑτέρᾳ ψυχῇ τῇ
καθαρᾷ οὐδὲν φαῦλον δίδωσιν, ἃ δὲ γίνεται εἰς τὸ

---

[1] Cp. I 1. 7. 17 ff.
[2] *Republic* X. 617E3.

emotions, coming from a disposition which is liable to emotion. So what is left which is " we "? Surely, just that which we really are, we to whom nature gave power to master our passions.[1] Yes, and God gave us too, in the midst of all these evils which we receive through the body, "virtue who is no man's slave."[2] For we do not need virtue when we are in peace but when there is a risk of being in evils if virtue is not there. So we must "fly from here"[3] and "separate"[4] ourselves from what has been added to us, and not be the composite thing, the ensouled body in which the nature of body (which has some trace of soul) has the greater power, so that the common life belongs more to the body; for everything that pertains to this common life is bodily. But to the other soul, which is outside the body, belongs the ascent to the higher world, to the fair and divine which no one masters, but either makes use of it that he may be it and live by it, withdrawing himself; or else he is bereft of this higher soul and lives under destiny, and then the stars do not only show him signs but he also becomes himself a part, and follows along with the whole of which he is a part. For every man is double, one of him is the sort of compound being and one of him is himself; and the whole universe is, one part the composite of body and a sort of soul bound to body, and one the soul of the All which is not in body but makes a trace of itself shine on that which is in body. And the sun and the other heavenly bodies are double in this way; they communicate no evil to the other pure soul, but what comes into the All

---

[3] Plato, *Theaetetus* 176A8–B1.
[4] Plato, *Phaedo* 67C6.

πᾶν παρ' αὐτῶν, καθ' ὃ μέρος εἰσὶ τοῦ παντός
καὶ σῶμα[1] ἐψυχωμένον, τὸ σῶμα μέρος μέρει
δίδωσι προαιρέσεως τοῦ ἄστρου καὶ ψυχῆς τῆς
ὄντως αὐτοῦ πρὸς τὸ ἄριστον βλεπούσης. Παρακο-
40 λουθεῖ δ' αὐτῷ τὰ ἄλλα, μᾶλλον δ' οὐκ αὐτῷ,
ἀλλὰ τοῖς περὶ αὐτόν, οἷον ἐκ πυρὸς θερμότητος
εἰς τὸ ὅλον ἰούσης, καὶ εἴ τι παρὰ ψυχῆς τῆς ἄλλης
εἰς ψυχὴν ἄλλην συγγενῆ οὖσαν· τὰ δὲ δυσχερῆ
διὰ τὴν μῖξιν. Μεμιγμένη γὰρ οὖν δὴ ἡ τοῦδε
τοῦ παντὸς φύσις, καὶ εἴ τις τὴν ψυχὴν τὴν
45 χωριστὴν αὐτοῦ χωρίσειε, τὸ λοιπὸν οὐ μέγα.
Θεὸς μὲν οὖν ἐκείνης συναριθμουμένης, τὸ δὲ
λοιπὸν δαίμων, φησί, μέγας καὶ τὰ πάθη τὰ ἐν
αὐτῷ δαιμόνια.

10. Εἰ δ' οὕτω, τὰς σημασίας καὶ νῦν δοτέον·
τὰς δὲ ποιήσεις οὐ πάντως οὐδὲ τοῖς ὅλοις αὐτῶν,
ἀλλὰ ὅσα τοῦ παντὸς πάθη, καὶ ὅσον τὸ λοιπὸν
αὐτῶν. Καὶ ψυχῇ μὲν καὶ πρὶν ἐλθεῖν εἰς γένεσιν
5 δοτέον ἥκειν τι φερούσῃ παρ' αὑτῆς· οὐ γὰρ ἂν
ἔλθοι εἰς σῶμα μὴ μέγα τι παθητικὸν ἔχουσα.
Δοτέον δὲ καὶ τύχας εἰσιούσῃ [τὸ κατ' αὐτὴν τὴν
φορὰν εἰσιέναι]· δοτέον δὲ καὶ αὐτὴν τὴν φορὰν
ποιεῖσθαι συνεργοῦσαν καὶ ἀποπληροῦσαν παρ'
αὑτῆς, ἃ δεῖ τελεῖν τὸ πᾶν, ἑκάστου τῶν ἐν αὐτῇ
10 τάξιν μερῶν λαβόντος.

----

[1] καὶ σῶμα Müller, H-S²: σῶμα καὶ codd.

----

[1] Plato Timaeus 47E5.
[2] The distinction of θεός and δαίμων comes from Symposium
202D5–E1 (the demonstration that Eros is a daemon, not a

from them, in so far as they are part of the All
and ensouled body, their body, which is a part,
gives to another part—while the star's intention
and the soul which is really itself is looking to the
Best. The other effects happen in sequence upon
it (or rather not upon it but upon its environment),
like heat from a fire spreading through the whole—
and perhaps something comes from the star's other
soul to another soul which is akin to it. The bad
effects are because of the mixture. For the nature
of " this All " is " mixed," [1] and if anyone separates
from him the separable soul, what is left is not much.
The universe is a god if the separable soul is reckoned
as part of it; the rest, Plato says, is a " great
daemon " [2] and what happens in it is daemonic.

10. If this is so, we must grant even at this stage of
the discussion the power of signifying to the stars, but
action not completely nor to their whole natures, but
only in so far as affections of the All are concerned
and as regards what is left of them [when their separable souls are left out of account]. And we must
admit that the soul, even before it enters the realm
of becoming, brings something [lower] of itself when
it comes: for it would not have come into body unless
it had a large part subject to affections. And we
must grant, too, that it enters into the domain of
chance. And we must grant that the heavenly circuit does act of itself, co-operating and completing
by its own power what the All must accomplish; and
in its action each individual heavenly body in it has
the status of a part.

god), but Plato does not apply it there or anywhere else to the
universe.

11. Χρὴ δὲ κἀκεῖνο ἐνθυμεῖσθαι, ὡς τὸ ἀπ᾽ ἐκείνων ἰὸν οὐ τοιοῦτόν εἰσιν[1] εἰς τοὺς λαβόντας, οἷον παρ᾽ ἐκείνων ἔρχεται· οἷον εἰ πῦρ, ἀμυδρὸν τοῦτο, καὶ εἰ φιλιακὴ διάθεσις, ἀσθενὴς γενομένη 5 ἐν τῷ λαβόντι οὐ μάλα καλὴν τὴν φίλησιν εἰργάσατο, καὶ θυμὸς δὴ οὐκ ἐν μέτρῳ τυχόντος, ὡς ἀνδρεῖον γενέσθαι, ἢ ἀκροχολίαν ἢ ἀθυμίαν εἰργάσατο, καὶ τὸ τιμῆς ἐν ἔρωτι ὂν καὶ περὶ τὸ καλὸν ἔχον τῶν δοκούντων καλῶν ἔφεσιν εἰργάσατο, καὶ νοῦ ἀπόρροια πανουργίαν· καὶ γὰρ ἡ πανουργία ἐθέλει 10 νοῦς εἶναι τυχεῖν οὗ ἐφίεται οὐ δυνάμενος. Γίνεται οὖν κακὰ ἕκαστα τούτων ἐν ἡμῖν ἐκεῖ οὐ τούτων ὄντων· ἐπεὶ καὶ τὰ ἐλθόντα, καίτοι οὐκ ἐκεῖνα ὄντα, οὐ μένει οὐδὲ ταῦτα οἷα ἦλθε σώμασι μιγνύμενα καὶ ὕλῃ καὶ ἀλλήλοις.

12. Καὶ δὴ καὶ τὰ ἰόντα εἰς ἓν συμπίπτει καὶ κομίζεται ἕκαστον τῶν γινομένων τι ἐκ τούτου τοῦ κράματος, ὥστε ὅ ἐστι καὶ ποιόν τι γενέσθαι. Οὐ γὰρ τὸν ἵππον ποιεῖ, ἀλλὰ τῷ ἵππῳ τι δίδωσιν· 5 ὁ γὰρ ἵππος ἐξ ἵππου καὶ ἐξ ἀνθρώπου ἄνθρωπος· συνεργὸς δὲ ἥλιος τῇ πλάσει· ὁ δὲ ἐκ τοῦ λόγου τοῦ ἀνθρώπου γίνεται. Ἀλλ᾽ ἔβλαψέ ποτε ἢ ὠφέλησε τὸ ἔξω· ὁμοίως γὰρ τῷ πατρί, ἀλλὰ πρὸς τὸ βέλτιον πολλάκις, ἔστι δ᾽ ὅτε πρὸς τὸ

---

[1] εἰσιν Kirchhoff, H-S²: ἐστιν codd.

---

[1] Cp. Aristotle, *Physics* B. 2. 194b13. "Man begets man and so does the sun." Cp. *De Gen. et Corr.* B. 10, where it is explained that the movement of the sun in the eclip-

11. We must consider, too, that what comes from the stars will not reach the recipients in the same state in which it left them. If it is fire, for instance, the fire down here is dim [by comparison with that of the stars], and if it is a loving disposition it becomes weak in the recipient and produces a rather unpleasant kind of loving; and manly spirit, when the receiver does not take it in due measure, so as to become brave, produces violent temper or spiritlessness; and that which belongs to honour in love and is concerned with beauty produces desire of what only seems to be beautiful, and the efflux of intellect produces knavery; for knavery wants to be intellect, only it is unable to attain what it aims at. So all these things become evil in us, though they are not so up in heaven; since even the things which have come down, though they are not that which they were in heaven, do not remain what they were when they came since they are mingled with bodies and matter and each other.

12. And, further, the influences which come from the stars combine into one, and each thing that comes into being takes something from the mixture, so that what it already is acquires a certain quality. The star-influences do not make the horse; they give something to the horse. Horse comes from horse and man from man: the sun co-operates in their making;[1] but man comes from the formative principle of man. The outside influence sometimes harms or helps. A man is like his father, but often he turns out better, sometimes worse. But the

tic is the " cause of the rhythm of generation and decay " (Cornford).

χεῖρον συνέπεσεν. Ἀλλ᾽ οὐκ ἐκβιβάζει τοῦ ὑπο-
10 κειμένου· ὁτὲ δὲ καὶ ἡ ὕλη κρατεῖ, οὐχ ἡ φύσις,
ὡς μὴ τέλεον γενέσθαι ἡττωμένου τοῦ εἴδους.

[Τὸ δὲ πρὸς ἡμᾶς τῆς σελήνης ἀφώτιστόν ἐστι
πρὸς τὰ ἐπὶ γῆς, οὐ τὸ ἄνω λυπεῖ. Οὐκ ἐπικου-
ροῦντος δὲ ἐκείνου τῷ πόρρω χεῖρον εἶναι δοκεῖ·
15 ὅταν δὲ πλήρης ᾖ, ἀρκεῖ τῷ κάτω, κἂν ἐκεῖνος
πόρρωθεν ᾖ. Πρὸς δὲ τὸν πυρώδη ἀφώτιστος
οὖσα πρὸς ἡμᾶς ἔδοξεν εἶναι ἀγαθή· ἀνταρκεῖ γὰρ
τὸ ἐκείνου πυρωδεστέρου ἢ πρὸς ἐκεῖνον ὄντος.
Τὰ δὲ ἰόντα ἐκεῖθεν σώματα ἐμψύχων ἄλλα ἄλλων
ἐπὶ τὸ μᾶλλον καὶ ἧττον θερμά, ψυχρὸν δὲ οὐδέν·
20 μαρτυρεῖ δὲ ὁ τόπος. Δία δὲ ὃν λέγουσιν, εὔκρατος
πυρί· καὶ ὁ Ἑῷος οὕτως·[1] διὸ καὶ σύμφωνοι
δοκοῦσιν ὁμοιότητι, πρὸς δὲ τὸν Πυρόεντα καλού-
μενον τῇ κράσει, πρὸς δὲ Κρόνον ἀλλοτρίως τῷ
πόρρω· Ἑρμῆς δ᾽ ἀδιάφορος πρὸς ἅπαντας, ὡς
δοκεῖ, ὁμοιούμενος. Πάντες δὲ πρὸς τὸ ὅλον
25 σύμφοροι· ὥστε πρὸς ἀλλήλους οὕτως, ὡς τῷ
ὅλῳ συμφέρει, ὡς ἐφ᾽ ἑνὸς ζῴου ἕκαστα τῶν
μερῶν ὁρᾶται. Τούτου γὰρ χάριν μάλιστα, οἷον
χολὴ καὶ τῷ ὅλῳ καὶ πρὸς τὸ ἐγγύς· καὶ γὰρ ἔδει
καὶ θυμὸν ἐγείρειν καὶ τὸ πᾶν καὶ τὸ πλησίον μὴ

---

[1] οὕτως Creuzer, H-S: οὗτος codd.

---

[1] The planets mentioned in this passage are Jupiter, Venus, Mars, Saturn and Mercury.

outside influence does not force anything out of its fundamental nature; sometimes, however, the matter, not the nature, gets the upper hand, so that, as a result of the defeat of the form, the thing does not come to perfection.

[The side of the moon which is towards us is un-lighted in relation to the regions of earth, but does no harm to that which is above it. But since that which is above does not help because it is far away, this conjunction is thought to be worse. But when the moon is full, it is sufficient for what is below even if the star above is far away. But when the moon is unlighted on the side towards the fiery star she is thought to be good in relation to us: for the power of that star persists which is fierier than it needs to be for itself [?]. The bodies of living things which come from that upper region differ from each other according to their degrees of heat, but none of them is cold. Their place is evidence of this. The planet that people call Zeus [1] is of fire in a well-balanced mixture; and so is the Morning Star; so these two because of their likeness are considered as " harmoni-ous," but are alien in disposition to the star called Fiery because of its composition and to Cronos be-cause of its distance. Hermes, however, is indif-ferent and is, it is thought, like all. But all contri-bute to the whole, and are therefore related to each other in a way that brings advantage to the whole, as we see that all the parts individually are of a living thing. For they are there precisely for the sake of the whole living thing, as, for instance, the gall is to serve the whole and in relation to the part next to it: for it has to stir up the manly spirit and keep the

ἐᾶν ὑβρίζειν. Καὶ δὴ καὶ ἐν τῷ παντελεῖ ἔδει
30 τινὸς τοιούτου καί τινος ἄλλου πρὸς τὸ ἡδὺ
ἀνημμένου· τὰ δὲ ὀφθαλμοὺς εἶναι· συμπαθῆ δὲ
πάντα τῷ ἀλόγῳ αὐτῶν εἶναι· οὕτω γὰρ ἓν καὶ
μία ἁρμονία.]

13. Δεῖ τοίνυν τὸ ἐντεῦθεν, ἐπειδὴ τὰ μὲν καὶ
παρὰ τῆς φορᾶς γίνεται, τὰ δὲ οὔ, διαλαβεῖν καὶ
διακρῖναι καὶ εἰπεῖν, πόθεν ἕκαστα ὅλως. Ἀρχὴ
δὲ ἥδε· ψυχῆς δὴ τὸ πᾶν τόδε διοικούσης κατὰ
5 λόγον, οἷα δὴ καὶ ἐφ᾽ ἑκάστου ζῴου ἡ ἐν αὐτῷ
ἀρχή, ἀφ᾽ ἧς ἕκαστα τὰ τοῦ ζῴου μέρη καὶ
πλάττεται καὶ πρὸς τὸ ὅλον συντέτακται, οὗ μέρη
ἐστίν, ἐν μὲν τῷ ὅλῳ ἐστὶ τὰ πάντα, ἐν δὲ τοῖς
μέρεσι τοσοῦτον μόνον, ὅσον ἐστὶν ἕκαστον. Τὰ
δὲ ἔξωθεν προσιόντα, τὰ μὲν καὶ ἐναντία τῇ
10 βουλήσει τῆς φύσεως, τὰ δὲ καὶ πρόσφορα· τῷ
δὲ ὅλῳ πάντα ἅτε μέρη ὄντα αὐτοῦ τὰ πάντα
συντέτακται φύσιν μὲν λαβόντα ἣν ἔχει καὶ
συμπληροῦντα τῇ οἰκείᾳ ὅμως ὁρμῇ πρὸς τὸν ὅλον
τοῦ παντὸς βίον. Τὰ μὲν οὖν ἄψυχα τῶν ἐν αὐτῷ
πάντῃ ὄργανα καὶ οἷον ὠθούμενα ἔξω εἰς τὸ
15 ποιεῖν· τὰ δὲ ἔμψυχα, τὰ μὲν τὸ κινεῖσθαι ἀορίστως
ἔχει, ὡς ὑφ᾽ ἅρμασιν ἵπποι πρὶν τὸν ἡνίοχον
ἀφορίσαι αὐτοῖς τὸν δρόμον, ἅτε δὴ πληγῇ
νεμόμενα· λογικοῦ δὲ ζῴου φύσις ἔχει παρ᾽

---

[1] On this passage see Introductory Note.

[2] Again a reminiscence of the *Phaedrus* (246C2; cp. note on ch. 8).

[3] The phrase is taken from Plato, *Critias* 109C1, where it is used in a context relevant to the argument here. But

whole and the part next to it from excess. So, too, in the complete whole [of the universe] there is need of some organ like the gall and of some other directed to producing sweetness; others are the eyes of the universe; all are united in feeling by their irrational part. So the universe is one and a single melody.][1]

13. We must, then, in consequence of this discussion (since some things do happen as a result of the movement of the heavens, but others do not) distinguish and discriminate and say from what cause in general each particular happening results. Our starting-point is this: since soul directs this All according to a rational order [2] (as with each individual living thing the principle in it does, from which the formation of the individual parts of the living thing and their ordering to the whole derive), it is altogether present in the whole, but in the parts only proportionately to the being of the individual. The influences which come from outside [to each individual thing] are sometimes opposed to the intention of its nature and sometimes favourable to it. But all are ordered to the whole because they are all parts of it; they received the nature which they have, but all the same they contribute, each by its own individual impulse, to the whole life of the All. The lifeless things in the All are altogether instruments and are, so to speak, pushed from outside to act. As for living things, some have unlimited movement, like horses harnessed to chariots before the driver marks off their course, in that he " controls them with the whip." [3] But the nature of a rational

Plotinus also still has in mind the *Phaedrus* myth, with its image of the charioteer and his horses.

ἑαυτῆς τὸν ἡνίοχον· καὶ ἐπιστήμονα μὲν ἔχουσα
κατ᾽ ἰθὺ φέρεται, μὴ δέ, ὡς ἔτυχε πολλάκις.
20 Ἄμφω δὲ εἴσω τοῦ παντὸς καὶ συντελοῦντα πρὸς
τὸ ὅλον· καὶ τὰ μὲν μείζω αὐτῶν καὶ ἐν πλείονι
τῇ ἀξίᾳ πολλὰ ποιεῖ καὶ μεγάλα καὶ πρὸς τὴν τοῦ
ὅλου ζωὴν συντελεῖ τάξιν ποιητικὴν μᾶλλον ἢ
παθητικὴν ἔχοντα, τὰ δὲ πάσχοντα διατελεῖ μικρὰν
δύναμιν πρὸς τὸ ποιεῖν ἔχοντα· τὰ δὲ μεταξὺ
25 τούτων, πάσχοντα μὲν παρ᾽ ἄλλων, ποιοῦντα δὲ
πολλὰ καὶ ἐν πολλοῖς ἀρχὴν παρ᾽ αὐτῶν εἰς
πράξεις καὶ ποιήσεις ἔχοντα. Καὶ γίνεται τὸ πᾶν
ζωὴ παντελὴς τῶν μὲν ἀρίστων ἐνεργούντων τὰ
ἄριστα, καθ᾽ ὅσον τὸ ἄριστον ἐν ἑκάστῳ· ὃ δὴ
30 καὶ τῷ ἡγεμονοῦντι συνακτέον, ὥσπερ στρατιώτας
στρατηγῷ, οἳ δὴ λέγονται καὶ ἕπεσθαι Διὶ ἐπὶ
φύσιν τὴν νοητὴν ἱεμένῳ. Τὰ δὲ ἥττονι τῇ φύσει
κεχρημένα δεύτερα τοῦ παντός, οἷα καὶ τὰ ἐν
ἡμῖν ψυχῆς δεύτερα· τὰ δ᾽ ἄλλα ἀνάλογον τοῖς ἐν
ἡμῖν μέρεσιν· οὐδὲ γὰρ ἐφ᾽ ἡμῶν πάντα ἴσα.
35 Ζῷα μὲν οὖν πάντα κατὰ λόγον τὸν τοῦ παντὸς
ὅλον, τά τε ἐν οὐρανῷ πάντα καὶ τὰ ἄλλα, ὅσα
εἰς τὸ ὅλον μεμέρισται, καὶ οὐδὲν τῶν μερῶν, οὐδ᾽
εἰ μέγα, δύναμιν ἔχει τοῦ ἐξαλλαγὴν ἐργάσασθαι
τῶν λόγων οὐδὲ τῶν κατὰ τοὺς λόγους γενομένων·
ἀλλοίωσιν δὲ ἐπ᾽ ἀμφότερα, χείρονός τε καὶ
40 βελτίονος, ἐργάσασθαι, ἀλλ᾽ οὐκ ἐκστῆσαί γε τῆς
οἰκείας φύσεως δύναται. Χεῖρον δὲ ἐργάζεται ἢ
κατὰ σῶμα ἀσθένειαν διδὸν ἢ τῇ ψυχῇ τῇ συμπαθεῖ
καὶ παρ᾽ αὐτοῦ δοθείσῃ εἰς τὸ κάτω κατὰ συμβεβηκὸς φαυλότητος αἴτιον γινόμενον ἢ σώματος

creature has its driver of itself; and if it has a skilled
one it goes straight, but if not, then often just as it
chances. But both are within the All, and contribute
to the whole. The greater living things which are
higher in rank do much that is important, and contribute to the life of the whole in an active rather than
a passive capacity; others continue passive, having
little power to act; others are between the two, acted
upon by others, but doing much and in many things
having a principle of doing and making which is their
own. And the All becomes a complete life when the
best parts do the best, according to the best in each
of them: and each has to subordinate its best to the
ruling principle, as soldiers to the general; so they
are said to " follow Zeus "[1] in his progress towards
the nature of Intellect. The things which are equip-
ped with a lower nature hold second place in the All,
as we, too, have a second part of soul; the rest are
like our parts; not everything in us is equal either.
So then living things are all conformed to the complete pattern of the All, both the ones in heaven and
the rest which have been made parts in the whole,
and no part, even if it is a great one, has power to
bring about a complete change in the patterns or the
things which happen according to the patterns.
It can bring about a non-essential alteration in either
direction, for better or worse, but it cannot make
anything abandon its own proper nature. It makes
a thing worse either by giving it bodily infirmity, or
by becoming responsible for an incidental badness in
the soul which is in sympathy with it and was given
out by it into the lower region, or, when the body is

---

[1] Cp. *Phaedrus* 246E6.

κακῶς συντεθέντος ἐμπόδιον τὴν εἰς αὐτὸ ἐνέργειαν
45 δι᾿ αὐτὸ ποιῆσαι· οἷον οὐχ οὕτως ἁρμοσθείσης
λύρας, ὡς δέξασθαι τὸ ἀκριβὲς ἁρμονίας εἰς τὸ
μουσικοὺς ἀποτελεῖν τοὺς φθόγγους.

14. Περὶ δὲ πενίας καὶ πλούτους καὶ δόξας καὶ
ἀρχὰς πῶς; Ἢ, εἰ μὲν παρὰ πατέρων οἱ πλοῦτοι,
ἐσήμηναν τὸν πλούσιον, ὥσπερ καὶ εὐγενῆ τὸν ἐκ
τοιούτων διὰ τὸ γένος τὸ ἔνδοξον ἔχοντα ἐδήλωσαν
5 μόνον· εἰ δ᾿ ἐξ ἀνδραγαθίας, εἰ σῶμα συνεργὸν
γεγένηται, συμβάλλοιντο ἂν οἱ τὴν σώματος ἰσχὺν
ἐργασάμενοι, γονεῖς μὲν πρῶτον, εἶτα, εἴ τι παρὰ [1]
τῶν τόπων ἔσχε, τὰ οὐράνια καὶ ἡ γῆ· εἰ δὲ ἄνευ
σώματος ἡ ἀρετή, αὐτῇ μόνῃ δοτέον τὸ πλεῖστον
καί, ὅσα παρὰ τῶν ἀμειψαμένων, συνεβάλλετο.
10 Οἱ δὲ δόντες εἰ μὲν ἀγαθοί, εἰς ἀρετὴν ἀνακτέον
καὶ οὕτω τὴν αἰτίαν· εἰ δὲ φαῦλοι, δικαίως δὲ
δόντες, τῷ ἐν αὐτοῖς βελτίστῳ ἐνεργήσαντι τοῦτο
γεγονέναι. Εἰ δὲ πονηρὸς ὁ πλουτήσας, τὴν μὲν
πονηρίαν προηγουμένην καὶ ⟨ὅ⟩τι [2] τὸ αἴτιον τῆς
πονηρίας, προσληπτέον δὲ καὶ τοὺς δόντας συναι-
15 τίους ὡσαύτως γενομένους. Εἰ δ᾿ ἐκ πόνων, οἷον
ἐκ γεωργίας, ἐπὶ τὸν γεωργόν, συνεργὸν τὸ
περιέχον γεγενημένον. Εἰ δὲ θησαυρὸν εὗρε,
συμπεσεῖν τι τῶν ἐκ τοῦ παντός· εἰ δέ, σημαίνεται·

---

[1] τι παρὰ Bury, H-S: τις ἄρα codd.
[2] ⟨ὅ⟩τι nunc proponunt Henry et Schwyzer: τί codd.
τι edd.

---

[1] For the metaphor of the body as lyre, cp. I4. 16. 23 ff.

badly put together, it may by means of it hinder the activity of the soul which is directed towards it: as when a lyre is not so tuned that it takes the melody accurately so as to make its sounds musical.[1]

14. But how about poverty and wealth and reputations and offices? If people are rich by inheritance from their fathers, the stars announce the rich man, just as they do no more than declare the man of good birth who comes of well-born parents and owes his distinction to his family. But if the wealth comes from manly virtue, then if the body has helped in producing this, those who have produced the body's vigour will have contributed, the parents first, then, if any place contributed anything, the heavenly regions and the earth. But if the virtue arose without the body, then the greatest part must be attributed to virtue alone, and it contributed all that was given by those who rewarded it. If the people who gave the riches were good, in this way, too, the cause must be referred back to virtue; but if they were bad, but were justified in giving the wealth, we must say that this happened by the activity of that which was best in them. But if the man who became rich was wicked his wealth must be attributed to his pre-existent wickedness and whatever was responsible for that wickedness, and we must include also those who gave the wealth, who also share in the responsibility. If a man's riches come from hard work, from farming, for instance, the cause is to be referred to the farmer, with the environment helping. If he found a treasure, we must say that something from the All cooperated; if so, it is indicated [in the heavens]; for

πάντως γὰρ ἀκολουθεῖ ἀλλήλοις πάντα· διὸ καὶ
20 πάντως. Εἰ δ' ἀπέβαλέ τις πλοῦτον, εἰ ἀφαιρεθείς,
ἐπὶ τὸν ἀφελόμενον, κἀκεῖνον ἐπὶ τὴν οἰκείαν
ἀρχήν· εἰ δ' ἐν θαλάττῃ, τὰ συμπεσόντα. Τὸ δ'
ἔνδοξον ἢ δικαίως ἢ οὔ. Εἰ οὖν δικαίως, τὰ ἔργα
καὶ τὸ παρὰ τοῖς δοξάζουσι βέλτιον· εἰ δ' οὐ
δικαίως, ἐπὶ τὴν τῶν τιμώντων ἀδικίαν. Καὶ
25 ἀρχῆς δὲ πέρι ὁ αὐτὸς λόγος· ἢ γὰρ προσηκόντως
ἢ οὔ· καὶ θάτερον μὲν ἐπὶ τὸ βέλτιον τῶν ἑλομένων,
ἢ ἐπ' αὐτὸν διαπραξάμενον ἑτέρων συστάσει καὶ
ὁπωσοῦν ἄλλως. Περὶ δὲ γάμων ἢ προαίρεσις ἢ
συντυχία καὶ σύμπτωσις ἐκ τῶν ὅλων. Παίδων
30 δὲ γενέσεις ἀκόλουθοι τούτοις, καὶ ἢ πέπλασται
κατὰ λόγον ἐμποδίσαντος οὐδενός, ἢ χεῖρον ἔσχε
γενομένου ἔνδον κωλύματός τινος ἢ παρ' αὐτὴν τὴν
κύουσαν ἢ τοῦ περιέχοντος οὕτω διατεθέντος ὡς
ἀσυμμέτρως πρὸς τήνδε τὴν κύησιν ἐσχηκότος.

15. Ὁ δὲ Πλάτων πρὸ τῆς περιφορᾶς τοῦ
ἀτράκτου δοὺς κλήρους καὶ προαιρέσεις συνεργοὺς
ὕστερον δίδωσι τοὺς ἐν τῷ ἀτράκτῳ, ὡς πάντως
τὰ αἱρεθέντα συναποτελοῦντας· ἐπεὶ καὶ ὁ δαίμων
5 συνεργὸς εἰς πλήρωσιν αὐτῶν. Ἀλλ' οἱ κλῆροι
τίνες; Ἢ ⟨τὸ⟩[1] τοῦ παντὸς ἔχοντος οὕτως, ὡς τότε

----
[1] ⟨τὸ⟩ Müller, H-S².

----
[1] *Republic* X. 617D–E.
[2] Ibid. 620D–E.

all things without exception are connected with each other; so everything without exception is indicated. If someone loses his wealth, then if it is taken away, the taker is responsible, and his own principle is responsible for him: if it is lost in the sea, the circumstances are responsible. And as for fame, a man is either rightly famous or not. If rightly, then it is his achievements that are responsible and that which is better in those who glorify him; but if not rightly, it is the unrighteousness of those who honour him that is responsible. The same argument applies to office: it is either appropriately conferred or not—in the one case the conferment is to be attributed to that which is better in the selectors; in the other to the man himself who has managed to succeed in getting it by the co-operation of others, or in some kind of other way. About marriages, the causes are free choice, or chance coming together with some incidental influence from the universal order. And births of children follow upon marriages, and the child is either formed according to pattern, when there is no hindrance, or it is in a worse state when some obstacle has occurred within, either due to the mother herself or because the environment is so disposed as to be out of harmony with this particular birth.

15. Plato gives the souls lots and choices before the circling of the Spindle,[1] and afterwards gives them the beings on the Spindle as helpers, to bring to accomplishment in every way what they have chosen: since the guardian spirit also co-operates in the fulfilment of their choices.[2] But what are the lots? Being born when the All was in the state in which it

εἶχεν, ὅτε εἰσήεσαν εἰς τὸ σῶμα, γενέσθαι, καὶ τὸ
εἰσελθεῖν εἰς τόδε τὸ σῶμα καὶ τῶνδε γονέων καὶ
ἐν τοιούτοις τόποις γίγνεσθαι καὶ ὅλως, ὡς
εἴπομεν, τὰ ἔξω. Πάντα δὲ ὁμοῦ γενόμενα καὶ
10 οἷον συγκλωσθέντα διὰ τῆς μιᾶς τῶν λεγομένων
Μοιρῶν δεδήλωται ἐπί τε ἑκάστων ἐπί τε τῶν
ὅλων· ἡ δὲ Λάχεσις τοὺς κλήρους· καὶ τὰ
συμπεσόντα τάδε πάντως ἀναγκαῖον τὴν Ἄτροπον
ἐπάγειν. Τῶν δ' ἀνθρώπων οἱ μὲν γίγνονται τῶν
ἐκ τοῦ ὅλου καὶ τῶν ἔξω, ὥσπερ γοητευθέντες, καὶ
15 ὀλίγα ἢ οὐδὲν αὐτοί· οἱ δὲ κρατοῦντες τούτων καὶ
ὑπεραίροντες οἷον τῇ κεφαλῇ πρὸς τὸ ἄνω καὶ ἐκτὸς
ψυχῆς ἀποσῴζουσι τὸ ἄριστον καὶ ⟨τὸ⟩[1] ἀρχαῖον
τῆς ψυχικῆς οὐσίας. Οὐ γὰρ δὴ νομιστέον τοιοῦτον
εἶναι ψυχήν, οἷον, ὅ τι ἂν ἔξωθεν πάθῃ, ταύτην
φύσιν ἴσχειν, μόνην τῶν πάντων οἰκείαν φύσιν
20 οὐκ ἔχουσαν· ἀλλὰ χρὴ πολὺ πρότερον αὐτὴν ἢ
τὰ ἄλλα, ἅτε ἀρχῆς λόγον ἔχουσαν, πολλὰς οἰκείας
δυνάμεις πρὸς ἐνεργείας τὰς κατὰ φύσιν ἔχειν· οὐ
γὰρ δὴ οἷόν τε οὐσίαν οὖσαν μὴ μετὰ τοῦ εἶναι
καὶ ὀρέξεις καὶ πράξεις καὶ τὸ πρὸς τὸ εὖ κεκτῆσθαι.
Τὸ μὲν οὖν συναμφότερον ἐκ τοῦ συναμφοτέρου
25 τῆς φύσεως καὶ τοιόνδε καὶ ἔργα ἔχει τοιάδε·

---

[1] ⟨τὸ⟩ Kirchhoff, H-S².

---

[1] For the allegorical interpretation of the names of the
Fates, cp. Cornutus *Theologiae Graecae Compendium* ch. 13
(p. 13, Lang). Here, as in Cornutus, they stand for different
aspects of the same power of destiny, Clotho (only indirectly

was when they came into the body, and coming into
this particular body and being born of these particular parents, and in such and such a place, and in
general what we call the external circumstances.
That all happenings form a unity and are as it were
spun together, in the cases of individuals as well as
wholes, is signified by one of the Fates, as they are
called. Lachesis signifies the lots. And it is altogether necessary that it should be Atropos who
brings in these concurrent circumstances.[1] Of men
some are born belonging to the powers that come
from the whole and to external circumstances, as if
under an enchantment, and are in few things or
nothing themselves. Others master these powers
and circumstances and rise above them, so to speak,
by their heads,[2] towards the upper world and beyond
soul, and so preserve the best and ancient part of the
soul's substance. For we must not think of the soul
as of such a kind that the nature which it has is just
whatever affection it receives from outside, and that
alone of all things it has no nature of its own; but it,
far before anything else, since it has the status of a
principle, must have many powers of its own for its
natural activities. It is certainly not possible for it,
since it is a substance, not to possess along with its
being desires and actions and the tendency towards
its good. The compound entity results from a composition of its nature and is of this particular [com-
posite] kind and has these particular works. But any

referred to here) for the way things are " spun together,"
Lachesis for destiny as " lot," Atropos for the way our circumstances are unchangeably determined.

[2] The *Phaedrus* myth again (248A1–3).

ψυχὴ δὲ εἴ τις χωρίζεται, χωριστὰ καὶ ἴδια ἐνεργεῖ
τὰ τοῦ σώματος πάθη οὐκ αὐτῆς τιθεμένη, ἅτε
ἤδη ὁρῶσα, ὡς τὸ μὲν ἄλλο, τὸ δὲ ἄλλο.

16. Ἀλλὰ τί τὸ μικτὸν καὶ τί τὸ μὴ καὶ τί τὸ
χωριστὸν καὶ ἀχώριστον, ὅταν ἐν σώματι ᾖ, καὶ
ὅλως τί τὸ ζῷον ἀρχὴν ἑτέραν ὕστερον λαβοῦσι
ζητητέον· οὐ γὰρ ἅπαντες τὴν αὐτὴν δόξαν ἔσχον
5 περὶ τούτου. Νῦν δὲ ἔτι λέγωμεν πῶς τὸ [1] "κατὰ
λόγον ψυχῆς διοικούσης τὸ πᾶν" εἴπομεν. Πότερα
γὰρ ἕκαστα οἷον ἐπ' εὐθείας ποιοῦσα, ἄνθρωπον,
εἶτα ἵππον καὶ ἄλλο ζῷον καὶ δὴ καὶ θηρία, πῦρ
δὲ καὶ γῆν πρότερον, εἶτα συμπεσόντα ταῦτα
ἰδοῦσα καὶ φθείροντα ἄλληλα ἢ καὶ ὠφελοῦντα,
10 τὴν συμπλοκὴν τὴν ἐκ τούτων ἰδοῦσα μόνον καὶ
τὰ ὕστερον συμβαίνοντα ἀεὶ γίγνεσθαι, οὐδὲν ἔτι
συμβαλλομένη πρὸς τὰ ἐφεξῆς, ἀλλ' ἢ μόνον ζῴων
γενέσεις τῶν ἐξ ἀρχῆς πάλιν ποιοῦσα καὶ τοῖς
πάθεσι τοῖς δι' ἀλλήλων αὐτὰ συγχωροῦσα; Ἢ
αἰτίαν λέγοντες καὶ τῶν οὕτω γινομένων, ὅτι παρ'
15 αὐτῆς γενόμενα τὰ ἐφεξῆς ἐργάζεται; Ἢ καὶ τὸ
τόδε τόδε ποιῆσαι ἢ παθεῖν ἔχει ὁ λόγος οὐκ εἰκῇ
οὐδὲ κατ' ἐπιτυχίαν οὐδὲ [2] τῶνδε γιγνομένων, ἀλλ'

---

[1] πῶς τὸ Creuzer, H-S: τὸ πῶς codd.
[2] οὐδὲ Kirchhoff, H-S²: οὐδὲν codd.

---

[1] An announcement of the next treatise (I 1).
[2] Cp. ch. 13. 3–4 and *Phaedrus* 246C1–2.
[3] Harder rejects πῦρ δὲ καὶ γῆν πρότερον, perhaps rightly;
it seems oddly inconsequent and inappropriate; but Plotinus

soul which is separating itself has separate activities of its own and does not consider the body's affections as belonging to itself, because it already sees that body is one thing and soul is another

16. But what the mixed is and what the unmixed, and what the separated is and what the unseparated, when the soul is in the body, and in general what the living being is, are questions which we must enquire into afterwards, taking a different starting-point; [1] for everyone does not hold the same opinion on this subject. But now, continuing our present discussion, let us state in what sense we speak of " soul directing the All according to rational plan." [2] Does soul, then, make individual things, so to speak, in a straight line one after another, man, then horse and some other living being, and wild beasts too, and fire and earth first,[3] and then see these coming together and destroying or benefiting each other, only seeing their interweaving and the continual succession of its consequences, making no new contribution to what happens after but only again causing the births of living creatures from the original ones and giving them up to what they experience from their action upon each other? Or do we mean that soul is the cause of the things which happen in this way, because the beings produced by it accomplish what happens in consequence of their production? Or does the " rational plan " include this particular thing's acting or being acted on in this particular way, so that not even these particular events happen at random or by chance but occur in the way they do

is sometimes inconsequent and it seems safer to keep the words in the text.

ἐξ ἀνάγκης οὕτως; Ἄρ' οὖν τῶν λόγων αὐτὰ
ποιούντων; Ἢ ὄντων μὲν τῶν λόγων, οὐχ ὡς
ποιούντων δέ, ἀλλ' ὡς εἰδότων, μᾶλλον δὲ τῆς
20 ψυχῆς τῆς τοὺς λόγους τοὺς γεννητικοὺς ἐχούσης
εἰδυίας τὰ ἐκ τῶν ἔργων συμβαίνοντα αὐτῆς ἀπάν-
των· τῶν γὰρ αὐτῶν συμπιπτόντων καὶ περιεστη-
κότων τὰ αὐτὰ πάντως προσήκει ἀποτελεῖσθαι· ἃ
δὴ παραλαβοῦσα ἢ προϊδοῦσα ἡ ψυχὴ ἐπὶ τούτοις
25 τὰ ἐφεξῆς περαίνει καὶ συνείρει, προηγούμενα οὖν
καὶ ἐπακολουθοῦντα πάντως καὶ πάλιν ἐπὶ τούτοις
τὰ ἐφεξῆς προηγούμενα, ὡς ἐκ τῶν παρόντων·
ὅθεν ἴσως ἀεὶ χείρω τὰ ἐφεξῆς· οἷον ἄνδρες ἄλλοι
πάλαι, νῦν δὲ ἄλλοι, τῷ μεταξὺ καὶ ἀεὶ ἀναγκαίῳ
τῶν λόγων εἰκόντων τοῖς τῆς ὕλης παθήμασι.
30 Συνορῶσα οὖν ἀεὶ ἄλλα, τὰ δ' ἄλλα, καὶ παρα-
κολουθοῦσα τοῖς τῶν αὐτῆς ἔργων παθήμασι τὸν
βίον τοιοῦτον ἔχει καὶ οὐκ ἀπήλλακται τῆς ἐπὶ τῷ
ἔργῳ φροντίδος τέλος ἐπιθεῖσα τῷ ποιήματι καὶ
ὅπως ἕξει καλῶς καὶ εἰς ἀεὶ ἅπαξ μηχανησαμένη,
οἷα δέ τις γεωργὸς σπείρας ἢ καὶ φυτεύσας ἀεὶ
35 διορθοῦται, ὅσα χειμῶνες ἔβλαψαν ὑέτιοι ἢ κρυμῶν
συνέχεια ἢ ἀνέμων ζάλαι. Ἀλλ' εἰ ταῦτα ἄτοπα,
ἐκεῖνο δεῖ λέγειν, ὅτι ἤδη ἔγνωσται ἢ καὶ κεῖται
ἐν τοῖς λόγοις καὶ ἡ φθορὰ καὶ τὰ ἀπὸ κακίας
ἔργα; Ἀλλ' εἰ τοῦτο, καὶ τὰς κακίας τοὺς λόγους

by necessity? Is it, then, the rational forming principles which cause these happenings? The forming principles certainly exist, but not as causing but as knowing—or rather the soul which contains the generative rational principles knows the consequences which come from all its works; when the same things come together, the same circumstances arise, then it is altogether appropriate that the same results should follow. Soul takes over or foresees these antecedent conditions and taking account of them accomplishes what follows and links up the chain of consequences, bringing antecedents and consequents into complete connection, and again linking to the antecedents the causes which precede them in order, as far as it can in the existing circumstances. This is, perhaps, why what comes later in the series is always worse. Men, for instance, were quite different once from what they are now, since by reason of the space between them and their origins and the continual pressure of necessity their forming principles have yielded to the affections of matter. So soul sees the continual succession of different events and, following what happens to its works, has a corresponding kind of life, and is not freed from care for its work when it has set the crown on its achievement and has arranged once for all that it shall be in a good state for ever; but it is like a farmer who, when he has sown or planted, is always putting right what rainstorms or continuous frosts or gales of wind have spoiled. But if this account is absurd, then must we maintain the alternative, that corruption and the works that come from evil are known and already present in the forming principles? But if this is so, then we shall be

ποιεῖν φήσομεν, καίτοι ἐν ταῖς τέχναις καὶ τοῖς
40 λόγοις αὐτῶν οὐκ ἔνι ἁμαρτία οὐδὲ παρὰ τὴν
τέχνην οὐδ' ἡ φθορὰ τοῦ κατὰ τέχνην. Ἀλλ'
ἐνταῦθά τις ἐρεῖ μὴ εἶναι μηδὲν παρὰ [1] φύσιν μηδὲ
κακὸν τῷ ὅλῳ· ἀλλ' ὅμως τὸ χεῖρον καὶ τὸ
βέλτιον συγχωρήσεται. Τί οὖν, εἰ τῷ ὅλῳ καὶ τὸ
χεῖρον συνεργόν, καὶ οὐ δεῖ πάντα καλὰ εἶναι;
45 Ἐπεὶ καὶ τὰ ἐναντία συντελεῖ καὶ οὐκ ἄνευ τούτων
κόσμος· καὶ γὰρ ἐπὶ τῶν καθ' ἕκαστα ζῴων οὕτω·
καὶ τὰ μὲν βελτίω ἀναγκάζει καὶ πλάττει ὁ λόγος,
ὅσα δὲ μὴ τοιαῦτα, δυνάμει κεῖται ἐν τοῖς λόγοις,
ἐνεργείᾳ δὲ ἐν τοῖς γενομένοις, οὐδὲν ἔτι δεομένης
50 ἐκείνης ποιεῖν οὐδ' ἀνακινεῖν τοὺς λόγους ἤδη τῆς
ὕλης τῷ σεισμῷ τῷ ἐκ τῶν προηγουμένων λόγων
καὶ τὰ παρ' αὐτῆς ποιούσης τὰ χείρω, κρατουμένης
δ' αὖ οὐδὲν ἧττον πρὸς τὰ βελτίω· ὥστε ἓν ἐκ
πάντων ἄλλως ἑκατέρως γινομένων καὶ ἄλλως αὖ
ἐν τοῖς λόγοις.

17. Πότερα δὲ οἱ λόγοι οὗτοι οἱ ἐν ψυχῇ
νοήματα; Ἀλλὰ πῶς κατὰ τὰ νοήματα ποιήσει;
Ὁ γὰρ λόγος ἐν ὕλῃ ποιεῖ, καὶ τὸ ποιοῦν φυσικῶς
οὐ νόησις οὐδὲ ὅρασις, ἀλλὰ δύναμις τρεπτικὴ τῆς
5 ὕλης, οὐκ εἰδυῖα ἀλλὰ δρῶσα μόνον, οἷον τύπον καὶ
σχῆμα ἐν ὕδατι, [ὥσπερ κύκλος], ἄλλου ἐνδόντος

---

[1] παρὰ Ficinus, H-S: κατὰ codd.

---

[1] Cp. Plato, *Republic* 342B3.

asserting that the forming principles are the causes of evil, though in the arts and their principles there is no error and nothing contrary to the art or any corruption of the work of art.[1] But here someone will say that there is nothing contrary to nature or evil in the Whole; all the same, he will admit that there is worse and better. Suppose, then, the worse helps towards the completion of the Whole, and everything ought not to be good? For the opposites, too, co-operate for the perfection of the universe, and without them there is no universal order; yes, and it is so with particular living beings too. The forming principle compels the better things to exist and shapes them; the things which are not so, are present potentially in the principles, but actually in what comes to be; there is no need then any more for soul to make or to stir up the forming principles as matter is already, by the disturbance which comes from the preceding principles, making the things which come from it, the worse ones; though it is none the less overruled towards the production of the better. So there is one universe composed of all the things that have come to be, differently in each of these two ways, and that exist differently again in the forming principles.

17. Are these forming principles which are in soul thoughts? But, then, how will it make things in accordance with these thoughts? For it is in matter that the forming principle makes things, and that which makes on the level of nature is not thought or vision, but a power which manipulates matter, which does not know but only acts, like an impression or a figure in water; something else, different from what

97

εἰς τοῦτο τῆς φυτικῆς δυνάμεως καὶ γεννητικῆς
λεγομένης τὸ ποιεῖν. Εἰ τοῦτο, ποιήσει τὸ ἡγού-
μενον τῆς ψυχῆς τῷ τρέπειν¹ τὴν ἔννυλον καὶ
γεννητικὴν ψυχήν. Τρέψει οὖν λογισαμένη αὐτή;
10 Ἀλλ' εἰ λογισαμένη, ἀναφορὰν ἕξει πρότερον εἰς
ἄλλο ἢ εἰς τὰ ἐν αὐτῇ. Ἀλλ' εἰς τὰ ἐν αὐτῇ
οὐδὲν δεῖ λογισμῶν· οὐ γὰρ οὗτος τρέψει, ἀλλὰ τὸ
ἐν αὐτῇ ἔχον τοὺς λόγους· τοῦτο γὰρ καὶ δυνατώτε-
ρον καὶ ποιεῖν ἐν ψυχῇ δυνάμενον. Κατ' εἴδη ἄρα
ποιεῖ. Δεῖ τοίνυν καὶ αὐτὴν παρὰ νοῦ ἔχουσαν
15 διδόναι. Νοῦς δὴ ψυχῇ δίδωσι τῇ τοῦ παντός,
ψυχὴ δὲ παρ' αὐτῆς ἡ μετὰ νοῦν τῇ μετ' αὐτὴν
ἐλλάμπουσα καὶ τυποῦσα, ἡ δὲ ὡσπερεὶ ἐπιταχθεῖσα
ἤδη ποιεῖ· ποιεῖ δὲ τὰ μὲν ἀνεμποδίστως, τὰ δὲ
ἐμποδισθεῖσα χείρω. Ἅτε δὲ δύναμιν εἰς τὸ ποιεῖν
20 λαβοῦσα καὶ λόγων οὐ τῶν πρώτων πληρωθεῖσα
οὐ μόνον καθ' ἃ ἔλαβε ποιήσει, ἀλλὰ γένοιτο ἄν τι
καὶ παρ' αὐτῆς καὶ τοῦτο δηλονότι χεῖρον· καὶ
ζῷον μέν, ζῷον δὲ ἀτελέστερον καὶ δυσχεραῖνον
τὴν αὐτοῦ ζωήν, ἅτε χείριστον καὶ δύσκολον δὴ
καὶ ἄγριον καὶ ἐξ ὕλης χείρονος οἷον ὑποστάθμης
τῶν προηγουμένων πικρᾶς καὶ πικρὰ ποιούσης·
25 καὶ ταῦτα παρέξει καὶ αὐτὴ τῷ ὅλῳ.

¹ τρέπειν Ficinus, H-S²: τρέφειν codd.

¹ If the text is sound this translation, suggested by Henry–
Schwyzer in their critical note, is probably right, but the word-
order is extraordinarily unnatural and there is a good deal to

ON WHETHER THE STARS ARE CAUSES

is called the power of growth and generation, gives it what is required for this making.[1] If this is so, the ruling principle of the soul will make by manipulating the generative soul in matter. Will it, then, manipulate it as the result of having reasoned? But if it is after having reasoned, it will first refer to something else, or to what it has in itself. But if it refers to what it has in itself, there is no need of reasoning. For it is not reasoning that manipulates, but the part of the soul which possesses the forming principles: for this is both more powerful, and is able to make in the soul. It makes, then, according to forms: that is, it must give what it receives from Intellect. Intellect gives to the Soul of the All, and Soul (the one which comes next after Intellect) gives from itself to the soul next after it, enlightening it and impressing form on it, and this last soul immediately makes, as if under orders. It makes some things without hindrance, but in others, the worse ones, it meets obstruction. Since its power to make is derived, and it is filled with forming principles which are not the original ones, it will not simply make according to the forms which it has received but there would be a contribution of its own, and this is obviously worse. Its product is a living being, but a very imperfect one, and one which finds its own life disgusting since it is the worst of living things, ill-conditioned and savage, made of inferior matter, a sort of sediment of the prior realities, bitter and embittering. This is the lowest soul's contribution to the Whole.

be said for Kirchhoff's deletion of τῆς . . . λεγομένης as a gloss, which is accepted by Cilento.

18. Ἆρ᾽ οὖν τὰ κακὰ τὰ ἐν τῷ παντὶ ἀναγκαῖα,
ὅτι ἕπεται τοῖς προηγουμένοις; Ἢ ὅτι, καὶ εἰ μὴ
ταῦτα ἦν, ἀτελὲς ἂν ἦν τὸ πᾶν. Καὶ γὰρ χρείαν
τὰ πολλὰ αὐτῶν ἢ καὶ πάντα παρέχεται τῷ ὅλῳ,
5 οἷον τὰ τῶν ἰοβόλων, λανθάνει δὲ τὰ πλεῖστα διὰ τί·
ἐπεὶ καὶ τὴν κακίαν αὐτὴν ἔχειν πολλὰ χρήσιμα
καὶ πολλῶν ποιητικὴν ⟨εἶναι⟩ [1] καλῶν, οἷον κάλλους
τεχνητοῦ παντός, καὶ κινεῖν εἰς φρόνησιν μὴ ἐῶσαν
ἐπ᾽ ἀδείας εὕδειν. Εἰ δὴ ταῦτα ὀρθῶς εἴρηται,
δεῖ τὴν τοῦ παντὸς ψυχὴν θεωρεῖν μὲν τὰ ἄριστα
10 ἀεὶ ἱεμένην πρὸς τὴν νοητὴν φύσιν τὸν θεόν,
πληρουμένης δὲ αὐτῆς καὶ πεπληρωμένης οἷον
ἀπομεστουμένης αὐτῆς τὸ ἐξ αὐτῆς ἴνδαλμα καὶ
τὸ ἔσχατον αὐτῆς πρὸς τὸ κάτω τὸ ποιοῦν τοῦτο
εἶναι. Ποιητὴς οὖν ἔσχατος οὗτος· ἐπὶ δ᾽ αὐτῷ
τῆς ψυχῆς τὸ πρώτως πληρούμενον παρὰ νοῦ· ἐπὶ
15 πᾶσι δὲ νοῦς δημιουργός, ὃς καὶ τῇ ψυχῇ τῇ μετ᾽
αὐτὸν δίδωσιν ὧν ἴχνη ἐν τῇ τρίτῃ. Εἰκότως οὖν
λέγεται οὗτος ὁ κόσμος εἰκὼν ἀεὶ εἰκονιζόμενος,
ἑστηκότων μὲν τοῦ πρώτου καὶ δευτέρου, τοῦ δὲ
τρίτου ἑστηκότος μὲν καὶ αὐτοῦ, ἀλλ᾽ ἐν τῇ ὕλῃ
20 καὶ κατὰ συμβεβηκὸς κινουμένου. Ἕως γὰρ ἂν
ᾖ νοῦς καὶ ψυχή, ῥεύσονται οἱ λόγοι εἰς τοῦτο τὸ
εἶδος ψυχῆς, ὥσπερ, ἕως ἂν ᾖ ἥλιος, πάντα τὰ ἀπ᾽
αὐτοῦ φῶτα.

---

[1] ⟨εἶναι⟩ Müller, H-S².

ON WHETHER THE STARS ARE CAUSES

18. Then are the evils in the All necessary, because they follow on the prior realities? Rather because if they did not exist the All would be imperfect. Most of them, even all of them, contribute something useful to the Whole—poisonous snakes do, for instance—though generally the reason why remains obscure. Even moral evil itself has many advantages and is productive of much excellence, for example, all the beauty of art,[1] and rouses us to serious thought about our way of living, not allowing us to slumber complacently. If this is correct, it must be that the Soul of the All contemplates the best, always aspiring to the intelligible nature and to God, and that when it is full, filled right up to the brim, its trace, its last and lowest expression, is this productive principle that we are discussing. This, then, is the ultimate maker; over it is that part of soul which is primarily filled from Intellect: over all is Intellect the Craftsman, who gives to the soul which comes next those gifts whose traces are in the third. This visible universe, then, is properly called an image [2] always in process of being made; its first and second principles are at rest, the third at rest too, but also in motion, incidentally and in matter. As long as Intellect and Soul exist, the forming principles will flow into this lower form of soul, just as, as long as the sun exists, all its rays will shine from it.

---

[1] Is Plotinus thinking here, perhaps, of tragic poetry? If so, the argument shows a startling reversal of Plato's standpoint. Plato in *Republic* II refused to allow poets to portray moral evil; Plotinus here seems to be justifying the existence of moral evil in the universe because it produces art.

[2] Cp. the end of the *Timaeus* 92C7.

ENNEAD II. 4

II. 4. ON MATTER

Introductory Note

THE title of this treatise (No. 12 in Porphyry's chronological order) is given by Porphyry in the *Life* as περὶ τῶν δύο ὑλῶν (On the Two Kinds of Matter); in the MSS of the *Enneads* and the ancient tables of contents (*Pinax, Summarium*) it appears simply as *On Matter*. It is referred to by Plotinus himself in I. 8. 15. 2 . . . δεικτέον αὐτῷ ἐκ τῶν περὶ ὕλης λόγων . . . but Harder is surely right in saying that there is no question of a title there—the phrase simply means "from our discussions about matter." Plotinus in fact, we know (*Life* ch. 4), gave no titles to his treatises: and the title given in the *Life* to this one seems preferable, because it describes the contents better, since the first part of the treatise is devoted to intelligible matter, the second to the matter of the sense-world. The treatise is a good example of Plotinus's method of work at its most professional and technical, a close and critical discussion of the views of the Stoics and of Aristotle. As often, he is particularly concerned to carry through a critical rethinking of Aristotle's doctrine designed to adapt it to Platonism as he understood it. The main points on which he differs from Aristotle in this treatise are: (1) he accepts matter in the intelligible world; the objections to belief in its existence stated in ch. 2. and refuted in the following chapters are in substance Aristotelian; (2) he identifies matter in the sense-world with privation; this is established against Aristotle in chs. 14–end, as is essential if Plotinus is to maintain his doctrine that matter is the principle of evil, the ultimate negativity,

ON MATTER

which appears clearly at the end of the treatise. On the other hand, Plotinus is maintaining Aristotle's doctrine against the Stoics when he argues that matter is incorporeal and without any sort of dimension (chs. 1, 8–12).

Synopsis

Matter is the substrate and receptacle of forms. Diverse views of its nature; corporeal (Stoics) incorporeal (Platonists and Aristotelians). The Platonist doctrine of intelligible matter (ch. 1). Objections to the existence of intelligible matter (ch. 2). Refutation of the objections and explanation of the true nature and function of intelligible matter (chs. 3–5). Matter in the sense-world, Aristotelian arguments for its existence (ch. 6). Criticism of pre-Socratic conceptions, also from Aristotle (ch. 7). Arguments to show that matter is incorporeal and without size, and that the conception of a sizeless incorporeal matter has a real meaning and philosophical value (chs. 8–12). Neither is matter quality, either positive or negative (ch. 13). As against Aristotle, it is identical with privation, (chs. 14–16), and so is absolute negativity and evil (ch. 16).

II. 4. (12) ΠΕΡΙ ΥΛΗΣ

1. Τὴν λεγομένην ὕλην ὑποκείμενόν τι καὶ ὑποδοχὴν εἰδῶν λέγοντες εἶναι κοινόν τινα τοῦτον λόγον περὶ αὐτῆς πάντες λέγουσιν, ὅσοι εἰς ἔννοιαν ἦλθον τῆς τοιαύτης φύσεως, καὶ μέχρι τούτου τὴν 5 αὐτὴν φέρονται· τίς δέ ἐστιν αὕτη ἡ ὑποκειμένη φύσις καὶ πῶς δεκτικὴ καὶ τίνων, τὸ ἐντεῦθεν ἤδη ζητοῦντες διέστησαν. Καὶ οἱ μὲν σώματα μόνον τὰ ὄντα εἶναι θέμενοι καὶ τὴν οὐσίαν ἐν τούτοις μίαν τε τὴν ὕλην λέγουσι καὶ τοῖς στοιχείοις ὑποβεβλῆσθαι καὶ αὐτὴν εἶναι τὴν οὐσίαν, τὰ δ' 10 ἄλλα πάντα οἷον πάθη ταύτης καί πως ἔχουσαν αὐτὴν καὶ τὰ στοιχεῖα εἶναι. Καὶ δὴ καὶ τολμῶσι καὶ μέχρι θεῶν αὐτὴν ἄγειν καὶ τέλος δὴ καὶ αὐτὸν αὐτῶν τὸν θεὸν ὕλην ταύτην πως ἔχουσαν εἶναι. Διδόασι δὲ καὶ σῶμα αὐτῇ ἄποιον αὐτὸ σῶμα λέγοντες καὶ μέγεθος δέ. Οἱ δὲ ἀσώματον

---

[1] ὑποκείμενον is Aristotle's word (cp., e.g., *Physics* A. 9. 192a33), ὑποδοχή Plato's (*Timaeus* 49A6). The two conceptions, of course, differ from each other considerably more than this summary definition would suggest.

II. 4. ON MATTER

1. What is called " matter " is said to be some sort of " substrate " and " receptacle " of forms;[1] this account is common to all those who have arrived at a conception of a nature of this kind, and as far as this they all go the same way. But they disagree as soon as they begin to pursue the further investigation into what this underlying nature is and how it is receptive and what of. Those who adopt the position that realities are exclusively bodies and that substance consists in bodies say there is one matter and that it underlies the elements and is itself substance; all other things are, so to speak, affections of matter, and the elements, too, are matter in a certain state. They even dare to take matter as far as the gods, and finally, even [to say] that their God himself is this matter in a certain state.[2] And they give it a body too, for they say that it is a body without quality and a magnitude.[3] But others [4] say that

---

[2] εἶναι cannot be dependent on τολμῶσι: a verb of saying is required. Henry and Schwyzer tentatively suggest ἀντεῖν for αὐτῶν. But this is rather far-fetched, and it seems to me possible that this is a piece of careless writing by Plotinus himself.

[3] These are the Stoics: cp. Stoicorum Veterum Fragmenta II. 316, 309, 326.

[4] Platonists and Aristotelians.

15 λέγουσι καὶ ταύτην οὐ μίαν τινὲς αὐτῶν, ἀλλὰ
ταύτην μὲν τοῖς σώμασιν ὑποβεβλῆσθαι καὶ αὐτοὶ
περὶ ἧς οἱ πρότεροι λέγουσιν, ἑτέραν μέντοι προτέ-
ραν ἐν τοῖς νοητοῖς ὑποβεβλημένην τοῖς ἐκεῖ εἴδεσι
καὶ ταῖς ἀσωμάτοις οὐσίαις.

2. Διὸ πρότερον ζητητέον περὶ ταύτης εἰ ἔστι,
καὶ τίς οὖσα τυγχάνει, καὶ πῶς ἐστιν. Εἰ δὴ
ἀόριστόν τι καὶ ἄμορφον δεῖ τὸ τῆς ὕλης εἶναι, ἐν
δὲ τοῖς ἐκεῖ ἀρίστοις οὖσιν οὐδὲν ἀόριστον οὐδὲ
5 ἄμορφον, οὐδ' ἂν ὕλη ἐκεῖ εἴη· καὶ εἰ ἁπλοῦν
ἕκαστον, οὐδ' ἂν δέοι ὕλης, ἵν' ἐξ αὐτῆς καὶ ἄλλου
τὸ σύνθετον· καὶ γινομένοις μὲν ὕλης δεῖ καὶ ἐξ
ἑτέρων ἕτερα ποιουμένοις, ἀφ' ὧν καὶ ἡ τῶν
αἰσθητῶν ὕλη ἐνοήθη, μὴ γινομένοις δὲ οὔ. Πόθεν
δὲ ἐλήλυθε καὶ ὑπέστη; Εἰ γὰρ ἐγένετο, καὶ ὑπό
10 τινος· εἰ δὲ ἀίδιος, καὶ ἀρχαὶ πλείους καὶ κατὰ
συντυχίαν τὰ πρῶτα. Κἂν εἶδος δὲ προσέλθῃ, τὸ
σύνθετον ἔσται σῶμα· ὥστε κἀκεῖ σῶμα.

3. Πρῶτον οὖν λεκτέον ὡς οὐ πανταχοῦ τὸ
ἀόριστον ἀτιμαστέον, οὐδὲ ὃ ἂν ἄμορφον ᾖ τῇ

---

[1] It seems probable that Plotinus is making a distinction
between Platonists and Aristotelians here. The only incorporeal beings whose existence was recognised by Aristotle
were pure forms (intelligences), not composites of form and
matter (cp. Met. Λ. 6. 1071b2). Aristotle speaks of ὕλη νοητή
in the *Metaphysics* (Z. 10. 1036a9–12, 11. 1037a4–5, H. 6.
1045a33–37), and Plotinus may have taken the term from
these passages. But the senses in which Aristotle uses it (see

matter is incorporeal, and some of them [1] that this incorporeal matter is not one, but they, too, maintain that the same kind of matter underlies bodies which the people mentioned before speak of, but that there is another, prior, kind in the intelligible world which underlies the forms there and the incorporeal substances.

2. So first we must enquire about this second matter, whether it exists, and what sort of thing it is, and how it exists. If what is of the matter kind must be something undefined and shapeless, and there is nothing undefined or shapeless among the beings there, which are the best, there would not be matter there. And if every intelligible being is simple, there would be no need of matter, so that the composite being might come from it and from something else. And there is need of matter for beings that come into existence and are made into one thing after another—this was what led people to conceive the matter of beings perceived by the senses—but not for beings that do not come into existence. And where did it come from, from where did it get its being? If it came to be, it was by some agency; but if it was eternal, there would be several principles and the primary beings would exist by chance. And if form comes to matter, the composite being will be a body; so that there will be body in the intelligible world too.

3. First, then, we must say that we should not in every case despise the undefined or anything of which

Ross's note on the passages from Z. in his edition of the *Metaphysics*, Vol. II, pp. 199–200) are very remote from that in which Plotinus understands it.

ἑαυτοῦ ἐπινοίᾳ, εἰ μέλλοι παρέχειν αὐτὸ τοῖς πρὸ
αὐτοῦ καὶ τοῖς ἀρίστοις· οἷόν τι καὶ ψυχὴ πρὸς
5 νοῦν καὶ λόγον πέφυκε μορφουμένη παρὰ τούτων
καὶ εἰς εἶδος βέλτιον ἀγομένη· ἔν τε τοῖς νοητοῖς
τὸ σύνθετον ἑτέρως, οὐχ ὡς τὰ σώματα· ἐπεὶ καὶ
λόγοι σύνθετοι καὶ ἐνεργείᾳ δὲ σύνθετον ποιοῦσι
τὴν ἐνεργοῦσαν εἰς εἶδος φύσιν. Εἰ δὲ καὶ πρὸς
ἄλλο καὶ παρ' ἄλλου, καὶ μᾶλλον. Ἡ δὲ τῶν
10 γιγνομένων ὕλη ἀεὶ ἄλλο καὶ ἄλλο εἶδος ἴσχει, τῶν
δὲ ἀιδίων ἡ αὐτὴ ταὐτὸν ἀεί. Τάχα δὲ ἀνάπαλιν
ἡ ἐνταῦθα. Ἐνταῦθα μὲν γὰρ παρὰ μέρος πάντα
καὶ ἐν ἑκάστοτε· διὸ οὐδὲν ἐμμένει ἄλλου ἄλλο
ἐξωθοῦντος· διὸ οὐ ταὐτὸν ἀεί. Ἐκεῖ δὲ ἅμα
πάντα· διὸ οὐκ ἔχει εἰς ὃ μεταβάλλοι, ἤδη γὰρ
15 ἔχει πάντα. Οὐδέποτ' οὖν ἄμορφος οὐδὲ [1] ἐκεῖ ἡ
ἐκεῖ, ἐπεὶ οὐδ' ἡ ἐνταῦθα, ἀλλ' ἕτερον τρόπον
ἑκατέρα. Τὸ δὲ εἴτε ἀίδιος, εἴτε γενομένη, ἐπειδὰν
ὅ τί ποτ' ἐστὶ λάβωμεν, δῆλον ἔσται.

4. Ὁ δὴ λόγος ἡμῖν ὑποθεμένοις τὸ νῦν εἶναι τὰ
εἴδη—δέδεικται γὰρ ἐν ἄλλοις—προΐτω. Εἰ οὖν
πολλὰ τὰ εἴδη, κοινὸν μέν τι ἐν αὐτοῖς ἀνάγκη

---

[1] οὐδὲ Volkmann, H-S²: οὔτε codd.

---

[1] The reference is probably to the earlier treatise V. 9 (5) 3–4.

the very idea implies shapelessness, if it is going to offer itself to the principles before it and to the best beings. Soul, for instance, is naturally disposed like this to Intellect and Reason; it is shaped by them and brought to a better form. And in the intelligible world the composite being is differently constituted, not like bodies: since forming principles, too, are composite, and by their actuality make composite the nature which is active towards the production of form. But if this nature both works on and derives from something other than itself, it is composite to an even higher degree. The matter, too, of the things that came into being is always receiving different forms, but the matter of eternal things is always the same and always has the same form. With matter here, it is pretty well exactly the other way round; for here it is all things in turn and only one thing at each particular time; so nothing lasts because one thing pushes out another; so it is not the same for ever. But in the intelligible world matter is all things at once; so it has nothing to change into, for it has all things already. Therefore, intelligible matter is certainly not ever shapeless in the intelligible world, since even the matter here is not, but each of them has shape in a different way. The question whether matter is eternal or came into being will be cleared up when we grasp what sort of a thing it is.

4. Let us assume for the present that the Forms exist—for it has been demonstrated elsewhere [1]— and continue our discussion on this assumption. If, then, the Forms are many, there must be something in them common to them all; and also something

εἶναι· καὶ δὴ καὶ ἴδιον, ᾧ διαφέρει ἄλλο ἄλλου.
5 Τοῦτο δὴ τὸ ἴδιον καὶ ἡ διαφορὰ ἡ χωρίζουσα ἡ
οἰκεία ἐστὶ μορφή. Εἰ δὲ μορφή, ἔστι τὸ μορφούμε-
νον, περὶ ὃ ἡ διαφορά. Ἔστιν ἄρα καὶ ὕλη ἡ τὴν
μορφὴν δεχομένη καὶ ἀεὶ τὸ ὑποκείμενον. Ἔτι εἰ
κόσμος νοητὸς ἔστιν ἐκεῖ, μίμημα δὲ οὗτος ἐκείνου,
οὗτος δὲ σύνθετος καὶ ἐξ ὕλης, κἀκεῖ δεῖ ὕλην
10 εἶναι. Ἢ πῶς προσερεῖς κόσμον μὴ εἰς εἶδος
ἰδών; Πῶς δὲ εἶδος μὴ ἐφ' ᾧ τὸ εἶδος λαβών;
Ἀμερὲς μὲν γὰρ παντελῶς πάντη αὐτό, μεριστὸν
δὲ ὁπωσοῦν. Καὶ εἰ μὲν διασπασθέντα ἀπ'
ἀλλήλων τὰ μέρη, ἡ τομὴ καὶ ἡ διάσπασις ὕλης
ἐστὶ πάθος· αὕτη γὰρ ἡ τμηθεῖσα· εἰ δὲ πολλὰ
15 ὂν ἀμέριστόν ἐστι, τὰ πολλὰ ἐν ἑνὶ ὄντα ἐν ὕλῃ
ἐστὶ τῷ ἑνὶ αὐτὰ μορφαὶ αὐτοῦ ὄντα· τὸ γὰρ ἓν
τοῦτο [τὸ ποικίλον] νόησον ποικίλον καὶ πολύμορφον.
Οὐκοῦν ἄμορφον αὐτὸ πρὸ τοῦ ποικίλον· εἰ γὰρ
τῷ νῷ ἀφέλοις τὴν ποικιλίαν καὶ τὰς μορφὰς καὶ
τοὺς λόγους καὶ τὰ νοήματα, τὸ πρὸ τούτων
20 ἄμορφον καὶ ἀόριστον καὶ τούτων οὐδὲν τῶν ἐπ'
αὐτῷ καὶ ἐν αὐτῷ.

5. Εἰ δ', ὅτι ἀεὶ ἔχει ταῦτα καὶ ὁμοῦ, ἐν ἄμφω
καὶ οὐχ ὕλη ἐκεῖνο, οὐδ' ἐνταῦθα ἔσται τῶν
σωμάτων ὕλη· οὐδέποτε γὰρ ἄνευ μορφῆς, ἀλλ'
ἀεὶ ὅλον σῶμα, σύνθετον μὴν ὅμως. Καὶ νοῦς

individual, by which one differs from another. Now this something individual, this separating difference, is the shape which belongs to each. But if there is shape, there is that which is shaped, about which the difference is predicated. Therefore, there is matter which receives the shape, and is the substrate in every case. Further, if there is an intelligible universal order There, and this universe here is an imitation of it, and this is composite, and composed of matter, then there must be matter There too. Or else how can you call it a universal order except with regard to its form? And how can you have form without something on which the form is imposed? Intelligible reality is certainly altogether absolutely without parts, yet it has parts in a kind of way. If the parts are torn apart from each other, then the cutting and tearing apart is an affection of matter: for it is matter that is cut. But if intelligible reality is at once many and partless, then the many existing in one are in matter which is that one, and they are its shapes: conceive this unity as varied and of many shapes. So, then, it must be shapeless before it is varied; for if you take away in your mind its variety and shapes and forming principles and thoughts, what is prior to these is shapeless and undefined and is none of these things that are on it and in it.

5. But if it is objected that, because intelligible matter always has these forms and has them all together, both are one and that underlying reality is not matter, then the matter of the bodies here will not exist in this world either: for it is never without shape but is always a complete body, but all the same a composite one. Intellect finds out its doubleness,

5 εὑρίσκει τὸ διττόν· οὗτος γὰρ διαιρεῖ, ἕως εἰς
ἁπλοῦν ἥκῃ μηκέτι αὐτὸ ἀναλύεσθαι δυνάμενον·
ἕως δὲ δύναται, χωρεῖ αὐτοῦ εἰς τὸ βάθος. Τὸ δὲ
βάθος ἑκάστου ἡ ὕλη· διὸ καὶ σκοτεινὴ πᾶσα, ὅτι
τὸ φῶς ὁ λόγος. Καὶ ὁ νοῦς λόγος· διὸ τὸν ἐφ᾽
ἑκάστου λόγον ὁρῶν τὸ κάτω ὡς ὑπὸ τὸ φῶς
10 σκοτεινὸν ἥγηται, ὥσπερ ὀρθαλμὸς φωτοειδὴς ὢν
πρὸς τὸ φῶς βαλὼν καὶ χρόας φῶτα ὄντα τὰ
ὑπὸ τὰ χρώματα σκοτεινὰ καὶ ὑλικὰ εἶναι λέγει
κεκρυμμένα τοῖς χρώμασι. Διάφορόν γε μὴν τὸ
σκοτεινὸν τό τε ἐν τοῖς νοητοῖς τό τε ἐν τοῖς
15 αἰσθητοῖς ὑπάρχει διάφορός τε ἡ ὕλη, ὅσῳ καὶ τὸ
εἶδος τὸ ἐπικείμενον ἀμφοῖν διάφορον· ἡ μὲν γὰρ
θεία λαβοῦσα τὸ ὁρίζον αὐτὴν ζωὴν ὡρισμένην καὶ
νοερὰν ἔχει, ἡ δὲ ὡρισμένον μέν τι γίγνεται, οὐ
μὴν ζῶν οὐδὲ νοοῦν, ἀλλὰ νεκρὸν κεκοσμημένον.
Καὶ ἡ μορφὴ δὲ εἴδωλον· ὥστε καὶ τὸ ὑποκείμενον
20 εἴδωλον. Ἐκεῖ δὲ ἡ μορφὴ ἀληθινόν· ὥστε καὶ
τὸ ὑποκείμενον. Διὸ καὶ τοὺς λέγοντας οὐσίαν τὴν
ὕλην, εἰ περὶ ἐκείνης ἔλεγον, ὀρθῶς ἔδει ὑπολαμβάνειν λέγειν· τὸ γὰρ ὑποκείμενον ἐκεῖ οὐσία,
μᾶλλον δὲ μετὰ τοῦ ἐπ᾽ αὐτῇ νοουμένη καὶ ὅλη
οὖσα πεφωτισμένη οὐσία. Πότερα δὲ ἀίδιος ἡ
25 νοητὴ ὁμοίως ζητητέον, ὡς ἄν τις καὶ τὰς ἰδέας
ζητοῖ· γενητὰ μὲν γὰρ τῷ ἀρχὴν ἔχειν, ἀγένητα
δέ, ὅτι μὴ χρόνῳ τὴν ἀρχὴν ἔχει, ἀλλ᾽ ἀεὶ παρ᾽

---

[1] This is an allusion to Plato's theory of vision. Cp.
Timaeus 45B.

for it divides till it comes to something simple which cannot itself be resolved into parts; but as long as it can it advances into the depth of body. And the depth of each individual thing is matter: so all matter is dark, because the light [in each thing] is the rational forming principle. Now intellect too is rational principle. So intellect sees the forming principle in each thing and considers that what is under it is dark because it lies below the light; just as the eye, which has the form of light,[1] directs its gaze at the light and at colours (which are lights) and reports that what lies below the colours is dark and material, hidden by the colours. The darkness, however, in intelligible things differs from that in the things of sense, and so does the matter, by just as much as the form superimposed on both is different. The divine matter when it receives that which defines it has a defined and intelligent life, but the matter of this world becomes something defined, but not alive or thinking, a decorated corpse. Shape here is only an image; so that which underlies it is also only an image. But There the shape is true shape, and what underlies it is true too. So those who say that matter is substance must be considered to be speaking correctly if they are speaking of matter in the intelligible world. For that which underlies form There is substance, or rather, considered along with the form imposed upon it, it makes a whole which is illuminated substance. As for the question whether intelligible matter is eternal, one must investigate it in the same way as one investigates the ideas: intelligible realities are originated in so far as they have a beginning, but unoriginated because they

ἄλλου, οὐχ ὡς γινόμενα ἀεί, ὥσπερ ὁ κόσμος, ἀλλὰ
ὄντα ἀεί, ὥσπερ ὁ ἐκεῖ κόσμος. Καὶ γὰρ ἡ
ἑτερότης ἡ ἐκεῖ ἀεί, ἣ τὴν ὕλην ποιεῖ· ἀρχὴ γὰρ
30 ὕλης αὕτη, καὶ ἡ κίνησις ἡ πρώτη· διὸ καὶ αὕτη
ἑτερότης ἐλέγετο, ὅτι ὁμοῦ ἐξέφυσαν κίνησις καὶ
ἑτερότης· ἀόριστον δὲ καὶ ἡ κίνησις καὶ ἡ ἑτερότης
ἡ ἀπὸ τοῦ πρώτου, κἀκείνου πρὸς τὸ ὁρισθῆναι
δεόμενα· ὁρίζεται δέ, ὅταν πρὸς αὐτὸ ἐπιστραφῇ·
πρὶν δὲ ἀόριστον καὶ ἡ ὕλη καὶ τὸ ἕτερον καὶ
35 οὔπω ἀγαθόν, ἀλλ' ἀφώτιστον ἐκείνου. Εἰ γὰρ
παρ' ἐκείνου τὸ φῶς, τὸ δεχόμενον τὸ φῶς, πρὶν
δέξασθαι, φῶς οὐκ ἔχει ἀεί, ἀλλὰ ἄλλο ὂν ἔχει,
εἴπερ τὸ φῶς παρ' ἄλλου. Καὶ περὶ μὲν τῆς ἐν
τοῖς νοητοῖς ὕλης πλείω τῶν προσηκόντων παρα-
γυμνωθέντα ταύτῃ.

6. Περὶ δὲ τῆς τῶν σωμάτων ὑποδοχῆς ὧδε
λεγέσθω. Ὅτι μὲν οὖν δεῖ τι τοῖς σώμασιν
ὑποκείμενον εἶναι ἄλλο ὂν παρ' αὐτά, ἥ τε εἰς
ἄλληλα μεταβολὴ τῶν στοιχείων δηλοῖ. Οὐ γὰρ

---

[1] Here we encounter Plotinus's interpretation of the
μέγιστα γένη of Plato, *Sophist* 254D ff. (Being, Motion, Rest,
Sameness and Otherness) as " categories of the intelligible
world," for which, cp. V. 1. 4 and the full exposition in VI. 2.
7–8.

[2] The doctrine briefly stated here is of cardinal importance
in the thought of Plotinus; it is that two moments are to be
distinguished in the timeless generation of Intellect from the
One; the first, in which it proceeds as an unformed potentiality;
the second, in which it returns upon the One in contemplation

have not a beginning in time; they always proceed from something else, not as always coming into being, like the universe, but as always existing, like the universe There. For Otherness There [1] exists always, which produces intelligible matter; for this is the principle of matter, this and the primary Movement. For this reason Movement, too, was called Otherness, because Movement and Otherness sprang forth together. The Movement and Otherness which came from the First are undefined, and need the First to define them; and they are defined when they turn to it.[2] But before the turning, matter, too, was undefined and the Other and not yet good, but unilluminated from the First. For if light comes from the First, then that which receives the light, before it receives it has everlastingly no light; but it has light as other than itself, since the light comes to it from something else. And now we have disclosed about the intelligible matter more than the occasion demanded.

6. About the receptacle of bodies, let this be our account.[3] That there must be something underlying bodies, which is different from the bodies themselves, is made clear by the changing of the elements into each other. For the destruction of that which

and is informed and actualised by him. For the basic doctrine, cp. V. 4. 2; for Plotinus's explanation of why the multiplicity of Forms results from Intellect's contemplation of the One, cp. V. 3. 11, V. 1. 7.

[3] What follows is an accurate exposition of Aristotle's doctrine of matter, in Aristotelian language: it reads like a Peripatetic commentary on *Met.* Λ 1-2. 1069b. The criticism of Pre-Socratic views in the following chapter is also entirely based on Aristotle; see the first note to ch. 7.

5 παντελὴς τοῦ μεταβάλλοντος ἡ φθορά· ἢ ἔσται τις
οὐσία εἰς τὸ μὴ ὂν ἀπολομένη· οὐδ' αὖ τὸ γενόμενον ἐκ τοῦ παντελῶς μὴ ὄντος εἰς τὸ ὂν ἐλήλυθεν,
ἀλλ' ἔστιν εἴδους μεταβολὴ ἐξ εἴδους ἑτέρου.
Μένει δὲ τὸ δεξάμενον τὸ εἶδος τοῦ γενομένου καὶ
ἀποβαλὸν θάτερον. Τοῦτό τε οὖν δηλοῖ καὶ ὅλως
10 ἡ φθορά· συνθέτου γάρ· εἰ δὲ τοῦτο, ἐξ ὕλης καὶ
εἴδους ἕκαστον. Ἥ τε ἐπαγωγὴ μαρτυρεῖ τὸ
φθειρόμενον σύνθετον δεικνῦσα· καὶ ἡ ἀνάλυσις
δέ· οἷον εἰ ἡ φιάλη εἰς τὸν χρυσόν, ὁ δὲ χρυσὸς εἰς
ὕδωρ, καὶ τὸ ὕδωρ δὲ φθειρόμενον τὸ ἀνάλογον
ἀπαιτεῖ. Ἀνάγκη δὲ τὰ στοιχεῖα ἢ εἶδος εἶναι ἢ
15 ὕλην πρώτην ἢ ἐξ ὕλης καὶ εἴδους. Ἀλλ' εἶδος
μὲν οὐχ οἷόν τε· πῶς γὰρ ἄνευ ὕλης ἐν ὄγκῳ καὶ
μεγέθει; Ἀλλ' οὐδὲ ὕλη ἡ πρώτη· φθείρεται γάρ.
Ἐξ ὕλης ἄρα καὶ εἴδους. Καὶ τὸ μὲν εἶδος κατὰ
τὸ ποιὸν καὶ τὴν μορφήν, ἡ δὲ κατὰ τὸ ὑποκείμενον
ἀόριστον, ὅτι μὴ εἶδος.

7. Ἐμπεδοκλῆς δὲ τὰ στοιχεῖα ἐν ὕλῃ θέμενος
ἀντιμαρτυροῦσαν ἔχει τὴν φθορὰν αὐτῶν. Ἀνα-
ξαγόρας δὲ τὸ μῖγμα ὕλην[1] ποιῶν, οὐκ ἐπιτηδειότητα
πρὸς πάντα, ἀλλὰ πάντα ἐνεργείᾳ ἔχειν λέγων ὂν
5 εἰσάγει νοῦν ἀναιρεῖ οὐκ αὐτὸν τὴν μορφὴν καὶ τὸ

---

[1] ὕλην Steinhart, H-S: ὕδωρ codd.

---

[1] The criticism of the Pre-Socratics in this chapter does not
indicate any independent study of them by Plotinus; it is
based on Aristotle (cp. *Physics* A. 4. 187a12 ff.; *Met.* A. 7.

changes is not complete; otherwise, there will be a
being which has totally perished into non-being;
nor has the engendered thing come to being from
absolute non-being, but there is a change from one
form into another. But if this is so there remains
that which has received the form of the engendered
thing and lost the other one. And then destruction
also makes this completely clear; for it is destruction
of a composite; but if each individual thing is a
composite, it is composed of matter and form. In-
duction demonstrates this by showing that what is
being destroyed is a composite; and the process of
reduction to a thing's elements shows it too; if, for
example, the cup is reduced to its gold and the gold to
water, the water in process of dissolution requires
something analogous to be reduced to. And the elements must be either form or first matter or composed
of matter and form. But it is not possible for them
to be form; for without matter how could they be in
a state of having bulk and dimension? But they are
not first matter either; for they are destroyed; so
they must be composed of matter and form: form
is in relation to their quality and shape, and matter
to their substrate, which is undefined because it is
not form.

7. Empedocles, who classes the elements as matter,
has their destruction as evidence against him.[1]
Anaxagoras, when he makes his mixture matter, and
says that it is not a capacity for everything but contains everything in actuality, does away with the
mind which he introduces by not making it the giver

988a27 ff.; Λ 2.. 1069b20–23), and is entirely Peripatetic in
spirit.

εἶδος διδόντα ποιῶν οὐδὲ πρότερον τῆς ὕλης ἀλλ'
ἅμα. Ἀδύνατον δὲ τὸ ἅμα. Εἰ γὰρ μετέχει τὸ
μῖγμα τοῦ εἶναι, πρότερον τὸ ὄν· εἰ δὲ καὶ τοῦτο
ὂν τὸ μῖγμα κἀκεῖνο, ἄλλου ἐπ' αὐτοῖς δεήσει
τρίτου. Εἰ οὖν πρότερον ἀνάγκη τὸν δημιουργὸν
10 εἶναι, τί ἔδει τὰ εἴδη κατὰ σμικρὰ ἐν τῇ ὕλῃ εἶναι,
εἶτα τὸν νοῦν διὰ πραγμάτων ἀνηνύτων διακρίνειν
ἐξὸν ἀποίῳ οὔσῃ τὴν ποιότητα καὶ τὴν μορφὴν
ἐπὶ πᾶσαν ἐκτεῖναι; Τό τε πᾶν ἐν παντὶ εἶναι πῶς
οὐκ ἀδύνατον; Ὁ δὲ τὸ ἄπειρον ὑποθεὶς τί ποτε
15 τοῦτο λεγέτω. Καὶ εἰ οὕτως ἄπειρον, ὡς ἀδιεξίτη-
τον, ὡς οὐκ ἔστι τοιοῦτόν τι ἐν τοῖς οὖσιν οὔτε
αὐτοάπειρον οὔτε ἐπ' ἄλλῃ φύσει ὡς συμβεβηκὸς
σώματί τινι, τὸ μὲν αὐτοάπειρον, ὅτι καὶ τὸ μέρος
αὐτοῦ ἐξ ἀνάγκης ἄπειρον, τὸ δὲ ὡς συμβεβηκός,
20 ὅτι τὸ ᾧ συμβέβηκεν ἐκεῖνο οὐκ ἂν καθ' ἑαυτὸ
ἄπειρον εἴη οὐδὲ ἁπλοῦν οὐδὲ ὕλη ἔτι, δῆλον.
Ἀλλ' οὐδὲ αἱ ἄτομοι τάξιν ὕλης ἕξουσιν αἱ τὸ
παράπαν οὐκ οὖσαι· τμητὸν γὰρ πᾶν σῶμα κατὰ
πᾶν· καὶ τὸ συνεχὲς δὲ τῶν σωμάτων καὶ τὸ
ὑγρὸν καὶ τὸ μὴ οἷόν τε ἄνευ νοῦ ἕκαστα καὶ
25 ψυχῆς, ἣν ἀδύνατον ἐξ ἀτόμων εἶναι—ἄλλην τε
φύσιν παρὰ τὰς ἀτόμους ἐκ τῶν ἀτόμων δημιουργεῖν

---

[1] This obscure criticism is less Peripatetic than the rest of
the chapter, as it seems to imply Plotinus's own equation of
Intellect and being.

[2] Anaximander. Plotinus's criticism shows how closely

of shape and form, and not prior to matter but simultaneous with it. But this simultaneity is impossible. For if the mixture participates in being the existent is prior; and if both this mixture and that other [i.e. being] are existent, there will be need of a third over them, different from them.[1] If, then, it is necessary for the maker to be prior, why did the forms have to be in small pieces in the matter, and why did mind have to separate them out with endless trouble, when it could, as matter is without quality, extend quality and shape over the whole of it? And how is it not impossible that everything should be in everything? And as for the man who posits the unbounded [as matter],[2] let him explain what it is. And if he means that it is unbounded in the sense that one cannot get to the end of it, it is clear that there is no such thing in existence, neither an unbounded-in-itself, nor an unbounded in another nature, as an accident of some body; there is no unbounded-in-itself, because its part, too, would be necessarily unbounded, and no accidental unbounded, because that of which it was an accident would not be unbounded in itself and would not be simple and not be matter any longer. Nor will the atoms hold the position of matter—they do not exist at all; for every body is altogether divisible: and the continuity and flexibility of bodies, and the inability of individual things to exist without mind and soul, which cannot be made of atoms (and it is impossible to make out of the atoms another kind of thing besides the atoms,

he is following Peripatetic tradition here; for he himself regards matter as ἄπειρον (below ch. 15), though in a very different sense from Anaximander.

οὐχ οἷόν τε, ἐπεὶ καὶ οὐδεὶς δημιουργὸς ποιήσει τι
ἐξ οὐχ ὕλης συνεχοῦς—καὶ μυρία ἂν λέγοιτο πρὸς
ταύτην τὴν ὑπόθεσιν καὶ εἴρηται· διὸ ἐνδιατρίβειν
περιττὸν ἐν τούτοις.

8. Τίς οὖν ἡ μία αὕτη καὶ συνεχὴς καὶ ἄποιος
λεγομένη; Καὶ ὅτι μὲν μὴ σῶμα, εἴπερ ἄποιος,
δῆλον· ἢ ποιότητα ἕξει. Λέγοντες δὲ πάντων
αὐτὴν εἶναι τῶν αἰσθητῶν καὶ οὐ τινῶν μὲν ὕλην,
5 πρὸς ἄλλα δὲ εἶδος οὖσαν—οἷον τὸν πηλὸν ὕλην
τῷ κεραμεύοντι, ἁπλῶς δὲ οὐχ ὕλην—οὐ δὴ οὕτως,
ἀλλὰ πρὸς πάντα λέγοντες, οὐδὲν ἂν αὐτῇ προσά-
πτοιμεν τῇ αὐτῆς φύσει, ὅσα ἐπὶ τοῖς αἰσθητοῖς
ὁρᾶται. Εἰ δὴ τοῦτο, πρὸς ταῖς ἄλλαις ποιότησιν,
οἷον χρώμασι καὶ θερμότησι καὶ ψυχρότησιν, οὐδὲ
10 τὸ κοῦφον οὐδὲ τὸ βάρος, οὐ πυκνόν, οὐχ ἀραιόν,
ἀλλ' οὐδὲ σχῆμα. Οὐ τοίνυν οὐδὲ μέγεθος· ἄλλο
γὰρ τὸ μεγέθει, ἄλλο τὸ μεμεγεθυσμένῳ εἶναι,
ἄλλο τὸ σχήματι, ἄλλο τὸ ἐσχηματισμένῳ. Δεῖ
δὲ αὐτὴν μὴ σύνθετον εἶναι, ἀλλ' ἁπλοῦν καὶ ἕν τι
τῇ αὐτῆς φύσει· οὕτω γὰρ πάντων ἔρημος. Καὶ
15 ὁ μορφὴν διδοὺς δώσει καὶ μορφὴν ἄλλην οὖσαν
παρ' αὐτὴν καὶ μέγεθος καὶ πάντα ἐκ τῶν ὄντων
οἷον προσφέρων· ἢ δουλεύσει τῷ μεγέθει αὐτῆς καὶ
ποιήσει οὐχ ἡλίκον θέλει, ἀλλ' ὅσον ἡ ὕλη βούλεται·
τὸ δὲ συντροχάζειν τὴν βούλησιν τῷ μεγέθει αὐτῆς
πλασματῶδες. Εἰ δὲ καὶ πρότερον τῆς ὕλης τὸ

since no maker will make anything out of discontinuous material), and innumerable other objections could be, and have been, alleged against this hypothesis; so there is no need to spend more time on this question.

8. What, then, is this one matter which is also continuous and without quality? It is clear that, if in fact it is without quality, it is not a body—if it was, it would have quality. But, since we say that it is the matter of all sense-objects and not the matter of some, but form in relation to others—as clay is matter to the potter, but not matter absolutely—since we do not mean that it is matter in this sense, but matter in relation to everything, we should not attribute to its nature any of the properties which are observed in sense-objects. Now if this is so, then besides the other qualities, colours and degrees of heat and cold, we must not attribute to it lightness or heaviness, density or rarity, and indeed not even shape: and so not size either. For it is one thing to be size and another to be given a size, one thing to be shape, another to be given a shape. And matter must not be composite, but simple and one thing in its own nature; for so it will be destitute of all qualities. And the giver of its shape will give it a shape which is different from matter itself, and a size, and everything, bringing them to matter, so to speak, from its store of realities. Otherwise, it will be enslaved to the size of matter and will make something, not as large as it wills, but of the size that matter wants: the idea that the will of the maker keeps in step with the size is a fiction. But if, too, the making principle is prior to the matter, matter will

20 ποιοῦν, ταύτῃ ἔσται ἡ ὕλη, ᾗ πάντῃ τὸ ποιοῦν
θέλει, καὶ εὐάγωγος εἰς ἅπαντα· καὶ εἰς μέγεθος
τοίνυν. Μέγεθός τε εἰ ἔχοι, ἀνάγκη καὶ σχῆμα
ἔχειν· ὥστε ἔτι μᾶλλον δύσεργος ἔσται. Ἔπεισι
τοίνυν τὸ εἶδος αὐτῇ πάντα ἐπ' αὐτὴν φέρον· τὸ
25 δὲ εἶδος πᾶν καὶ μέγεθος ἔχει καὶ ὁπόσον ἂν ᾖ
μετὰ τοῦ λόγου καὶ ὑπὸ τούτου. Διὸ καὶ ἐπὶ τῶν
γενῶν ἑκάστων μετὰ τοῦ εἴδους καὶ τὸ ποσὸν
ὥρισται· ἄλλο γὰρ ἀνθρώπου καὶ ἄλλο ὄρνιθος
καὶ ὄρνιθος τοιουτουί. Θαυμαστότερον τὸ ποσὸν
τῇ ὕλῃ ἄλλο ἐπάγειν τοῦ ποιὸν αὐτῇ προστιθέναι;
30 οὐδὲ τὸ μὲν ποιὸν λόγος, τὸ δὲ ποσὸν οὐκ, εἶδος
καὶ μέτρον καὶ ἀριθμὸς ὄν.

9. Πῶς οὖν τις λήψεταί τι τῶν ὄντων, ὃ μὴ
μέγεθος ἔχει; Ἤ πᾶν ὅπερ μὴ ταὐτὸν τῷ ποσῷ·
οὐ γὰρ δὴ τὸ ὂν καὶ τὸ ποσὸν ταὐτόν. Πολλὰ δὲ
καὶ ἄλλα ἕτερα τοῦ ποσοῦ. Ὅλως δὲ πᾶσαν
5 ἀσώματον φύσιν ἄποσον θετέον· ἀσώματος δὲ καὶ
ἡ ὕλη. Ἐπεὶ καὶ ἡ ποσότης αὐτὴ οὐ ποσόν, ἀλλὰ
τὸ μετασχὸν αὐτῆς· ὥστε καὶ ἐκ τούτου δῆλον,
ὅτι εἶδος ἡ ποσότης. Ὡς οὖν ἐγένετό τι λευκὸν
παρουσίᾳ λευκότητος, τὸ δὲ πεποιηκὸς τὸ λευκὸν
χρῶμα ἐν ζῴῳ καὶ τὰ ἄλλα δὲ χρώματα ποικίλα
10 οὐκ ἦν ποικίλον χρῶμα, ἀλλὰ ποικίλος, εἰ βούλει,

be exactly as the making principle wills it to be in every way, tractable to everything, and so to size too. And if it had size it would necessarily have shape as well; so that it would be still harder to work. So when the form comes to the matter it brings everything with it; the form has everything, the size and all that goes with and is caused by the formative principle. Therefore, in every natural kind the dimensions are determined along with the form; the dimensions of a man are different from those of a bird, and those of different kinds of birds from one another. Is there anything more surprising in the bringing of quantity to matter as something different from itself than in the addition to it of quality? It is not the case that quality is a rational formative principle and quantity is not, since quantity is form and measure and number.

9. How, then, is one to conceive an existing thing which has not size? Everything is without size which is not identical with that which has quantity; for, certainly, that which exists is not identical with that which has quantity: and there are many other things which are different from that which has quantity. One must regard all bodiless nature as altogether without quantity; but matter is also bodiless. For quantity itself, too, is not a thing which has quantity; that which has quantity is that which participates in quantity; so it is clear from this, too, that quantity is a form. As, then something becomes white by the presence of whiteness, but that which makes the white colour in a living thing, and the other varied colours too, is not varied colour itself but a various, if you like to put it that

λόγος, οὕτω καὶ τὸ ποιοῦν τὸ τηλικόνδε οὐ
τηλικόνδε, ἀλλ᾽ αὖ τὸ " τὶ πηλίκον " ἢ πηλικότης ἢ
ὁ λόγος τὸ ποιοῦν. Προσελθοῦσα οὖν ἡ πηλικότης
ἐξελίττει εἰς μέγεθος τὴν ὕλην; Οὐδαμῶς· οὐδὲ
γὰρ ἐν ὀλίγῳ συνεσπείρατο· ἀλλ᾽ ἔδωκε μέγεθος
15 τὸ οὐ πρότερον ὄν, ὥσπερ καὶ ποιότητα τὴν οὐ
πρότερον οὖσαν.

10. Τί οὖν νοήσω ἀμέγεθες ἐν ὕλῃ; Τί δὲ
νοήσεις ἄποιον ὁπωσοῦν; Καὶ τίς ἡ νόησις καὶ
τῆς διανοίας ἡ ἐπιβολή; Ἡ ἀοριστία· εἰ γὰρ τῷ
ὁμοίῳ τὸ ὅμοιον, καὶ τῷ ἀορίστῳ τὸ ἀόριστον.
5 Λόγος μὲν οὖν γένοιτο ἂν περὶ τοῦ ἀορίστου
ὡρισμένος, ἡ δὲ πρὸς αὐτὸ ἐπιβολὴ ἀόριστος. Εἰ
δ᾽ ἕκαστον λόγῳ καὶ νοήσει γινώσκεται, ἐνταῦθα
δὲ ὁ μὲν λόγος λέγει, ἃ δὴ λέγει περὶ αὐτῆς, ἡ δὲ
βουλομένη εἶναι νόησις οὐ νόησις, ἀλλ᾽ οἷον ἄνοια,
μᾶλλον νόθον ἂν εἴη τὸ φάντασμα αὐτῆς καὶ οὐ
10 γνήσιον, ἐκ θατέρου οὐκ ἀληθοῦς καὶ μετὰ τοῦ
ἑτέρου λόγου συγκείμενον. Καὶ τάχα εἰς τοῦτο
βλέπων ὁ Πλάτων νόθῳ λογισμῷ εἶπε ληπτὴν
εἶναι. Τίς οὖν ἡ ἀοριστία τῆς ψυχῆς; ῏Αρα
παντελὴς ἄγνοια ὡς ἀφασία; [1] Ἡ ἐν καταφάσει
τινὶ τὸ ἀόριστον, καὶ οἷον ὀρθαλμῷ τὸ σκότος ὕλη

---

[1] ἀφασία Heintz: ἀπουσία codd. H-S.

---

[1] *Timaeus* 52B2.

[2] ἐν καταφάσει in the next sentence strongly suggests that
Heintz's ἀφασία is the right reading here, and I translate it.
But the MSS ἀπουσία is not quite impossible; Dr. Schwyzer
suggests that the antithesis to ἐν καταφάσει is to be found in

way, formative principle; so that which makes a
thing a certain size is not a thing of certain size itself,
but the specific magnitude, or magnitude itself, or
the formative principle which makes magnitude.
Does magnitude, then, come to matter and unfold
it into size? By no means; for matter was not
shrunk together in a small space; but the formative
principle gave a size which was not there before,
just as it gave a quality which was not there before.

10. " What, then, shall I conceive this sizelessness
in matter to be? " What will you conceive anything
whatever without quality to be? What is the act of
thought, and how do you apply your mind to it?
By indefiniteness; for if like is known by like, the
indefinite is known by the indefinite. The concept,
then, of the indefinite may be defined, but the application of the mind to it is indefinite. If, then, each
thing is known by concept and thought, but in this
case the concept states about matter what it does in
fact state, that which wants to be a thought about it
will not be a thought but a sort of thoughtlessness; or
rather the mental representation of it will be spurious
and not genuine, compounded of an unreal part and
with the diverse kind of reasoning. And it was perhaps because he observed this that Plato said that
matter was apprehended by a " spurious reasoning." [1]
What, then is the indefiniteness of the soul? Is it
complete ignorance amounting to inability to say anything? [2] Rather, the indefiniteness is contained in
a positive statement, and, as with the eye we see

παντελὴς ἄγνοια and that ὡς introduces a comparison, " Is it
complete ignorance, like an absence? Rather, the indefiniteness is contained in a positive statement . . .".

15 ὂν παντὸς ἀοράτου χρώματος, οὕτως οὖν καὶ
ψυχὴ ἀφελοῦσα ὅσα ἐπὶ τοῖς αἰσθητοῖς οἷον φῶς
τὸ λοιπὸν οὐκέτι ἔχουσα ὁρίσαι ὁμοιοῦται τῇ ὄψει
τῇ ἐν σκότῳ ταυτόν πως γινομένη τότε τῷ ὃ οἷον
ὁρᾷ. Ἆρ' οὖν ὁρᾷ; Ἢ οὕτως ὡς ἀσχημοσύνην
καὶ ὡς ἄχροιαν καὶ ὡς ἀλαμπὲς καὶ προσέτι δὲ
20 ὡς οὐκ ἔχον μέγεθος· εἰ δὲ μή, εἰδοποιήσει ἤδη.
Ὅταν οὖν μηδὲν νοῇ, οὐ ταὐτὸ τοῦτο περὶ ψυχὴν
πάθος; Ἢ οὔ, ἀλλ' ὅταν μὲν μηδέν, λέγει μηδέν,
μᾶλλον δὲ πάσχει οὐδέν· ὅταν δὲ τὴν ὕλην, οὕτω
πάσχει πάθος οἷον τύπον τοῦ ἀμόρφου· ἐπεὶ καὶ
ὅταν τὰ μεμορφωμένα καὶ τὰ μεμεγεθυσμένα νοῇ,
25 ὡς σύνθετα νοεῖ· ὡς γὰρ κεχρωσμένα καὶ ὅλως
πεποιωμένα. Τὸ ὅλον οὖν νοεῖ καὶ τὸ συνάμφω·
καὶ ἐναργὴς μὲν ἡ νόησις ἢ ἡ αἴσθησις τῶν
ἐπόντων, ἀμυδρὰ δὲ ἡ τοῦ ὑποκειμένου, τοῦ
ἀμόρφου· οὐ γὰρ εἶδος. Ὁ οὖν ἐν τῷ ὅλῳ καὶ
συνθέτῳ λαμβάνει μετὰ τῶν ἐπόντων ἀναλύσασα
30 ἐκεῖνα καὶ χωρίσασα, ὃ καταλείπει ὁ λόγος, τοῦτο
νοεῖ ἀμυδρῶς ἀμυδρὸν καὶ σκοτεινῶς σκοτεινὸν καὶ
νοεῖ οὐ νοοῦσα. Καὶ ἐπειδὴ οὐκ ἔμεινεν οὐδ' αὐτὴ
ἡ ὕλη ἄμορφος, ἀλλ' ἐν τοῖς πράγμασίν ἐστι
μεμορφωμένη, καὶ ἡ ψυχὴ εὐθέως ἐπέβαλε τὸ
εἶδος τῶν πραγμάτων αὐτῇ ἀλγοῦσα τῷ ἀορίστῳ,
35 οἷον φόβῳ τοῦ ἔξω τῶν ὄντων εἶναι καὶ οὐκ
ἀνεχομένη ἐν τῷ μὴ ὄντι ἐπιπολὺ ἑστάναι.

darkness which is matter of every unseen colour, so, too, the soul, when it has taken away everything which corresponds to light in the objects of sense, being no longer able to define what is left, is made like sight in darkness, having become then somehow the same as what it, so to speak, sees. But does it really see? Only as if it was seeing absence of shape and absence of colour, and something lightless, and without size as well. If it does not see in this way, it will already be giving matter a form. Is not the soul, then, affected in this very same way when it thinks nothing? No, but when it thinks nothing, it says nothing, or rather is not affected at all; but when it thinks matter, it is affected in a way as if it received an impression of the shapeless; since, also when it thinks things that have received shape and size, it thinks them as composites; for it thinks them as things which have been given colour and, in general, quality. So it thinks the whole and the compound of both elements [matter and form]; and the thought or perception of the overlying elements is clear, but that of the substrate, the shapeless, is dim; for it is not form. That, then, which it apprehends in the composite whole along with the overlying elements, when it has analysed these out and separated them, that which reason leaves over, this is what it thinks, a dim thing dimly and a dark thing darkly, and it thinks it without thinking. And since matter itself does not remain shapeless, but is shaped in things, the soul, too, immediately imposes the form of the things on it because matter's indefiniteness distresses it, as if it were in fear of being outside the realm of being and could not endure to stay for long in non-being.

11. Καὶ τί δεῖ τινος ἄλλου πρὸς σύστασιν σωμάτων μετὰ μέγεθος καὶ ποιότητας ἁπάσας; Ἢ τοῦ ὑποδεξομένου πάντα. Οὐκοῦν ὁ ὄγκος· εἰ δὲ ὁ ὄγκος, μέγεθος δήπου. Εἰ δὲ ἀμέγεθες, οὐδ᾽ ὅπου
5 δέξεται ἔχει. Ἀμέγεθες δὲ ὂν τί ἂν συμβάλλοιτο, εἰ μήτε εἰς εἶδος καὶ τὸ ποιὸν μήτε εἰς τὴν διάστασιν καὶ τὸ μέγεθος, ὃ δὴ παρὰ τῆς ὕλης δοκεῖ, ὅπου ἂν ᾖ, ἔρχεσθαι εἰς τὰ σώματα; Ὅλως δὲ ὥσπερ πράξεις καὶ ποιήσεις καὶ χρόνοι καὶ κινήσεις ὑποβολὴν ὕλης ἐν αὐτοῖς οὐκ ἔχοντα ἔστιν
10 ἐν τοῖς οὖσιν, οὕτως οὐδὲ τὰ σώματα τὰ πρῶτα ἀνάγκη ὕλην ἔχειν, ἀλλὰ ὅλα ἕκαστα εἶναι ἅ ἐστι ποικιλώτερα ὄντα μίξει τῇ ἐκ πλειόνων εἰδῶν τὴν σύστασιν ἔχοντα· ὥστε τοῦτο τὸ ἀμέγεθες ὕλης ὄνομα κενὸν εἶναι. Πρῶτον μὲν οὖν οὐκ ἀνάγκη
15 τὸ ὑποδεχόμενον ὁτιοῦν ὄγκον εἶναι, ἐὰν μὴ μέγεθος ἤδη αὐτῷ παρῇ· ἐπεὶ καὶ ἡ ψυχὴ πάντα δεχομένη ὁμοῦ ἔχει πάντα· εἰ δὲ μέγεθος αὐτῇ συμβεβηκὸς ἦν, ἔσχεν ἂν ἕκαστα ἐν μεγέθει. Ἡ δὲ ὕλη διὰ τοῦτο ἐν διαστήματι ἃ δέχεται λαμβάνει, ὅτι διαστήματός ἐστι δεκτική· ὥσπερ καὶ τὰ ζῷα
20 καὶ τὰ φυτὰ μετὰ τοῦ μεγεθύνεσθαι καὶ τὸ ποιὸν ἀντιπαραγόμενον ἴσχει τῷ ποσῷ καὶ συστελλομένου

---

[1] The objector whose point of view is put here is presumably the same as the "person who says that matter does not exist" mentioned at the beginning of I. 8. 15 (where there is a reference back to this passage). The objection was probably one that Plotinus had really encountered, made by Platonists who interpreted *Timaeus* 52A8 ff. (probably correctly) as meaning that Plato identified the "receptacle" with space, and who therefore rejected the Aristotelian conception of a

ON MATTER

11. " And why is there any need of anything else for the composition of bodies besides size and all qualities? There is need of something to receive them all. This is, then, the mass. But if mass, then, presumably, size. But if it has no size, it will have nowhere to receive anything. If it is without size, what would it contribute, if it contributes neither to form and quality nor to extension and size, which appears, wherever it occurs, to come to bodies from their matter? But in general, just as actions and productions and times and movements exist in reality without having a foundation of matter in them, so there is no need for the primary bodies to have matter; they can each of them be what they are as wholes, with a more varied richness of content when they have their structure produced by the mixture of a greater number of forms: so that this sizelessness of matter is an empty name." [1] First of all, then, it is not necessary that what receives anything should be a mass, if size is not already present to it: since the soul which receives everything, contains everything together; but if size were one of its incidental attributes it would contain all individual things in their sizes. But matter does accept in extension what it receives, for this reason, that it is itself receptive of extension; just as animals and plants along with their growth in size have development of quality corresponding to their increase in quantity, and if the quantity decreased the quality

dimensionless ὕλη (cp. Bréhier's introduction to this treatise). The contention that there is no such thing as Aristotelian matter reappears in S. Basil *In Hexaem.* I. 21A–B(8E–9A); cp. S. Gregory of Nyssa *De Hom. Op.* 213C.

συσταλείη ἄν. Εἰ δ' ὅτι προϋπάρχει τι μέγεθος
ἐν τοῖς τοιούτοις ὑποκείμενον τῷ μορφοῦντι, κἀκεῖ
ἀπαιτεῖ, οὐκ ὀρθῶς· ἐνταῦθα γὰρ ἡ ὕλη οὐχ ἡ
ἁπλῶς, ἀλλ' ἡ τούτου· τὴν δ' ἁπλῶς δεῖ καὶ τοῦτο
25 παρ' ἄλλου ἔχειν. Οὐ τοίνυν ὄγκον δεῖ εἶναι τὸν
δεξόμενον τὸ εἶδος, ἀλλ' ὁμοῦ τῷ γενέσθαι ὄγκον
καὶ τὴν ἄλλην ποιότητα δέχεσθαι. Καὶ φάντασμα
μὲν ἔχειν ὄγκου ὡς ἐπιτηδειότητα τούτου ὥσπερ
πρώτην, κενὸν δὲ ὄγκον. Ὅθεν τινὲς ταὐτὸν τῷ
30 κενῷ τὴν ὕλην εἰρήκασι. Φάντασμα δὲ ὄγκου
λέγω, ὅτι καὶ ἡ ψυχὴ οὐδὲν ἔχουσα ὁρίσαι, ὅταν
τῇ ὕλῃ προσομιλῇ, εἰς ἀοριστίαν χεῖ ἑαυτὴν οὔτε
περιγράφουσα οὔτε εἰς σημεῖον ἰέναι δυναμένη·
ἤδη γὰρ ὁρίζει. Διὸ οὔτε μέγα λεκτέον χωρὶς οὔτε
σμικρὸν αὖ, ἀλλὰ μέγα καὶ μικρόν· καὶ οὕτως
35 ὄγκος καὶ ἀμέγεθες οὕτως, ὅτι ὕλη ὄγκου καὶ
συστελλόμενον ἐκ τοῦ μεγάλου ἐπὶ τὸ σμικρὸν καὶ
ἐκ τοῦ σμικροῦ ἐπὶ τὸ μέγα οἷον ὄγκον διατρέχει·
καὶ ἡ ἀοριστία αὐτῆς ὁ τοιοῦτος ὄγκος, ὑποδοχὴ
μεγέθους ἐν αὐτῇ· ἐν δὲ φαντασίᾳ ἐκείνως. Καὶ
γὰρ τῶν μὲν ἄλλων ἀμεγέθων ὅσα εἴδη ὥρισται

---

[1] Cp. Aristotle *Physics* Δ. 214a13. Aristotle is here
referring to Plato; cp. 209b11.

[2] Plato's term, as reported by Aristotle (*Physics* A4. 187a17,
Γ4. 203a16; *Metaphysics* A7. 988a26).

would decrease too. But if, because in things like these a certain size is present beforehand underlying the shaping principle, [our opponent] demands it there too [in the case of prime matter], the demand is incorrect; for in the case of plants and animals the matter is not simply matter, but the matter of this particular thing; matter which is simply matter must receive size too from something else. So, then, that which is going to receive the form must not be a mass, but it must receive the rest of its qualities as well at the same time as it becomes a mass. And it does, indeed, have an imaginary appearance of mass because the first, so to speak, of its capacities is a capacity for mass, but the mass is void. For this reason some people have said that matter is identical with the void.[1] I say " an imaginary appearance of mass " because the soul, too, when it is keeping company with matter, having nothing to delimit, spills itself into indefiniteness, neither drawing a line round it nor able to arrive at a point; for if it did it would already be delimiting it. For this reason matter should not be called " great " separately or again " small " separately, but " great-and-small."[2] It is " mass " in this sense and " without size " in this sense, that it is the matter of mass, and when mass is contracted from the great to the small and expands from the small to the great, matter, so to speak, runs through the whole range of mass: and its indefiniteness is mass in this sense, that it has the capacity of receiving size in itself; but in imaginary representation it is mass in the sense we have described. For in the case of the other things without size, those of them that are forms are each of them

40 ἕκαστον· ὥστε οὐδαμῇ ἔννοια ὄγκου· ἡ δὲ ἀόριστος οὖσα καὶ μήπω στᾶσα παρ' αὑτῆς ἐπὶ
πᾶν εἶδος φερομένη δεῦρο κἀκεῖσε καὶ πάντη
εὐάγωγος οὖσα πολλή τε γίνεται τῇ ἐπὶ πάντα
ἀγωγῇ καὶ γενέσει καὶ ἔσχε τοῦτον τὸν τρόπον
φύσιν ὄγκου.

12. Συμβάλλεται οὖν τὰ μέγιστα τοῖς σώμασι·
τά τε γὰρ εἴδη τῶν σωμάτων ἐν μεγέθεσι. Περὶ
δὲ μέγεθος οὐκ ἂν ἐγένετο ταῦτα, ἀλλ' ἢ περὶ τὸ
μεμεγεθυσμένον· εἰ γὰρ περὶ μέγεθος, οὐ περὶ
5 ὕλην, ὁμοίως ἂν ἀμεγέθη καὶ ἀνυπόστατα ἦν ἢ
λόγοι μόνοι ἂν ἦσαν—οὗτοι δὲ περὶ ψυχήν—καὶ
οὐκ ἂν ἦν σώματα. Δεῖ οὖν ἐνταῦθα περὶ ἕν τι τὰ
πολλά· τοῦτο δὲ μεμεγεθυσμένον· τοῦτο δὲ ἕτερον
τοῦ μεγέθους. Ἐπεὶ καὶ νῦν ὅσα μίγνυται τῷ
ὕλην ἔχειν εἰς ταὐτὸν ἔρχεται καὶ οὐ δεῖται ἄλλου
10 του περὶ ὅ, ὅτι ἕκαστον τῶν μιγνυμένων ἥκει
φέρον τὴν αὐτοῦ ὕλην. Δεῖται δὲ [ὅμως] καὶ ὡς
ἑνός τινος τοῦ δεξομένου ἢ ἀγγείου ἢ τόπου· ὁ δὲ
τόπος ὕστερος τῆς ὕλης καὶ τῶν σωμάτων, ὥστε
πρότερον ἂν δέοιτο τὰ σώματα ὕλης. Οὐδέ, ὅτι
αἱ ποιήσεις καὶ αἱ πράξεις ἄυλοι, διὰ τοῦτο καὶ τὰ
σώματα· σύνθετα γὰρ τὰ σώματα, αἱ δὲ πράξεις
15 οὔ. Καὶ τοῖς πράττουσιν ἡ ὕλη ὅταν πράττωσι τὸ
ὑποκείμενον δίδωσι μένουσα ἐν αὐτοῖς, εἰς τὸ
πράττειν οὐχ αὑτὴν δίδωσιν· οὐδὲ γὰρ οἱ πράτ-

clearly defined, so that there is no room anywhere in their case for a conception of mass. But matter is indefinite and not yet stable by itself, and is carried about here and there into every form, and since it is altogether adaptable becomes many by being brought into everything and becoming everything, and in this way acquires the nature of mass.

12. Matter, then, makes the greatest contribution to the formation of bodies; for the forms of bodies are in sizes. But these corporeal forms could not come into being in size but only in that which has been given size; for if in size, they would not come into being in matter and would be the same as before, without size and without underlying material substantiality, or they would only be rational principles— but these are in soul—and would not be bodies. So here in the material world the many forms must be in something which is one; and this is what has been given size; but this is different from size. We can see that this is so because in our present experience things that are mixed together come to identity by having matter, and there is no need for any other medium, because each constituent of the mixture comes bringing its own matter. All the same, there is need of some one kind of vessel or place to receive bodies; but place is posterior to matter and bodies, so that bodies would need matter before they need place. Nor, because actions and productions are without matter, are bodies without matter too: for bodies are composite, but actions are not. And matter does provide the substrate for those who act, whenever they act, by its continuing presence in themselves, but does not give itself to the action; nor

τοντες τοῦτο ζητοῦσι. Καὶ οὐ μεταβάλλει ἄλλη
πρᾶξις εἰς ἄλλην, ἵνα ἂν ἦν καὶ αὐταῖς ὕλη, ἀλλ' ὁ
20 πράττων ἐπ' ἄλλην μεταβάλλει πρᾶξιν ἐξ ἄλλης·
ὥστε ὕλην αὐτὸν εἶναι ταῖς πράξεσιν. Ἔστι
τοίνυν ἀναγκαῖον ἡ ὕλη καὶ τῇ ποιότητι καὶ τῷ
μεγέθει· ὥστε καὶ τοῖς σώμασι· καὶ οὐ κενὸν
ὄνομα, ἀλλ' ἔστι τι ὑποκείμενον κἂν ἀόρατον κἂν
ἀμέγεθες ὑπάρχῃ. Ἢ οὕτως οὐδὲ τὰς ποιότητας
25 φήσομεν οὐδὲ τὸ μέγεθος τῷ αὐτῷ λόγῳ· ἕκαστον
γὰρ τῶν τοιούτων λέγοιτο ἂν οὐδὲν εἶναι ἐφ'
ἑαυτοῦ μόνον λαμβανόμενον. Εἰ δὲ ταῦτα ἔστι
καίπερ ἀμυδρῶς ὂν ἕκαστον, πολὺ μᾶλλον ἂν εἴη
ὕλη, κἂν μὴ ἐναργὴς ὑπάρχῃ αἱρετὴ οὖσα οὐ ταῖς
αἰσθήσεσιν· οὔτε γὰρ ὄμμασιν, ἄχρους γὰρ· οὔτε
30 ἀκοῇ, οὐ γὰρ ψόφος· οὐδὲ χυμοί, διὸ οὐδὲ ῥῖνες
οὐδὲ γλῶσσα. Ἆρ' οὖν ἁφῇ; Ἢ οὔ, ὅτι μηδὲ
σῶμα· σώματος γὰρ ἡ ἁφή, ὅτι ἢ πυκνοῦ ἢ
ἀραιοῦ, μαλακοῦ σκληροῦ, ὑγροῦ ξηροῦ· τούτων
δὲ οὐδὲν περὶ τὴν ὕλην· ἀλλὰ λογισμῷ οὐκ ἐκ νοῦ,
ἀλλὰ κενῶς· διὸ καὶ νόθος, ὡς εἴρηται. Ἀλλ'
35 οὐδὲ σωματότης περὶ αὐτήν· εἰ μὲν λόγος ἡ
σωματότης, ἕτερος αὐτῆς· αὕτη οὖν ἄλλο· εἰ δ'
ἤδη ποιήσασα καὶ οἷον κραθεῖσα, σῶμα φανερῶς
ἂν εἴη καὶ οὐχ ὕλη μόνον.

13. Εἰ δὲ ποιότης τις τὸ ὑποκείμενον κοινή τις
οὖσα ἐν ἑκάστῳ τῶν στοιχείων, πρῶτον μὲν τίς

---

[1] In ch. 10 (the reference to the *Timaeus*).

do those who are acting even want it to. And one action does not change into another—if it did then actions, too, would have matter—but the person acting changes from one action to another, so that he himself is matter to his actions. So, then, matter is necessary both to quality and to size, and therefore to bodies; and it is not an empty name but it is something underlying, even if it is invisible and sizeless. If we do deny the existence of matter we shall by the same argument be prevented from asserting the existence of qualities and size; for everything of this kind could be said to be nothing taken alone by itself. But if these have an existence, though in each case an obscure one, still more would matter exist, though it is not obvious since it is not by the senses that it is apprehended: not by the eyes, for it is without colour; not by the hearing, since it makes no noise; nor has it taste or smell, so it is not nostrils or tongue that perceive it. Is it touch, then? No, because it is not a body, for touch apprehends body, because it apprehends density and rarity, hardness and softness, wetness and dryness; and none of these apply to matter. It is apprehended by a process of reasoning, which does not come from mind but works emptily; so it is spurious reasoning, as has been said.[1] But even corporeality does not belong to it; for if corporeality is a rational formative principle it is different from matter, and so matter is something else; but if corporeality has already come into action and is so to speak mixed, it would clearly be body and not matter alone.

13. If the substrate is to be some quality, a common one which exists in each and every one of the

αὕτη λεκτέον. Ἔπειτα πῶς ποιότης ὑποκείμενον
ἔσται; Πῶς δὲ ἐν ἀμεγέθει ποιὸν θεωρηθήσεται
5 μὴ ἔχον ὕλην μηδὲ μέγεθος; Ἔπειτα εἰ μὲν
ὡρισμένη ἡ ποιότης, πῶς ὕλη; Εἰ δ' ἀόριστόν τι,
οὐ ποιότης, ἀλλὰ τὸ ὑποκείμενον καὶ ἡ ζητουμένη
ὕλη. Τί οὖν κωλύει ἄποιον μὲν εἶναι τῷ τῶν
ἄλλων μηδεμιᾶς τῇ αὐτῆς φύσει μετέχειν, αὐτῷ
δὲ τούτῳ τῷ μηδεμιᾶς μετέχειν ποιὰν εἶναι ἰδιότητα
10 πάντως τινὰ ἔχουσαν καὶ τῶν ἄλλων διαφέρουσαν,
οἷον στέρησίν τινα ἐκείνων; Καὶ γὰρ ὁ ἐστερημένος
ποιός· οἷον ὁ τυφλός. Εἰ οὖν στέρησις τούτων
περὶ αὐτήν, πῶς οὐ ποιά; Εἰ δὲ καὶ ὅλως στέρησις
περὶ αὐτήν, ἔτι μᾶλλον, εἴ γε δὴ καὶ στέρησις
ποιόν τι. Ὁ δὴ ταῦτα λέγων τί ἄλλο ἢ ποιὰ καὶ
15 ποιότητας πάντα ποιεῖ; Ὥστε καὶ ἡ ποσότης
ποιότης ἂν εἴη καὶ ἡ οὐσία δέ. Εἰ δὲ ποιόν,
πρόσεστι ποιότης. Γελοῖον δὲ τὸ ἕτερον τοῦ
ποιοῦ καὶ μὴ ποιὸν ποιὸν ποιεῖν. Εἰ δ', ὅτι ἕτερον,
ποιόν, εἰ μὲν αὐτοετερότης, οὐδ' ὡς ποιόν· ἐπεὶ
οὐδ' ἡ ποιότης ποιά· εἰ δ' ἕτερον μόνον, οὐχ
20 ἑαυτῇ, ἀλλ' ἑτερότητι ἕτερον καὶ ταυτότητι ταὐτόν.
Οὐδὲ δὴ ἡ στέρησις ποιότης οὐδὲ ποιόν, ἀλλ'
ἐρημία ποιότητος ἢ ἄλλου, ὡς ἡ ἀψοφία οὐ ψόφου
ἢ ὁτουοῦν ἄλλου· ἄρσις γὰρ ἡ στέρησις, τὸ δὲ

---

[1] I.e. you cannot classify soundlessness as a special sort of
sound or any other sort of positive quality; a quality is always
something positive, a privation, never.

elements, first of all it must be stated what this quality is. Next, how can a quality be a substrate? How is a quality in something without size to be conceived, when it does not have matter or size? Then, if the quality is defined, how is it matter? But if it is something indefinite, it is not a quality but the substrate and the matter we were looking for. " What, then, prevents it from being something qualified by participating, by its own nature, in none of the other qualities, but by this very fact of participating in none of them being qualified, since it has a thoroughly distinctive characteristic, different from the others, a sort of privation of those other qualities? For anyone who is deprived has a quality—a blind man, for instance. If then privation of the qualities belongs to it, how is it not qualified? But if complete privation belongs to it, it is qualified still more, if privation, too, is really something qualified." But what else is the person who says this doing than making everything qualified and qualities? So that even quantity would be a quality, and substance too. But if something is qualified, quality is present to it. But it is absurd to make qualified what is other than the qualified and so not qualified. But if it is qualified because it is other, if it is absolute otherness, it is not so as being qualified, since quality [the form] is not qualified; but if it is simply other, it is not so by itself, but other by otherness and the same by sameness. And privation is certainly not quality or qualified, but lack of quality or of something else, as soundlessness does not belong to sound or anything else [positive];[1] for privation is a taking away, but qualification is a matter of positive assertion. The

ποιὸν ἐν καταφάσει. Ἥ τε ἰδιότης τῆς ὕλης οὐ
μορφή· τῷ γὰρ μὴ ποιὰ εἶναι μηδ' εἶδός τι ἔχειν·
25 ἄτοπον δή, ὅτι μὴ ποιά, ποιὰν λέγειν καὶ ὅμοιον
τῷ, ὅτι ἀμέγεθες, αὐτῷ τούτῳ μέγεθος ἔχειν.
Ἔστιν οὖν ἡ ἰδιότης αὐτῆς οὐκ ἄλλο τι ἢ ὅπερ
ἔστι, καὶ οὐ πρόσκειται ἡ ἰδιότης, ἀλλὰ μᾶλλον ἐν
σχέσει τῇ πρὸς τὰ ἄλλα, ὅτι ἄλλο αὐτῶν. Καὶ τὰ
μὲν ἄλλα οὐ μόνον ἄλλα, ἀλλὰ καί τι ἕκαστον ὡς
30 εἶδος, αὕτη δὲ πρεπόντως ἂν λέγοιτο μόνον ἄλλο·
τάχα δὲ ἄλλα, ἵνα μὴ τῷ " ἄλλο " ἑνικῶς ὁρίσῃς,
ἀλλὰ τῷ " ἄλλα " τὸ ἀόριστον ἐνδείξῃ.

14. Ἀλλ' ἐκεῖνο ζητητέον. πότερα στέρησις, ἢ
περὶ αὐτῆς ἡ στέρησις. Ὁ τοίνυν λέγων λόγος
ὑποκειμένῳ μὲν ἓν ἄμφω, λόγῳ δὲ δύο, δίκαιος ἦν
διδάσκειν καὶ τὸν λόγον ἑκατέρου ὄντινα δεῖ
5 ἀποδιδόναι, τῆς μὲν ὕλης ὃς ὁριεῖται αὐτὴν οὐδὲν
προσαπτόμενος τῆς στερήσεως, τῆς τε αὖ στερήσεως ὡσαύτως. Ἢ γὰρ οὐδέτερον ἐν οὐδετέρῳ τῷ
λόγῳ ἢ ἑκάτερον ἐν ἑκατέρῳ ἢ θάτερον ἐν θατέρῳ
μόνον ὁποτερονοῦν. Εἰ μὲν οὖν ἑκάτερον χωρὶς
καὶ οὐκ ἐπιζητεῖ οὐδέτερον, δύο ἔσται ἄμφω καὶ
10 ἡ ὕλη ἕτερον στερήσεως, κἂν συμβεβήκῃ αὐτῇ ἡ
στέρησις. Δεῖ δ' ἐν τῷ λόγῳ μηδὲ δυνάμει
ἐνορᾶσθαι θάτερον. Εἰ δὲ ὡς ἡ ῥὶς ἡ σιμὴ καὶ τὸ

---

[1] To say that something is " other " than something else
is a way of helping to define it, to show it as a distinctive
unity; this remarkable plural is an attempt to exclude all
definition, to speak of matter as absolutely indefinite and
incoherent with no sort of distinctive unity.

[2] Cp. for Aristotle's view here criticised *Physics* A9. 192a2 ff.

distinctive characteristic, too, of matter is not shape:
for it consists in not being qualified and not having
any form; it is surely fantastic to call it qualified
because it has no quality; it is like saying that because it is sizeless, by this very fact it has a size. So,
then, its distinctive characteristic is not something
else other than what it is; it is not an addition to it
but rather consists in its relationship to other things,
its being other than they. Other things are not
only other but each of them is something as form, but
this would appropriately be called nothing but other;
or perhaps others, so as not to define it as a unity by
the term " other " but to show its indefiniteness by
calling it " others." [1]

14. But we must investigate this further point,
whether it is privation or the subject of privation.
Now the argument which says that in the substrate
both are one, but that in rational definition they are
two,[2] is under an obligation to instruct us what
rational definition of each of these two things one
must give, one of matter which will define it without
applying to it any term belonging to privation, and an
exactly similar one of privation. For there are three
possibilities; neither of them is contained in the
definition of the other, or both are in each other's
definitions, or one only is in the definition of the other,
whichever one it is. If, then, each of the two things
is separate and neither of them requires the other,
the pair of them will be two distinct things and matter
will be other than privation, even if privation is
incidentally predicated of it. But, then, the other
must not appear even potentially in the definition of
one of them. But if they are related as the snub

σιμόν, καὶ οὕτω διπλοῦν ἑκάτερον καὶ δύο. Εἰ δὲ
ὡς τὸ πῦρ καὶ ἡ θερμότης, ἐν μὲν τῷ πυρὶ τῆς
θερμότητος οὔσης, ἐν δὲ τῇ θερμότητι οὐ λαμ-
15 βανομένου τοῦ πυρός, καὶ ἡ ὕλη οὕτω στέρησις,
ὡς τὸ πῦρ θερμόν, οἷον εἶδος αὐτῆς ἔσται ἡ
στέρησις, τὸ δ' ὑποκείμενον ἄλλο, ὃ δεῖ τὴν ὕλην
εἶναι. Καὶ οὐδ' οὕτως ἕν. Ἆρα οὖν οὕτως ἓν
τῷ ὑποκειμένῳ, δύο δὲ τῷ λόγῳ, τῆς στερήσεως
20 οὐ σημαινούσης τι παρεῖναι, ἀλλὰ μὴ παρεῖναι,
καὶ οἷον ἀπόφασις ἡ στέρησις τῶν ὄντων; ὥσπερ
ἂν εἴ τις λέγοι οὐκ ὄν, οὐ γὰρ προστίθησιν ἡ
ἀπόφασις, ἀλλά φησιν οὐκ εἶναι· καὶ οὕτω
στέρησις ὡς οὐκ ὄν. Εἰ μὲν οὖν οὐκ ὄν, ὅτι μὴ
τὸ ὄν, ἀλλ' ἄλλο ὄν τί ἐστι, δύο οἱ λόγοι, ὁ μὲν τοῦ
ὑποκειμένου ἁπτόμενος, ὁ δὲ τῆς στερήσεως τὴν
25 πρὸς τὰ ἄλλα σχέσιν δηλῶν. Ἢ ὁ μὲν τῆς ὕλης
πρὸς τὰ ἄλλα καὶ ὁ τοῦ ὑποκειμένου δὲ πρὸς τὰ
ἄλλα, ὁ δὲ τῆς στερήσεως εἰ τὸ ἀόριστον αὐτῆς
δηλοῖ, τάχα ἂν αὐτὸς αὐτῆς ἐφάπτοιτο· πλὴν ἕν
γε ἑκατέρως τῷ ὑποκειμένῳ, λόγῳ δὲ δύο. Εἰ
μέντοι τῷ ἀορίστῳ εἶναι καὶ ἀπείρῳ εἶναι καὶ
30 ἀποίῳ εἶναι τῇ ὕλῃ ταὐτόν, πῶς ἔτι δύο οἱ λόγοι;

15. Πάλιν οὖν ζητητέον, εἰ κατὰ συμβεβηκὸς τὸ
ἄπειρον καὶ τὸ ἀόριστον ἐπ' ἄλλῃ φύσει καὶ πῶς

---

[1] A stock Aristotelian example, cp., e.g., *Metaphysics* Z5.
1030b30–31. Was this philosophical snub nose originally
Socrates's?

nose is to snubness,[1] in this way also they are each
of them double and each two things. But if they are
related as fire and heat, where heat is in fire but fire
is not included in the definition of heat, and matter is
privation in the way in which fire is hot, privation
will be a sort of form of matter, and the substrate will
be something else, which must be the matter. And
they will not be one thing in this way either. Is,
then, this unity in substrate and duality in definition
to be understood in this way, that privation does not
indicate that anything is there but that it is not there;
privation being a kind of denial of realities? It
would be just as if someone said " not being," for his
denial does not make any addition but asserts that
something does not exist; and it would be privation
in this way, as not existing. If then it is non-
existent because it is not being, but some other
existing thing different from being, the definitions
are two, one comprising the substrate, and that of
privation making clear its relationship to the other
existing things. Or perhaps the definition of matter
shows its relationship to other things and that of the
substrate also shows its relationship to other things,
but that of privation, if it makes clear the indefiniteness of matter, might actually grasp it in itself [and
not only its relationship to other things]; but in this
case they are both one in substratum, but two in
rational definition. But if privation, by being indefinite and unlimited and without qualities, is the
same thing as matter, how do the definitions still
remain two?

15. We must enquire, therefore, again whether the
unlimited and indefinite are incidentally predicated

συμβεβηκὸς καὶ εἰ στέρησις συμβέβηκεν. Εἰ δὴ
ὅσα μὲν ἀριθμοὶ καὶ λόγοι ἀπειρίας ἔξω—ὅροι γὰρ
5 καὶ τάξεις καὶ τὸ τεταγμένον καὶ τοῖς ἄλλοις παρὰ
τούτων, τάττει δὲ ταῦτα οὐ τὸ τεταγμένον οὐδὲ
τάξις, ἀλλὰ ἄλλο τὸ ταττόμενον παρὰ τὸ τάττον,
τάττει δὲ τὸ πέρας καὶ ὅρος καὶ λόγος—ἀνάγκη τὸ
ταττόμενον καὶ ὁριζόμενον τὸ ἄπειρον εἶναι. Τάτ-
10 τεται δὲ ἡ ὕλη καὶ ὅσα δὲ μὴ ὕλη τῷ μετέχειν ἢ
ὕλης λόγον ἔχειν· ἀνάγκη τοίνυν τὴν ὕλην τὸ
ἄπειρον εἶναι, οὐχ οὕτω δὲ ἄπειρον, ὡς κατὰ
συμβεβηκὸς καὶ τῷ συμβεβηκέναι τὸ ἄπειρον
αὐτῇ. Πρῶτον μὲν γὰρ τὸ συμβαῖνόν τῳ δεῖ
λόγον εἶναι· τὸ δὲ ἄπειρον οὐ λόγος· ἔπειτα τίνι
ὄντι τὸ ἄπειρον συμβήσεται; Πέρατι καὶ πεπε-
15 ρασμένῳ. Ἀλλ' οὐ πεπερασμένον οὐδὲ πέρας ἡ
ὕλη. Καὶ τὸ ἄπειρον δὲ προσελθὸν τῷ πεπερασ-
μένῳ ἀπολεῖ αὐτοῦ τὴν φύσιν· οὐ τοίνυν συμβεβηκὸς τῇ ὕλῃ τὸ ἄπειρον· αὐτὴ τοίνυν τὸ ἄπειρον.
Ἐπεὶ καὶ ἐν τοῖς νοητοῖς ἡ ὕλη τὸ ἄπειρον καὶ
εἴη ἂν γεννηθὲν ἐκ τῆς τοῦ ἑνὸς ἀπειρίας ἢ
20 δυνάμεως ἢ τοῦ ἀεί, οὐκ οὔσης ἐν ἐκείνῳ ἀπειρίας
ἀλλὰ ποιοῦντος. Πῶς οὖν ἐκεῖ καὶ ἐνταῦθα; Ἢ
διττὸν καὶ τὸ ἄπειρον. Καὶ τί διαφέρει; Ὡς
ἀρχέτυπον καὶ εἴδωλον. Ἐλαττόνως οὖν ἄπειρον

of another nature, and how they are incidental attributes, and if privation is an incidental attribute. Now if all things that are number and proportion are outside limitlessness—for they are bounds and orders, and other things derive their being set in order from them, but it is not being ordered or order that orders them, but that which is set in order is different from that which orders it, and that which orders is limit and bound and proportion—that which is set in order and bounded must be the unlimited. But matter is set in order, as are all things which are not matter in so far as they participate in it or are reckoned as matter; so matter must be the unlimited, but not unlimited in the sense that it is so incidentally and that the unlimited is an incidental attribute of it. For, first, the incidental attribute of anything must be a rational concept; but the unlimited is not a concept. Then what will the subject be of which the unlimited is incidentally predicated? Limit and something limited. But matter is not something limited, nor is it limit. And the unlimited when it comes to that which is limited will destroy its nature. So the unlimited is not an incidental attribute of matter; matter itself, then is the unlimited. For in the intelligible world, too, matter is the unlimited, and it would be produced from the unlimitedness or the power or the everlastingness of the One; unlimitedness is not in the One, but the One produces it. How, then, is matter both there and here? The unlimited is double, too. And what is the difference between the two unlimiteds? They differ as the archetype differs from the image. Is the unlimited here, then, less unlimited? More, rather;

τοῦτο; Ἢ μᾶλλον· ὅσῳ γὰρ εἴδωλον πεφευγὸς τὸ
εἶναι ⟨καὶ⟩ [1] τὸ ἀληθές, μᾶλλον ἄπειρον. Ἡ γὰρ
25 ἀπειρία ἐν τῷ ἧττον ὁρισθέντι μᾶλλον· τὸ γὰρ
ἧττον ἐν τῷ ἀγαθῷ μᾶλλον ἐν τῷ κακῷ. Τὸ ἐκεῖ
οὖν μᾶλλον ὂν εἴδωλον ὡς ἄπειρον, τὸ δ' ἐνταῦθα
ἧττον, ὅσῳ πέφευγε τὸ εἶναι καὶ τὸ ἀληθές, εἰς δὲ
εἰδώλου κατερρύη φύσιν, ἀληθεστέρως ἄπειρον.
Τὸ αὐτὸ οὖν τὸ ἄπειρον καὶ τὸ ἀπείρῳ εἶναι; Ἢ
30 ὅπου λόγος καὶ ὕλη ἄλλο ἑκάτερον, ὅπου δὲ ὕλη
μόνον ἢ ταὐτὸν λεκτέον ἢ ὅλως, ὃ καὶ βέλτιον,
οὐκ εἶναι ἐνθάδε τὸ ἀπείρῳ εἶναι· λόγος γὰρ
ἔσται, ὃς οὐκ ἔστιν ἐν τῷ ἀπείρῳ, ἵν' ᾖ ἄπειρον.
Ἄπειρον μὲν δὴ παρ' αὐτῆς τὴν ὕλην λεκτέον
ἀντιτάξει τῇ πρὸς τὸν λόγον. Καὶ γάρ, ὥσπερ ὁ
35 λόγος οὐκ ἄλλο τι ὢν ἐστι λόγος, οὕτω καὶ τὴν
ὕλην ἀντιτεταγμένην τῷ λόγῳ κατὰ τὴν ἀπειρίαν
οὐκ ἄλλο τι οὖσαν λεκτέον ἄπειρον.

16. Ἆρ' οὖν καὶ ἑτερότητι ταὐτόν; Ἢ οὔ,
ἀλλὰ μορίῳ ἑτερότητος ἀντιταττομένῳ πρὸς τὰ
ὄντα κυρίως, ἃ δὴ λόγοι. Διὸ καὶ μὴ ὂν οὕτω τι
ὂν καὶ στερήσει ταὐτόν, εἰ ἡ στέρησις ἀντίθεσις
5 πρὸς τὰ ἐν λόγῳ ὄντα. Οὐκοῦν φθαρήσεται ἡ
στέρησις προσελθόντος τοῦ οὗ στέρησις; Οὐδαμῶς·

---

[1] ⟨καὶ⟩ Harder, H-S².

---

[1] Cp. Aristotle, *Physics* Γ5. 204a23 ff.

for in so far as it is an image which has escaped from being and truth, it is more unlimited. For unlimitedness is present in a higher degree in that which is less defined; and less in the good is more in the bad. That which is there, which has a greater degree of existence, is unlimited [only] as an image, that which is here has a less degree of existence, and in proportion as it has escaped from being and truth, and sunk down into the nature of an image, it is more truly unlimited. Are, then, the unlimited and essential unlimitedness the same?[1] Where there is a formative principle and matter the two are different, but where there is only matter they must be said to be the same, or, which is better, that there is no essential unlimitedness here; for it will be a rational formative principle, the absence of which from the unlimited is the condition of its being unlimited. So matter must be called unlimited of itself, by opposition to the forming principle; and just as the forming principle is forming principle without being anything else, so the matter which is set over against the forming principle by reason of its unlimitedness must be called unlimited without being anything else.

16. Is matter, then, the same thing as otherness? No, rather it is the same thing as the part of otherness which is opposed to the things which in the full and proper sense exist, that is to say rational formative principles. Therefore, though it is non-existent, it has a certain sort of existence in this way, and is the same thing as privation, if privation is opposition to the things that exist in rational form. Will privation, then, be destroyed by the accession of that of which

ὑποδοχὴ γὰρ ἕξεως οὐχ ἕξις, ἀλλὰ στέρησις, καὶ
πέρατος οὐ τὸ πεπερασμένον οὐδὲ τὸ πέρας, ἀλλὰ
τὸ ἄπειρον καὶ καθ' ὅσον ἄπειρον. Πῶς οὖν [οὐκ]
ἀπολεῖ αὐτοῦ τὴν φύσιν τοῦ ἀπείρου προσελθὸν τὸ
10 πέρας καὶ ταῦτα οὐ κατὰ συμβεβηκὸς ὄντος
ἀπείρου; Ἢ εἰ μὲν κατὰ τὸ ποσὸν ἄπειρον,
ἀνῄρει· νῦν δὲ οὐχ οὕτως, ἀλλὰ τοὐναντίον σῴζει
αὐτὸ ἐν τῷ εἶναι· ὃ γὰρ πέφυκεν, εἰς ἐνέργειαν καὶ
τελείωσιν ἄγει, ὥσπερ τὸ ἄσπαρτον, ὅταν σπείρη-
ται· καὶ ὅταν τὸ θῆλυ τοῦ ἄρρενος † καὶ οὐκ
15 ἀπόλλυται τὸ θῆλυ, ἀλλὰ μᾶλλον θηλύνεται· τοῦτο
δέ ἐστιν· ὃ ἐστι μᾶλλον γίγνεται. Ἆρ' οὖν καὶ
κακὸν ἡ ὕλη μεταλαμβάνουσα ἀγαθοῦ; Ἢ διὰ
τοῦτο, ὅτι ἐδεήθη· οὐ γὰρ εἶχε. Καὶ γὰρ ὃ μὲν
ἂν δέηταί τινος, τὸ δ' ἔχῃ, μέσον ἂν ἴσως γίγνοιτο
ἀγαθοῦ καὶ κακοῦ, εἰ ἰσάζοι πως ἐπ' ἄμφω· ὃ δ'
20 ἂν μηδὲν ἔχῃ ἅτε ἐν πενίᾳ ὄν, μᾶλλον δὲ πενία ὄν,
ἀνάγκη κακὸν εἶναι. Οὐ γὰρ πλούτου πενία τοῦτο
[οὐδὲ ἰσχύος], ἀλλὰ πενία μὲν φρονήσεως, πενία δὲ
ἀρετῆς, κάλλους, ἰσχύος, μορφῆς, εἴδους, ποιοῦ.
Πῶς οὖν οὐ δυσειδές; Πῶς δὲ οὐ πάντη αἰσχρόν;
25 Πῶς δὲ οὐ πάντη κακόν; Ἐκείνη δὲ ἡ ὕλη ἡ ἐκεῖ
ὄν· τὸ γὰρ πρὸ αὐτῆς ἐπέκεινα ὄντος. Ἐνταῦθα
δὲ τὸ πρὸ αὐτῆς ὄν. Οὐκ ὂν ἄρα αὐτή, ἕτερον ὄν,
πρὸς τῷ καλῷ τοῦ ὄντος.

---

¹ L. A. Post suggests that the MSS text can be accepted
here if we understand <σπέρματι σπείρηται>: this is not per-

it is privation? Not at all; for that which receives a state is not a state but a privation, and the recipient of limit is not what is limited or limit, but the unlimited and that in so far as it is unlimited. How, then, can limit, when it has come to it, possibly destroy the nature of the absolutely unlimited, especially when it is not only incidentally unlimited? If it was quantitatively unlimited, limit would do away with it; but as it is, it does not do so; on the other hand, it keeps it in being; for it brings what it naturally is to actuality and perfection, like the unsown field when it is sown, and as when the female conceives by the male,[1] and does not lose its femaleness but becomes still more female: and that is, becomes more what it is. Is matter, then, also evil because it participates in good? Rather, because it lacks it; for this means that it does not have it. Anything which lacks something, but has something else, might perhaps hold a middle position between good and evil, if its lack and its having more or less balance; but that which has nothing because it is in want, or rather is want, must necessarily be evil. For this thing is not want of wealth but want of thought, want of virtue, of beauty, strength, shape, form, quality. Must it not then be ugly? Must it not be utterly vile, utterly evil? But the matter There is something real, for that which is before it is beyond being. Here, however, that which is before matter is real, and so matter itself is not real; it is something other, over and above the excellence of real being.

haps too much of an ellipsis for Plotinus, and is certainly the best suggestion so far.

ENNEAD II. 5

II. 5. ON WHAT EXISTS POTENTIALLY
AND WHAT ACTUALLY

Introductory Note

THIS treatise (No. 25 in Porphyry's chronological order) is, like most of II. 4, concerned with the close discussion of technical Aristotelian concepts: it is less explicitly critical of Aristotle than the preceding treatise, but the conception of matter which it presents is Plotinus's own and not that of Aristotle. The main purpose of the treatise is in fact to show clearly what Plotinus means by matter in the intelligible world, and how he conceives of matter in the sense-world as potentiality which never can be actualised, essential negation, " that which is really unreal "; this paradoxical conception is stated more clearly, perhaps, in the last chapter of this treatise than anywhere else in the *Enneads*.

Synopsis

What is meant by potential and actual existence, and by potentiality and actuality; a discussion designed to bring out clearly the meaning of these Aristotelian concepts (ch. 1–2). How these concepts are to be applied to the intelligible world; there is no matter there in the sense of a principle of change, but the something like matter which our analysis detects is form, one aspect of the unchanging actuality (ch. 3). How they apply to the matter of the sense-world; it is a potentiality which never becomes or can become anything actual (chs. 4–5).

II. 5. (25) ΠΕΡΙ ΤΟΥ ΔΥΝΑΜΕΙ ΚΑΙ ΕΝΕΡΓΕΙΑΙ

1. Λέγεται τὸ μὲν δυνάμει, τὸ δὲ ἐνεργείᾳ εἶναι·
λέγεται δέ τι καὶ ἐνέργεια ἐν τοῖς οὖσι. Σκεπτέον
οὖν τί τὸ δυνάμει καὶ τί τὸ ἐνεργείᾳ. ᾽Αρα τὸ
αὐτὸ τῷ ἐνεργείᾳ εἶναι ἡ ἐνέργεια, καὶ εἴ τί ἐστιν
5 ἐνέργεια, τοῦτο καὶ ἐνεργείᾳ, ἢ ἕτερον ἑκάτερον
καὶ τὸ ἐνεργείᾳ ὂν οὐκ ἀνάγκη καὶ ἐνέργειαν εἶναι;
῞Οτι μὲν οὖν ἐν τοῖς αἰσθητοῖς τὸ δυνάμει, δῆλον·
εἰ δὲ καὶ ἐν τοῖς νοητοῖς, σκεπτέον. ῍Η ἐκεῖ τὸ
ἐνεργείᾳ μόνον· καὶ εἰ ἔστι τὸ δυνάμει, τὸ δυνάμει
μόνον ἀεί, κἂν ἀεὶ ᾖ, οὐδέποτε ἂν ἔλθοι εἰς
10 ἐνέργειαν ⟨τῷ⟩ οὐ τῷ χρόνῳ[1] ἐξείργεσθαι. ᾽Αλλὰ
τί ἐστι τὸ δυνάμει πρῶτον λεκτέον, εἰ δὴ τὸ δυνάμει
δεῖ μὴ ἁπλῶς λέγεσθαι· οὐ γὰρ ἔστι τὸ δυνάμει
μηδενὸς εἶναι. Οἷον δυνάμει ἀνδριὰς ὁ χαλ-
κός· εἰ γὰρ μηδὲν ἐξ αὐτοῦ μηδ᾽ ἐπ᾽ αὐτῷ μηδ᾽
ἔμελλε μηθὲν ἔσεσθαι μεθ᾽ ὃ ἦν μηδ᾽ ἐνεδέχετο

---

[1] ⟨τῷ⟩ οὐ τῷ χρόνῳ Theiler: οὐ τῶ χρόνῳ codd: τῷ οὐ χρόνῳ
H-S¹: † οὐ τῷ χρόνῳ H-S².

---

[1] I accept Theiler's emendation and interpretation here:
see his note *ad loc.* (Plotins Schriften II. 6. p. 431).

[2] Aristotle, *Physics* Γ. 1. 201a30.

II. 5. ON WHAT EXISTS
POTENTIALLY AND WHAT
ACTUALLY

1. One speaks of potential and actual existence; and one speaks of actuality as something in the class of existing things. We must consider therefore what potential and what actual existence is. Is actuality the same as actual existence, and if anything is actuality is it also actually existent, or are the two different, and is it not necessary for that which is actually existing to be actuality? Further, it is clear that there is potential existence in the world of things perceived by the senses; but we must consider whether it is also in the intelligible world. Now, in that world there is only actual existence; even if there is potential existence, it is always only potential, and even if it always exists, it would never come to actuality because it is excluded from it by the fact that it is not in time.[1] But first we must say what potential existence is, if, as is indeed the case, we must not speak of potential existence simply; for it is not possible to exist potentially without being potentially anything. For instance, " the bronze is potentially statue ";[2] for if nothing was going to come out of a thing or come upon it, and it was not going to be anything subsequent to what it was and there was no possibility of its becoming anything,

15 γενέσθαι, ἦν ἂν ὃ ἦν μόνον. Ὃ δὲ ἦν, ἤδη παρῆν
καὶ οὐκ ἔμελλε· τί οὖν ἐδύνατο ἄλλο μετὰ τὸ
παρὸν αὐτό; Οὐ τοίνυν ἦν ἂν δυνάμει. Δεῖ
τοίνυν τὸ δυνάμει τι ὂν ἄλλο ἤδη τῷ τι καὶ ἄλλο
μετ’ αὐτὸ δύνασθαι, ἤτοι μένον μετὰ τοῦ ἐκεῖνο
ποιεῖν ἢ παρέχον αὐτὸ ἐκείνῳ ὃ δύναται φθαρὲν
20 αὐτό, δυνάμει λέγεσθαι· ἄλλως γὰρ τὸ “ δυνάμει
ἀνδριὰς ὁ χαλκός,” ἄλλως τὸ ὕδωρ δυνάμει
χαλκὸς καὶ ὁ ἀὴρ πῦρ. Τοιοῦτον δὴ ὂν τὸ
δυνάμει ἆρα καὶ δύναμις λέγοιτο ἂν πρὸς τὸ
ἐσόμενον, οἷον ὁ χαλκὸς δύναμις τοῦ ἀνδριάντος;
Ἤ, εἰ μὲν ἡ δύναμις κατὰ τὸ ποιεῖν λαμβάνοιτο,
25 οὐδαμῶς· οὐ γὰρ ἡ δύναμις ἡ κατὰ τὸ ποιεῖν
λαμβανομένη λέγοιτο ἂν δυνάμει. Εἰ δὲ τὸ
δυνάμει μὴ μόνον πρὸς τὸ ἐνεργείᾳ λέγεται, ἀλλὰ
καὶ πρὸς ἐνέργειαν, εἴη ἂν καὶ δύναμις δυνάμει.
Βέλτιον δὲ καὶ σαφέστερον τὸ μὲν δυνάμει πρὸς
τὸ ἐνεργείᾳ, τὴν δὲ δύναμιν πρὸς ἐνέργειαν λέγειν.
30 Τὸ μὲν δὴ δυνάμει τοιοῦτον ὥσπερ ὑποκείμενόν τι
πάθεσι καὶ μορφαῖς καὶ εἴδεσιν, ἃ μέλλει δέχεσθαι
καὶ πέφυκεν· ἢ καὶ σπεύδει ἐλθεῖν, καὶ τὰ μὲν ὡς
πρὸς τὸ βέλτιστον, τὰ δὲ πρὸς τὰ χείρω καὶ
λυμαντικὰ αὐτῶν, ὧν ἕκαστον καὶ ἐνεργείᾳ ἐστὶν
ἄλλο.

it would be what it was alone. But what it was, was there already, and was not going to be. What other potentiality, then, would it have after what was already there? It would not be potential at all. So one must speak of anything which is potential as already potentially something else by being able to become something after what it already is, either remaining along with its production of that other thing, or giving itself up to that which it is able to become and being destroyed itself; for " the bronze is potentially statue " in one sense, the water is potentially bronze and the air, fire, in another. Well, then, if this is the sort of thing which potential existence is, can it be called potentiality in regard to that which it is going to be? For instance, is the bronze the potentiality of the statue? If potentiality is taken in the sense of being able to make, certainly not; for potentiality understood in the sense of being able to make would not be described as existing potentially. But if the term " potential existence " is used not only in relation to actual existence but also in relation to actuality, then potentiality, too, would exist potentially. But it is better and clearer to use " potential existence " in relation to " actual existence," and " potentiality " in relation to " actuality." Potential existence in this sense is like something which underlies affections and shapes and forms, which it is going to receive and naturally disposed to receive: indeed, it even strives to come to them, and attains some of them with the best results, others with worse results, spoiling the individual things, of which each is actually something other [than what it is potentially].

2. Περὶ δὲ τῆς ὕλης σκεπτέον, εἰ ἕτερόν τι οὖσα
ἐνεργείᾳ δυνάμει ἐστὶ πρὸς ἃ μορφοῦται, ἢ οὐδὲν
ἐνεργείᾳ, καὶ ὅλως καὶ τὰ ἄλλα ἃ λέγομεν δυνάμει
λαβόντα τὸ εἶδος καὶ μένοντα αὐτὰ ἐνεργείᾳ
5 γίνεται, ἢ τὸ ἐνεργείᾳ κατὰ τοῦ ἀνδριάντος
λεχθήσεται ἀντιτιθεμένου μόνον τοῦ ἐνεργείᾳ
ἀνδριάντος πρὸς τὸν δυνάμει ἀνδριάντα, ἀλλ᾽ οὐ
τοῦ ἐνεργείᾳ κατηγορουμένου κατ᾽ ἐκείνου, καθ᾽
οὗ τὸ δυνάμει ἀνδριὰς ἐλέγετο. Εἰ δὴ οὕτως, οὐ
τὸ δυνάμει γίνεται ἐνεργείᾳ, ἀλλ᾽ ἐκ τοῦ δυνάμει
10 ὄντος πρότερον ἐγένετο τὸ ἐνεργείᾳ ὕστερον. Καὶ
γὰρ αὖ τὸ ὃ ἐνεργείᾳ ὂν τὸ συναμφότερον, οὐχ ἡ
ὕλη, τὸ δὲ εἶδος τὸ ἐπ᾽ αὐτῇ. Καὶ τοῦτο μέν, εἰ
ἑτέρα γίγνοιτο οὐσία, οἷον ἐκ χαλκοῦ ἀνδριάς·
ἄλλη γὰρ οὐσία ὡς τὸ συναμφότερον ὁ ἀνδριάς.
Ἐπὶ δὲ τῶν ὅλως οὐ μενόντων φανερόν, ὡς τὸ
15 δυνάμει παντάπασιν ἕτερον ἦν. Ἀλλ᾽ ὅταν ὁ
δυνάμει γραμματικὸς ἐνεργείᾳ γένηται, ἐνταῦθα
τὸ δυνάμει πῶς οὐ καὶ ἐνεργείᾳ τὸ αὐτό; Ὁ γὰρ
δυνάμει Σωκράτης ὁ αὐτὸς καὶ ἐνεργείᾳ σοφός.
Ἆρ᾽ οὖν καὶ ὁ ἀνεπιστήμων ἐπιστήμων; Δυνάμει
20 γὰρ ἦν ἐπιστήμων. Ἢ κατὰ συμβεβηκὸς ὁ ἀμαθὴς
ἐπιστήμων. Οὐ γὰρ ᾗ ἀμαθὴς δυνάμει ἐπιστήμων,

ON WHAT EXISTS POTENTIALLY

2. We must also consider the question of matter, whether it exists potentially in relation to the things which are given shape and is something else actually, or whether it is nothing actually; and in general, whether the other things which we say exist potentially come to exist actually when they receive the form while remaining themselves, or whether actual existence will be predicated of the statue, and the actual statue only opposed to the potential statue, but the predicate " actual " will not be applied to that of which the term " potential statue " was used. If this is so, it is not that which exists potentially which comes to exist actually, but the subsequent actually existing thing comes into being out of the prior potentially existing thing. Again, the actually existing thing is the compound of matter and form, not the matter on the one side, and on the other, the form imposed upon it. This is so when a different substance comes into existence, for instance, a statue from bronze; for the statue, as being the compound of matter and form is a different substance. And in the case of things of which no trace remains, it is obvious that what existed potentially was altogether different [from the actuality]. But when the man who is potentially educated becomes actually educated, surely in this case what existed potentially is the same as what exists actually. For it is the same Socrates who is potentially and actually wise. Then, is this true when the man without knowledge becomes a man of knowledge? For he was a man of knowledge potentially. It is only incidentally that the unlearned man becomes a man of knowledge. For it was not in so far as he was unlearned that he

PLOTINUS: ENNEAD II. 5.

ἀλλὰ συμβεβήκει αὐτῷ ἀμαθεῖ εἶναι, ἡ δὲ ψυχὴ
καθ' αὑτὴν ἐπιτηδείως ἔχουσα τὸ δυνάμει ἦν
ἧπερ καὶ ἐπιστήμων. Ἔτι οὖν σῴζει τὸ δυνάμει,
καὶ δυνάμει γραμματικὸς ἤδη γραμματικὸς ὤν;
25 Ἢ οὐδὲν κωλύει καὶ ἄλλον τρόπον· ἐκεῖ μὲν
δυνάμει μόνον, ἐνταῦθα δὲ τῆς δυνάμεως ἐχούσης
τὸ εἶδος. Εἰ οὖν ἐστι τὸ μὲν δυνάμει τὸ ὑποκείμενον, τὸ δ' ἐνεργείᾳ τὸ συναμφότερον, ὁ ἀνδριάς,
τὸ εἶδος τὸ ἐπὶ τοῦ χαλκοῦ τί ἂν λέγοιτο; Ἢ οὐκ
30 ἄτοπον τὴν ἐνέργειαν, καθ' ἣν ἐνεργείᾳ ἐστὶ καὶ
οὐ μόνον δυνάμει, τὴν μορφὴν καὶ τὸ εἶδος λέγειν,
οὐχ ἁπλῶς ἐνέργειαν, ἀλλὰ τοῦδε ἐνέργειαν· ἐπεὶ
καὶ ἄλλην ἐνέργειαν τάχα κυριώτερον ἂν λέγοιμεν,
τὴν ἀντίθετον τῇ δυνάμει τῇ ἐπαγούσῃ ἐνέργειαν.
Τὸ μὲν γὰρ δυνάμει τὸ ἐνεργείᾳ ἔχειν παρ' ἄλλου,
τῇ δὲ δυνάμει ὃ δύναται παρ' αὑτῆς ἡ ἐνέργεια·
35 οἷον ἕξις καὶ ἡ κατ' αὐτὴν λεγομένη ἐνέργεια,
ἀνδρία καὶ τὸ ἀνδρίζεσθαι. Ταῦτα μὲν οὖν οὕτως.

3. Οὗ δ' ἕνεκα ταῦτα προείρηται, νῦν λεκτέον,
ἐν τοῖς νοητοῖς πῶς ποτε τὸ ἐνεργείᾳ λέγεται καὶ
εἰ ἐνεργείᾳ μόνον ἢ καὶ ἐνέργεια ἕκαστον καὶ εἰ
ἐνέργεια πάντα καὶ εἰ τὸ δυνάμει κἀκεῖ. Εἰ δὴ
5 μήτε ὕλη ἐκεῖ ἐν ᾗ τὸ δυνάμει, μήτε τι μέλλει τῶν

160

was potentially a man of knowledge, but it was incidental to him that he was unlearned, and his soul
being appropriately disposed was the potential existence, and by it he became a man of knowledge. So,
then, does he still keep the potential existence, and is
he potentially educated when he is already educated?
There is no obstacle to this, and we can put it in a
different way: before he is educated he is only
potentially educated, when he is educated the potentiality has its form. If, then, the potential existence
is the substratum, and the actual existence the compound, the statue, what should the form imposed
on the bronze be called? It is not unreasonable to
call the shape and form, by which the statue exists
actually and not only potentially, the actuality, that
is, not simply actuality but the actuality of this
particular thing: since we might also apply the term
" actuality " more properly to something else, the
actuality contrasted with the potentiality that brings
it to the thing. For the potential existence has its
actual existence from something else, but for the
potentiality what it is capable of by itself is its
actuality; for instance, a moral disposition and the
activity called after it, courage and courageous
behaviour. So much, then, for this.

3. Now we must speak about the question to which
this preliminary discussion was directed, what is
really meant by actual existence in the intelligible
world, and whether each individual intelligible reality
is only actually existent or whether it is also actuality,
and if they are all together actuality, and if there is
potential existence There too. If, of course, there
is no matter there in which potential existence could

ἐκεῖ, ὃ μὴ ἤδη ἐστί, μηδ' ἔτι μεταβάλλον εἰς ἄλλο
ἢ μένον ἕτερόν τι γεννᾷ ἢ ἐξιστάμενον ἑαυτοῦ
ἔδωκεν ἄλλῳ ἀντ' αὐτοῦ εἶναι, οὐκ ἂν εἴη ἐκεῖ τὸ
δυνάμει ἐν ᾧ ἐστι, τῶν ὄντων καὶ αἰῶνα, οὐ
χρόνον ἐχόντων. Εἴ τις οὖν καὶ ἐπὶ τῶν νοητῶν
10 τοὺς τιθεμένους κἀκεῖ ὕλην ἔροιτο, εἰ μὴ κἀκεῖ τὸ
δυνάμει κατὰ τὴν ὕλην τὴν ἐκεῖ—καὶ γὰρ εἰ ἄλλον
τρόπον ἡ ὕλη, ἀλλ' ἔσται ἐφ' ἑκάστου τὸ μὲν ὡς
ὕλη, τὸ δὲ ὡς εἶδος, τὸ δὲ συναμφότερον—τί
ἐροῦσιν; Ἢ καὶ τὸ ὡς ὕλη ἐκεῖ εἶδός ἐστιν, ἐπεὶ
καὶ ἡ ψυχὴ εἶδος ὂν πρὸς ἕτερον ἂν εἴη ὕλη.
15 Οὐκοῦν πρὸς ἐκεῖνο καὶ δυνάμει; Ἢ οὔ· εἶδος
γὰρ ἦν αὐτῆς καὶ οὐκ εἰς ὕστερον δὲ τὸ εἶδος καὶ
οὐ χωρίζεται δὲ ἀλλ' ἢ λόγῳ, καὶ οὕτως ὕλην
ἔχον, ὡς διπλοῦν νοούμενον, ἄμφω δὲ μία φύσις·
οἷον καὶ Ἀριστοτέλης φησὶ τὸ πέμπτον σῶμα
ἄυλον εἶναι. Περὶ δὲ ψυχῆς πῶς ἐροῦμεν;
20 Δυνάμει γὰρ ζῷον, ὅταν μήπω, μέλλῃ δέ, καὶ
μουσικὴ δυνάμει καὶ τὰ ἄλλα ὅσα γίνεται οὐκ ἀεὶ
οὖσα· ὥστε καὶ ἐν νοητοῖς τὸ δυνάμει. Ἢ οὐ

---

[1] Aristotle never actually says this: it may perhaps be
taken as implicit in *De Caelo* A. 3. 270a–b, where he argues
that the celestial substance "the body that moves in a circle"
must be ageless, impassible, without any sort of quantitative
or qualitative change. Possibly Plotinus depends here on
some Peripatetic commentator on this passage, who drew
the conclusion that Aristotle thought that the quintessence

be, and nothing there is going to be that which it is
not already, and nothing, either in the process of
changing into another thing, or remaining what it is,
produces anything else, or, going out of itself, gives
another thing existence in its place: then there will
be nothing there in which potential existence can be,
among things which really exist and possess eternity,
not time. If, then, anyone were to ask those who
posit matter there, too, in the intelligible world, if
there is not potential existence There, too, in respect
of the matter There—for even if matter exists There
in a different way, there will be in each thing something like matter, something like form, and the
compound of the two—what will they say? The
answer is that the something like matter There is
form, since the soul too, which is form, can be matter
to something else. Then does it exist potentially in
relation to that something else? No; for then the
something else would be its form, and the form does
not come to it afterwards and is not separated except
by rational abstraction: it has matter in the sense
that it is thought of as double, but both form and
matter are one nature; just as Aristotle, too, says
that his quintessence is without matter.[1] But how
are we to speak about the soul? For it is potentially
a living being, when it is not one yet but is going to
be, and is potentially musical, and so with everything else that it becomes and is not always; so that
there is potential existence also in the intelligible
world. No, the soul is not these things potentially,

was without matter because he states so clearly that it is
absolutely unchanging, and there is therefore no need to
postulate any matter in it to be the substrate of change.

δυνάμει ταῦτα, ἀλλὰ δύναμις ἡ ψυχὴ τούτων. Τὸ
δὲ ἐνεργείᾳ πῶς ἐκεῖ; Ἆρα ὡς ὁ ἀνδριὰς τὸ
συναμφότερον ἐνεργείᾳ, ὅτι τὸ εἶδος ἕκαστον
25 ἀπείληφεν; Ἢ ὅτι εἶδος ἕκαστον καὶ τέλειόν ὅ
ἐστι. Νοῦς γὰρ οὐκ ἐκ δυνάμεως τῆς κατὰ τὸ
οἷόν τε νοεῖν εἰς ἐνέργειαν τοῦ νοεῖν—ἄλλου γὰρ
ἂν προτέρου τοῦ οὐκ ἐκ δυνάμεως δέοιτο—ἀλλ᾿
ἐν αὐτῷ τὸ πᾶν. Τὸ γὰρ δυνάμει βούλεται ἑτέρου
30 ἐπελθόντος εἰς ἐνέργειαν ἄγεσθαι, ἵνα ἐνεργείᾳ
γίνηταί τι, ὃ δ᾿ αὐτὸ παρ᾿ αὑτοῦ τὸ ἀεὶ οὕτως ἔχει,
τοῦτο ἐνέργεια ἂν εἴη. Πάντα οὖν τὰ πρῶτα
ἐνέργεια· ἔχει γὰρ ὃ δεῖ ἔχειν καὶ παρ᾿ αὑτῶν
καὶ ἀεί· καὶ ψυχὴ δὴ οὕτως ἡ μὴ ἐν ὕλῃ, ἀλλ᾿ ἐν
τῷ νοητῷ. Καὶ ἡ ἐν ὕλῃ δὲ ἄλλη ἐνέργεια· οἷον
ἡ φυτική· ἐνέργεια γὰρ καὶ αὕτη ὅ ἐστιν. Ἀλλ᾿
35 ἐνεργείᾳ μὲν πάντα καὶ οὕτως, ἐνέργεια δὲ πάντα;
Ἢ πῶς; Εἰ δὴ καλῶς εἴρηται ἐκείνη ἡ φύσις
ἄγρυπνος¹ εἶναι καὶ ζωὴ καὶ ζωὴ ἀρίστη, αἱ
κάλλισται ἂν εἶεν ἐκεῖ ἐνέργειαι. Καὶ ἐνεργείᾳ
ἄρα καὶ ἐνέργεια τὰ πάντα καὶ ζωαὶ τὰ πάντα καὶ
40 ὁ τόπος ὁ ἐκεῖ τόπος ἐστὶ ζωῆς καὶ ἀρχὴ καὶ πηγὴ
ἀληθοῦς ψυχῆς τε καὶ νοῦ.

4. Τὰ μὲν οὖν ἄλλα πάντα, ὅσα δυνάμει τί
ἐστιν, ἔχει καὶ τὸ ἐνεργείᾳ εἶναι ἄλλο τι, ὃ ἤδη
ὂν πρὸς ἄλλο δυνάμει εἶναι λέγεται· περὶ δὲ τῆς

¹ Cp. *Timaeus* 52B7. Plotinus speaks of the "sleepless
light" in Intellect in his fine description of its changeless,
eternal life and thought in VI. 2. 8. 7.

it is the potentiality of these things. But how are we
to understand actual existence there? Is it like the
way in which the statue, the compound of matter and
form, exists actually, because each intelligible thing
has already received its form? Rather because
each of them is form and is perfectly what it is. For
intellect does not move from a potentiality consisting
in being able to think to an actuality of thinking—
otherwise it would need another prior principle which
does not move from potentiality to actuality—but the
whole is in it. For potential existence wants to be
brought to actuality by the coming to it of something
else, so that it may become something actually, but
that which has itself from itself unchanging identity,
this will be actuality. So all the primary beings are
actuality; for they have what they need to have
from themselves and for ever: and soul is in this
state too, the soul which is not in matter but in the
intelligible. But the soul in matter, too, is another
actuality—the growth-soul for instance; for this, too,
is an actuality, what it is. But, granted that everything there exists actually in this way, is everything
there actuality? Why not? Certainly, if it is well
said that that nature there is sleepless,[1] and life, and
the best life, the noblest actualities would be there.
All things there, then, both exist actually and are
actualities, and all are lives, and the region there is
a region of life and the origin and spring of true soul
and intellect.

4. Everything else, then, which is potentially
something, has actual existence as something else;
and this something else which already exists is said
to exist potentially in relation to another thing.

λεγομένης εἶναι ὕλης, ἣν πάντα δυνάμει λέγομεν
5 τὰ ὄντα, πῶς ἔστιν εἰπεῖν ἐνεργείᾳ τι τῶν ὄντων
εἶναι; Ἤδη γὰρ οὐ πάντα τὰ ὄντα δυνάμει ἂν
εἴη. Εἰ οὖν μηδὲν τῶν ὄντων, ἀνάγκη μηδ' ὂν
αὐτὴν εἶναι. Πῶς οὖν ἂν ἐνεργείᾳ τι εἴη μηδὲν
τῶν ὄντων οὖσα; Ἀλλ' οὐδὲν τῶν ὄντων ἂν εἴη
τούτων, ἃ γίνεται ἐπ' αὐτῆς, ἄλλο δέ τι οὐδὲν
10 κωλύει εἶναι, εἴπερ μηδὲ πάντα τὰ ὄντα ἐπὶ τῇ
ὕλῃ. Ἡι μὲν δὴ οὐδέν ἐστι τούτων τῶν ἐπ' αὐτῇ,
ταῦτα δὲ ὄντα, μὴ ὂν ἂν εἴη. Οὐ μὲν δὴ ἀνείδεόν
τι φανταζομένη εἶδος ἂν εἴη· οὐ τοίνυν οὐδ' ἐν
ἐκείνοις ἂν[1] ἀριθμηθείη. Μὴ ὂν ἄρα καὶ ταύτῃ
ἔσται. Ἐπ' ἄμφω ἄρα μὴ ὂν οὖσα πλειόνως μὴ
15 ὂν ἔσται. Εἰ δὴ πέφευγε μὲν τὴν τῶν ὡς ἀληθῶς
ὄντων φύσιν, οὐ δύναται δὲ ἐφικέσθαι οὐδὲ τῶν
ψευδῶς λεγομένων εἶναι, ὅτι μηδὲ ἴνδαλμα λόγου
ἐστὶν ὡς ταῦτα, ἐν τίνι τῷ εἶναι ἂν ἁλοίη; Εἰ δὲ
ἐν μηδενὶ τῷ εἶναι, τί ἂν ἐνεργείᾳ εἴη;

5. Πῶς οὖν λέγομεν περὶ αὐτῆς; Πῶς δὲ τῶν
ὄντων ὕλη; Ἤ ὅτι δυνάμει. Οὐκοῦν, ὅτι ἤδη
δυνάμει, ἤδη οὖν ἔστι καθὸ μέλλει; Ἀλλὰ τὸ
εἶναι αὐτῇ μόνον τὸ μέλλον ἐπαγγελλόμενον· οἷον
5 τὸ εἶναι αὐτῇ εἰς ἐκεῖνο ἀναβάλλεται, ὃ ἔσται.
Τὸ τοίνυν δυνάμει οὔ τι, ἀλλὰ δυνάμει πάντα·

---

[1] ἂν Kirchhoff; H-S²: ὂν codd.

ON WHAT EXISTS POTENTIALLY

But as for matter, which is said to exist and which we say is all realities potentially, how is it possible to say that it is actually something real? For if it was, it would already have ceased to be potentially all realities. If, then, it is nothing real, it necessarily cannot be existent either. How could it, then, be actually something when it is nothing real? But, even if it is not any of the realities which come into being upon it, there is no obstacle to its being something else, since it is not all realities which have a material foundation. In so far, then, as it is none of these things which are founded upon it, and these are realities, it is non-existent. But certainly it could not be a form, since it is imagined as something formless; so it could not be numbered among those form-realities of the intelligible world. So it will be non-existent in this way too. If, then, it is non-existent in both these ways, it will be still more non-existent. If, then, it has made good its escape from the nature of the true realities, and cannot attain even to those which are falsely said to exist, because it is not even a phantasm of rational form as these are, in what sort of existence can it be grasped? And if in no sort of existence, how can it exist actually?

5. How, then, do we speak of it? How is it the matter of real things. Because it is they potentially. Then, because it is they already potentially, is it therefore just as it is going to be? But its being is no more than an announcement of what it is going to be: it is as if being for it was adjourned to that which it will be. So its potential existence is not being something, but being potentially everything;

167

μηδὲν δὲ ὂν καθ᾽ αὑτό, ἀλλ᾽ ὅ ἐστιν ὕλη ὄν, οὐδ᾽
ἐνεργείᾳ ἐστίν. Εἰ γὰρ ἔσται τι ἐνεργείᾳ, ἐκεῖνο
ὅ ἐστιν ἐνεργείᾳ, οὐχ ἡ ὕλη ἔσται· οὐ πάντη οὖν
ὕλη, ἀλλὰ οἷον ὁ χαλκός. Εἴη ἂν οὖν τοῦτο μὴ ὄν,
10 οὐχ ὡς ἕτερον τοῦ ὄντος, οἷον κίνησις· αὕτη γὰρ
καὶ ἐποχεῖται τῷ ὄντι οἷον ἀπ᾽ αὐτοῦ καὶ ἐν αὐτῷ
οὖσα, ἡ δέ ἐστιν οἷον ἐκριφεῖσα καὶ πάντη χωρισ-
θεῖσα καὶ μεταβάλλειν ἑαυτὴν οὐ δυναμένη, ἀλλ᾽
ὅπερ ἐξ ἀρχῆς ἦν—μὴ ὂν δὲ ἦν—οὕτως ἀεὶ ἔχουσα.
Οὔτε δὲ ἦν ἐξ ἀρχῆς ἐνεργείᾳ τι ἀποστᾶσα πάντων
15 τῶν ὄντων οὔτε ἐγένετο· ἃ γὰρ ὑποδῦναι ἠθέλησεν,
οὐδὲ χρωσθῆναι ἀπ᾽ αὐτῶν δεδύνηται, ἀλλὰ
μένουσα πρὸς ἄλλο δυνάμει οὖσα πρὸς τὰ ἐφεξῆς,
τῶν δ᾽ ὄντων ἤδη παυσαμένων ἐκείνων φανεῖσα
ὑπό τε τῶν μετ᾽ αὐτὴν γενομένων καταληφθεῖσα
ἔσχατον καὶ τούτων κατέστη. Ὑπ᾽ ἀμφοτέρων
20 οὖν καταληφθεῖσα ἐνεργείᾳ μὲν οὐδετέρων ἂν εἴη,
δυνάμει δὲ μόνον ἐγκαταλέλειπται εἶναι ἀσθενές τι
καὶ ἀμυδρὸν εἴδωλον μορφοῦσθαι μὴ δυνάμενον.
Οὐκοῦν ἐνεργείᾳ εἴδωλον· οὐκοῦν ἐνεργείᾳ ψεῦδος.
Τοῦτο δὲ ταὐτὸν τῷ ἀληθινῶς ψεῦδος· τοῦτο
25 δὲ ὄντως μὴ ὄν. Εἰ οὖν ἐνεργείᾳ μὴ ὄν, μᾶλλον
μὴ ὄν, καὶ ὄντως ἄρα μὴ ὄν. Πολλοῦ ἄρα δεῖ

---

[1] Cp. ch. 1. The bronze is already actually bronze, a
formed, actually existing thing; but it is potentially the
statue which can be made out of it, and so the matter of the
statue.

and since it is nothing in itself—except what it is, matter—it does not exist actually at all. For, if it is to be anything actually, it will be what it is actually and not matter: so it will not be altogether matter, but only matter in the way that the bronze is.[1] So then it must be non-existent not in the sense of being different from existence, like motion:[2] for this rides on existence, as if coming from it and being in it, but matter is as if cast out and utterly separated, and unable to change itself, but always in the state it was from the beginning—and it was non-existent. It was not anything actually from the beginning, since it stood apart from all realities, and it did not become anything; it has not been able to take even a touch of colour from the things that wanted to plunge into it, but remaining directed to something else it exists potentially to what comes next; when the realities of the intelligible world had already come to an end it appeared and was caught by the things that came into being after it and took its place as the last after these too. So, being caught by both, it could belong actually to neither class of realities; it is only left for it to be potentially a sort of weak and dim phantasm unable to receive a shape. So it is actually a phantasm: so it is actually a falsity: this is the same as " that which is truly a falsity "; this is " what is really unreal."[3] That, then, which has

---

[2] Motion is one of the " categories of the intelligible world," cp. ch. 5 of the preceding treatise, and the note there.

[3] The phrase τὸ ὡς ἀληθῶς ψεῦδος comes from Plato, *Republic* II. 382A4, but occurs there in a quite different context (the " lie in the soul "): ὄντως μὴ ὄν comes from *Sophist* 254D1, and again certainly does not refer to ὕλη.

αὐτῷ ἐνεργείᾳ τι τῶν ὄντων εἶναι τὸ ἀληθὲς ἔχοντι
ἐν τῷ μὴ ὄντι. Εἴπερ ἄρα δεῖ αὐτὸ εἶναι, δεῖ
αὐτὸ ἐνεργείᾳ μὴ εἶναι, ἵνα ἐκβεβηκὸς τοῦ ἀληθῶς
εἶναι ἐν τῷ μὴ εἶναι ἔχῃ τὸ εἶναι, ἐπείπερ τοῖς
30 ψευδῶς οὖσιν, ἐὰν ἀφέλῃς τὸ ψεῦδος αὐτῶν,
ἀφεῖλες αὐτῶν ἥντινα εἶχον οὐσίαν, καὶ τοῖς
δυνάμει τὸ εἶναι καὶ τὴν οὐσίαν ἔχουσιν εἰσαγαγὼν
τὴν ἐνέργειαν ἀπολώλεκας αὐτῶν τῆς ὑποστάσεως
τὴν αἰτίαν, ὅτι τὸ εἶναι αὐτοῖς ἐν δυνάμει ἦν.
Εἴπερ ἄρα δεῖ ἀνώλεθρον τὴν ὕλην τηρεῖν, ὕλην
35 αὐτὴν δεῖ τηρεῖν· δεῖ ἄρα δυνάμει, ὡς ἔοικεν,
εἶναι λέγειν μόνον, ἵνα ᾖ ὅ ἐστιν, ἢ τούτους τοὺς
λόγους ἐξελεγκτέον.

its truth in non-existence is very far from being actually any reality. If, then, it must exist, it must actually not exist, so that, having gone out of true being, it may have its being in non-being; for when you are dealing with things which exist falsely, if you take away their falsity, you have taken away what substance they have, and if you bring in actuality to things which have their being and substance in potentiality you have destroyed the ground of their existence, since their being was in their potentiality. If, then, we must keep matter as indestructible, we must keep it as matter. One must say, then, it would seem, only that it exists potentially, in order that it may be what it is, or else one must refute these arguments.

ENNEAD II. 6

II. 6. ON SUBSTANCE, OR ON QUALITY

Introductory Note

THIS treatise (No. 17 in Porphyry's chronological order) is a highly technical, and at times extremely obscure, criticism of Aristotle's doctrine of quality: it puts forward a view which is in all essentials the same as that which Plotinus much later expounds in his great treatise *On the Categories* (VI. 1–3. 42–44 in the chronological order). This is that the category of quality cannot be used in speaking of the intelligible world, where everything is substance; and even in the sense-world its use is severely restricted; the essential quality or *differentia* is not really a quality at all but an activity of the formative principle, and even accidental qualities, though they may still be called qualities, are traces or shadows of the activities of substances in the intelligible world.

Synopsis

In the intelligible world everything is substance. What place, then, can be found there for quality? The Aristotelian distinction between essential differentiations and accidental qualities does not work—the same quality appears in one thing as a *differentia*, in another as an accident, white, for instance, in " white lead " and " white man." We must say, rather, that what is quality here is substance in the intelligible world (ch. 1). Further critical examination of the Aristotelian doctrine of quality as applied to things in the sense-world, with the conclusion that the notion of *differentia* is unsatisfactory here too, and that essential differentiations should be regarded, not as qualities, but as activities of substance and formative principle; only non-essential, accidental qualities are to be called qualities (ch. 2).   In the intelligible world the origins and archetypes of even these non-essential qualities are substantial activities, of which quality here is a trace or shadow (ch. 3).

II. 6. (17) ΠΕΡΙ ΟΥΣΙΑΣ Η ΠΕΡΙ
ΠΟΙΟΤΗΤΟΣ

1. Ἆρα τὸ ὂν καὶ ἡ οὐσία ἕτερον, καὶ τὸ μὲν ὂν
ἀπηρημωμένον τῶν ἄλλων, ἡ δὲ οὐσία τὸ ὂν μετὰ
τῶν ἄλλων, κινήσεως, στάσεως, ταὐτοῦ, ἑτέρου,
καὶ στοιχεῖα ταῦτα ἐκείνης; Τὸ οὖν ὅλον οὐσία,
5 ἕκαστον δὲ ἐκείνων τὸ μὲν ὄν, τὸ δὲ κίνησις, τὸ
δὲ ἄλλο τι. Κίνησις μὲν οὖν κατὰ συμβεβηκὸς ὄν·
οὐσία δὲ ἆρα κατὰ συμβεβηκός, ἢ συμπληρωτικὸν
οὐσίας; Ἢ καὶ αὐτὴ [ἡ] οὐσία καὶ τὰ ἐκεῖ πάντα
οὐσία. Πῶς οὖν οὐ καὶ ἐνταῦθα; Ἢ ἐκεῖ, ὅτι ἓν
πάντα, ἐνθάδε δὲ διαληφθέντων τῶν εἰδώλων τὸ
10 μὲν ἄλλο, τὸ δὲ ἄλλο· ὥσπερ ἐν μὲν τῷ σπέρματι
ὁμοῦ πάντα καὶ ἕκαστον πάντα καὶ οὐ χεὶρ χωρὶς
καὶ χωρὶς κεφαλή, ἔνθα δὲ χωρίζεται ἀλλήλων·
εἴδωλα γὰρ καὶ οὐκ ἀληθῆ. Τὰς οὖν ποιότητας
ἐκεῖ φήσομεν οὐσίας διαφορὰς περὶ οὐσίαν οὔσας
15 ἢ περὶ ὄν, διαφορὰς δὲ ποιούσας ἑτέρας οὐσίας

---

[1] The " categories of the intelligible world ": cp. II. 4. 5
and II. 5. 5.

II. 6. ON SUBSTANCE, OR ON QUALITY

1. Are being and substance different, and is being stripped of everything else, while substance is being along with everything else, with motion, rest, sameness, otherness,[1] and are these elements of substance? The whole, then, is substance, and each of those others is, one of them being, another motion, and another something else. So, then, motion is incidentally being: is it, then, incidentally substance, or a constituent element essential to the completion of substance? Motion is certainly itself substance, and everything in the intelligible world is substance. Why, then, is everything not substance here below too? There, in the intelligible world, everything is substance because all are one; here below the images are separated, and one is one thing, one another: just as in the seed all things are together and each is all, and there is not a hand separately and a head separately, but here and now they are separated from each other; for they are images and not true realities.

Shall we, then, say that the qualities in the intelligible world are differentiations of substance applying to substance or to being, but differentiations in that they make substances distinct from each other and so are entirely responsible for making

πρὸς ἀλλήλας καὶ ὅλως οὐσίας; Ἢ οὐκ ἄτοπον,
ἀλλὰ περὶ τῶν τῇδε ποιοτήτων, ὧν αἱ μὲν διαφοραὶ
οὐσιῶν, ὡς τὸ δίπουν καὶ τὸ τετράπουν, αἱ δὲ οὐ
διαφοραὶ οὖσαι αὐτὸ τοῦτο μόνον ποιότητες λέγονται. Καίτοι τὸ αὐτὸ καὶ διαφορὰ γίγνεται
20 συμπληροῦσα καὶ οὐ διαφορὰ ἐν ἄλλῳ οὐ συμπληροῦσα τὴν οὐσίαν, συμβεβηκὸς δέ· οἷον τὸ λευκὸν
ἐν μὲν κύκνῳ ἢ ψιμυθίῳ συμπληροῦν, ἐν δὲ σοὶ
συμβεβηκός. Ἢ τὸ λευκὸν τὸ μὲν ἐν τῷ λόγῳ
συμπληροῦν καὶ οὐ ποιότης, τὸ δὲ ἐν τῇ ἐπιφανείᾳ
ποιόν. Ἢ διαιρετέον τὸ ποιόν, ὡς τὸ μὲν
25 οὐσιῶδες ἰδιότης τις οὖσα τῆς οὐσίας, τὸ δὲ μόνον
ποιόν, καθ᾽ ὃ ποιὰ οὐσία, τοῦ ποιοῦ οὐ διαλλαγὴν
εἰς τὴν οὐσίαν ποιοῦντος οὐδ᾽ ἐκ τῆς οὐσίας, ἀλλ᾽
οὔσης ἤδη καὶ πεπληρωμένης διάθεσίν τινα ἔξωθεν
ποιοῦντος καὶ μετὰ τὴν οὐσίαν τοῦ πράγματος
προσθήκην, εἴτε περὶ ψυχὴν εἴτε περὶ σῶμα
30 γίγνοιτο. Ἀλλ᾽ εἰ καὶ τὸ ὁρώμενον λευκὸν ἐπὶ τοῦ
ψιμυθίου συμπληρωτικὸν εἴη αὐτοῦ;—ἐπὶ μὲν γὰρ
τοῦ κύκνου οὐ συμπληρωτικόν· γένοιτο γὰρ ἂν
καὶ οὐ λευκός—ἀλλ᾽ ἐπὶ τοῦ ψιμυθίου· καὶ τοῦ
πυρὸς δὲ ἡ θερμότης. Ἀλλ᾽ εἴ τις λέγοι τὴν
πυρότητα τὴν οὐσίαν εἶναι καὶ ἐπὶ τοῦ ψιμυθίου

---

[1] White lead appears as a stock example of whiteness already
in Aristotle, *Nibomachean Ethics* A. 4. 1096b23, where it is
coupled with snow.   As for the swan, Plotinus's self-correction
below (1. 31–32) seems to confirm the correctness of the MSS
reading: cp. also Simplicius, *In Phys.* I. 3, p. 119, 16.

them substances? Now this view is not unreasonable in itself, but it is unreasonable when it is applied
to the qualities here, of which some are differentiations of substance, for instance, " two-footed " and
" four-footed," and some, which are not differentiations of substance are called just qualities, and nothing but qualities. And, in fact, the same thing
becomes a differentiation essential to the completion
of a substance, and in something else is not a differentiation and does not contribute to the completion
of the substance, but is an incidental attribute: as
for instance " white " is an essential completion in a
swan or white lead,[1] but in you it is an incidental attribute. The white which enters into the definition
is an essential completing element and not a quality,
that which appears on the surface is qualitative.
Perhaps we should make a distinction between two
kinds of quality, the substantial kind being a distinctive particularity of substance, and the other qualitative and nothing else, that by which a substance is
of a certain quality when the quality does not
change the thing either into or out of its substance,
but only puts it into a certain state from outside when
it exists already in fullness of substantial being, and
produces an addition posterior to the substance,
whether this happens in the case of body or of soul.
But what if the visible white in white lead was an
essential completion of it?—in the swan white is not
an essential completion, for there could be a swan
which was not white; but our question was about
white lead: and the same might be true of the heat
of fire. But suppose one said that " fireness " is the
substance of fire, and what corresponds to it the

35 τὸ ἀνάλογον; Ἀλλ' ὅμως τοῦ ὁρωμένου πυρὸς
[πυρότης] ἡ θερμότης συμπληροῦσα καὶ ἡ λευκότης
ἐπὶ τοῦ ἑτέρου. Αἱ αὐταὶ τοίνυν συμπληρώσουσι
καὶ οὐ ποιότητες, καὶ οὐ συμπληρώσουσι καὶ [οὐ]
ποιότητες. Καὶ ἄτοπον ἐν μὲν οἷς συμπληροῦσι
40 λέγειν ἄλλο εἶναι, ἐν δὲ οἷς μὴ ἄλλο, τῆς αὐτῆς
φύσεως οὔσης. Ἀλλ' ἄρα τοὺς μὲν λόγους τοὺς
ποιήσαντας αὐτὰ οὐσιώδεις ὅλους, τὰ δὲ ἀποτελέ-
σματα ἔχειν ἤδη τὰ ἐκεῖ τι ἐνταῦθα ποιά, οὐ τί.
Ὅθεν καὶ ἁμαρτάνειν ἡμᾶς ἀεὶ περὶ τὸ τι ἀπολισθά-
νοντας ἐν ταῖς ζητήσεσιν αὐτοῦ καὶ εἰς τὸ ποιὸν
45 καταφερομένους. Οὐ γὰρ εἶναι τὸ πῦρ ὃ λέγομεν
εἰς τὸ ποιὸν ἀφορῶντες, ἀλλὰ τὸ μὲν εἶναι οὐσίαν,
ἃ δὲ νῦν βλέπομεν, εἰς ἃ καὶ ἀφορῶντες λέγομεν,
ἀπάγειν ἡμᾶς ἀπὸ τοῦ τι καὶ ὁρίζεσθαι τὸ ποιόν.
Καὶ ἐπὶ τῶν αἰσθητῶν εὐλόγως· οὐδὲν γὰρ αὐτῶν
οὐσίαν εἶναι, ἀλλ' αὐτῆς πάθη. Ὅθεν κἀκεῖνο,
50 πῶς οὐκ ἐξ οὐσιῶν οὐσία. Ἐλέγετο μὲν οὖν, ὅτι
οὐ δεῖ τὸ αὐτὸ τὸ γινόμενον εἶναι τοῖς ἐξ ὧν· νῦν
δὲ λέγειν δεῖ ὅτι οὐδὲ τὸ γενόμενον οὐσία. Ἀλλὰ
πῶς ἐκεῖ ἦν ἐλέγομεν οὐσίαν οὐκ ἐξ οὐσίας

---

[1] Cp. Plato, *Seventh Letter* 343C1–6.

substance of white lead? Even so, the heat is an essential completion of the visible fire, and the whiteness in white lead. So, then, the same distinctive features will be essential completions and not qualities, and qualities and not essential completions. And it is unreasonable to say that they are one thing in what they complete and another in what they do not, when their nature is the same. But, then, one must say rather that the rational formative principles which made them are altogether substantial, but that the things produced by them have here and now what in the intelligible world is a " something " but here below qualitative and not a " something." This is the reason why we are always making mistakes in our investigations about the " something," and slipping off it and being carried away to the qualitative.[1] For fire is not what we say it is when we concentrate our gaze on the qualitative, but its being is substance, and what we see now, that which we concentrate our gaze on when we speak of it, leads us away from the " something " and we define only the qualitative. This is reasonable procedure when we are dealing with objects of sense; for there is nothing of them which is substance, but only affections of substance. This raises that other problem, how substance can come not from substances [but from something which is not substance]. Now it has already been said that what comes into being cannot be the same as that from which it comes; we must add at this stage that what has come into being is not substance. But how, then, does there come to be in the intelligible world what we said was substance, when we said it did not come from substance?

λέγοντες; Τὴν γὰρ οὐσίαν φήσομεν ἐκεῖ κυριώτε-
55 ρον καὶ ἀμιγέστερον ἔχουσαν τὸ ὂν εἶναι οὐσίαν—
ὡς ἐν διαφοραῖς—ὄντως, μᾶλλον δὲ μετὰ προσθή-
κης ἐνεργειῶν λεγομένην οὐσίαν, τελείωσιν μὲν
δοκοῦσαν εἶναι ἐκείνου, τάχα δ' ἐνδεεστέραν τῇ
προσθήκῃ καὶ τῷ οὐχ ἁπλῷ, ἀλλ' ἤδη ἀφισταμένην
τούτου.

2. Ἀλλὰ περὶ τῆς ποιότητος σκεπτέον τί ὅλως·
τάχα γὰρ γνωσθὲν ὅ τι ἐστὶ μᾶλλον παύσει τὰς
ἀπορίας. Πρῶτον οὖν ἐκεῖνο ζητητέον, εἰ τὸ αὐτὸ
θετέον ὁτὲ μὲν ποιὸν μόνον, ὁτὲ δὲ συμπληροῦν
5 οὐσίαν, οὐ δυσχεράναντας ποιὸν συμπληρωτικὸν
οὐσίας εἶναι, ἀλλὰ ποιᾶς μᾶλλον οὐσίας. Δεῖ
τοίνυν ἐπὶ τῆς ποιᾶς οὐσίας τὴν οὐσίαν πρὸ τοῦ
ποιὰν εἶναι καὶ τὸ τί ἐστι. Τί οὖν ἐπὶ τοῦ πυρὸς
πρὸ τῆς ποιᾶς οὐσίας ἡ οὐσία; Ἆρα τὸ σῶμα;
Τὸ γένος τοίνυν οὐσία ἔσται, τὸ σῶμα, τὸ δὲ πῦρ
10 σῶμα θερμὸν καὶ οὐκ οὐσία τὸ ὅλον, ἀλλ' οὕτω τὸ
θερμὸν ἐν αὐτῷ, ὡς καὶ ἐν σοὶ τὸ σιμόν. Ἀφαιρε-
θείσης τοίνυν θερμότητος καὶ τοῦ λαμπροῦ καὶ
κούφου, ἃ δὴ δοκεῖ ποιὰ εἶναι, καὶ ἀντιτυπίας τὸ
τριχῇ διαστατὸν καταλείπεται καὶ ἡ ὕλη οὐσία.
15 Ἀλλ' οὐ δοκεῖ· τὸ γὰρ εἶδος μᾶλλον οὐσία.
Ἀλλὰ τὸ εἶδος ποιότης. Ἢ οὐ ποιότης, ἀλλὰ

---

[1] Cp. Aristotle, *Metaphysics* Z3, 1029a16–19: Sextus
Empiricus, *Pyrrh. hyp.* III. 39.

ON SUBSTANCE, OR ON QUALITY

We shall assert that the substance There, because
it has a more authentic and purer being, is really
substance, as far as is possible in differentiations of
being, or rather that when we speak of substance
There we speak of it with the addition of its activities;
it seems to be a perfection of That [which is its
source], but is perhaps deficient in comparison with
it by this addition, and by not being simple but already moving away from this original simplicity.

2. But we must enquire what in itself quality is:
for perhaps the knowledge of what it is will more
effectively put an end to our difficulties. First of
all, then, we must enquire into the question already
raised, whether we are to assume that the same thing
is at one time only qualitative, and at another
essentially completing substance (we must not be
uneasy about what is qualitative being an essential
completing element of substance, but regard it
rather as a completing element of a substance of a
certain quality). Now in the substance of a certain
quality the substance, the specific essence, must be
there before it is qualified. What then, in the case of
fire, is the substance which is there before the
qualified substance. Is it the body? Then the
genus " body " will be the substance, and fire will
be a hot body, and the whole of it will not be substance but the hot will be in it in the same way as
the quality of snubnosedness is in you. So if the
heat and the brightness and the lightness—these
appear to be qualitative—are taken away, the three-
dimensionality is left and the matter is the substance.[1]
But we do not think it is: the form, rather, is substance. But the form is quality. No, the form is not

λόγος τὸ εἶδος. Τὰ οὖν ἐκ τοῦ λόγου καὶ τοῦ
ὑποκειμένου τί ἐστιν; Οὐ γὰρ τὸ ὁρώμενον καὶ τὸ
καῖον· τοῦτο δὲ ποιόν. Εἰ μή τις λέγοι τὸ καίειν
ἐνέργειαν ἐκ τοῦ λόγου· καὶ τὸ θερμαίνειν καὶ τὸ
λευκαίνειν τοίνυν καὶ τὰ ἄλλα ποιήσεις· ὥστε τὴν
20 ποιότητα οὐχ ἕξομεν ὅπου καταλείψομεν. Ἤ
ταύτας μὲν οὐ λεκτέον ποιότητας, ὅσαι λέγονται
συμπληροῦν οὐσίας, εἴπερ ἐνέργειαι αἱ αὐτῶν ἀπὸ
τῶν λόγων καὶ τῶν δυνάμεων τῶν οὐσιωδῶν
ἰοῦσαι, ἅ δ᾽ ἐστιν ἔξωθεν πάσης οὐσίας οὐ πῇ μὲν
ποιότητες, ἄλλοις δὲ οὐ ποιότητες φανταζόμεναι,
25 τὸ δὲ περιττὸν μετὰ τὴν οὐσίαν ἔχουσαι, οἷον καὶ
ἀρεταὶ καὶ κακίαι καὶ αἴσχη καὶ κάλλη καὶ
ὑγίειαι καὶ οὕτως ἐσχηματίσθαι. Καὶ τρίγωνον
μὲν καὶ τετράγωνον καθ᾽ αὑτὸ οὐ ποιόν, τὸ δὲ
τετριγωνίσθαι ᾗ μεμόρφωται ποιὸν λεκτέον, καὶ
οὐ τὴν τριγωνότητα, ἀλλὰ τὴν μόρφωσιν· καὶ τὰς
30 τέχνας δὲ καὶ τὰς ἐπιτηδειότητας· ὥστε εἶναι τὴν
ποιότητα διάθεσίν τινα ἐπὶ ταῖς οὐσίαις ἤδη
οὔσαις εἴτ᾽ ἐπακτὴν εἴτ᾽ ἐξ ἀρχῆς συνοῦσαν, ἢ εἰ
μὴ συνῆν, οὐδὲν ἔλαττον εἶχεν ἡ οὐσία. Ταύτην
δὲ καὶ εὐκίνητον καὶ δυσκίνητον εἶναι· ὡς διττὸν
εἶναι εἶδος, τὸ μὲν εὐκίνητον, τὸ δὲ ἔμμονον αὐτῆς.

3. Τὸ οὖν λευκὸν τὸ ἐπὶ σοὶ θετέον οὐ ποιότητα,
ἀλλ᾽ ἐνέργειαν δηλονότι ἐκ δυνάμεως τῆς τοῦ

[1] Cp. Aristotle, *Categories* 8, 10a14–16.

quality but rational formative principle. What, then, is the result of the combination of the formative principle and the underlying matter? Not what is seen and burns: for this is qualitative. Unless, perhaps, someone were to say that the burning is an activity which comes from the formative principle; then the heating, too, and the brightening and the rest would be activities of making; so we shall have no place to put quality. We ought not to call what are said to be essential completions of substance qualities, seeing that those of them which come from the formative principles and substantive powers are activities; we should call qualities only what are outside all substance and do not appear in one place as qualities but in other things as not qualities; they contain that which is extra and comes after substance, for instance, virtues and vices, and uglinesses and beauties, and states of health, and being of this and that shape. Triangularity and quadrangularity in themselves are not qualitative, but being made triangular in so far as it is being given shape must be called qualitative, not the triangularity, that is, but the shaping.[1] Arts and aptitudes should also be called qualities. So quality, we say, is a condition of substances which already exist, either brought about from outside or accompanying them from the beginning: [even in this latter case], if it was not there the substance would have nothing less. This quality can be sometimes easy to remove, sometimes hard; so that there are two kinds of it, the easily removable and the persistent.

3. The whiteness, therefore, in you must be assumed not to be a quality but an activity, obviously

λευκαίνειν, κἀκεῖ πάσας τὰς λεγομένας ποιότητας
ἐνεργείας τὸ ποιὸν λαβούσας παρὰ τῆς ἡμετέρας
5 δόξης τῷ ἰδιότητα εἶναι ἑκάστην οἷον διοριζούσας
τὰς οὐσίας πρὸς ἀλλήλας καὶ πρὸς ἑαυτὰς ἴδιον
χαρακτῆρα ἐχούσας. Τί οὖν διοίσει ποιότης ἡ
ἐκεῖ; Ἐνέργειαι γὰρ καὶ αὗται. Ἢ ὅτι μὴ οἷόν
τί ἐστι δηλοῦσιν οὐδὲ ἐναλλαγὴν τῶν ὑποκειμένων
οὐδὲ χαρακτῆρα, ἀλλ' ὅσον μόνον τὴν λεγομένην
10 ποιότητα ἐκεῖ ἐνέργειαν οὖσαν· ὥστε τὸ μέν,
ὅταν ἰδιότητα οὐσίας ἔχῃ, δῆλον αὐτόθεν ὡς οὐ
ποιόν, ὅταν δὲ χωρίσῃ ὁ λόγος τὸ ἐπ' αὐτοῖς ἴδιον
οὐκ ἐκεῖθεν ἀφελών, ἀλλὰ μᾶλλον λαβὼν καὶ
γεννήσας ἄλλο, ἐγέννησε ποιὸν οἷον μέρος οὐσίας
λαβὼν τὸ ἐπιπολῆς φανὲν αὐτῷ. Εἰ δὲ τοῦτο,
15 οὐδὲν κωλύει καὶ τὴν θερμότητα τῷ σύμφυτον
εἶναι τῷ πυρὶ εἶδός τι εἶναι τοῦ πυρὸς καὶ ἐνέργειαν
καὶ οὐ ποιότητα αὐτοῦ, καὶ αὖ ἄλλως ποιότητα,
μόνην δὲ ἐν ἄλλῳ ληφθεῖσαν οὐκέτι μορφὴν οὐσίας
οὖσαν, ἀλλὰ ἴχνος μόνον καὶ σκιὰν καὶ εἰκόνα
ἀπολιποῦσαν αὐτῆς τὴν οὐσίαν, ἧς ἡ ἐνέργεια,
20 ποιότητα εἶναι. Ὅσα οὖν συμβέβηκε καὶ μὴ
ἐνέργειαι καὶ εἴδη οὐσιῶν μορφάς τινας παρεχόμενα,
ποιὰ ταῦτα· οἷον καὶ αἱ ἕξεις καὶ διαθέσεις ἄλλαι

proceeding from the power of whitening; and in the intelligible world all qualities, as we call them, must be assumed to be activities, taking their qualitativeness from the way we think about them, because each and every one of them is an individual characteristic, that is, they mark off the substances in relation to each other and have their own individual character in relation to themselves. In what way, then, will quality in the intelligible world differ from qualities here? The qualities here are activities too. The qualities in the intelligible world do not indicate what sort of things their underlying realities are, or their alterations or their distinctive characters, but only just what we call quality, which is activity there: so that it is immediately clear that the reality there, when it possesses an individual characteristic of substance, is not qualitative, but when the process of rational thinking separates the distinctive individuality in these realities, not taking it away from the intelligible world but rather grasping it and producing something else, it produces the qualitative as a kind of part of substance, grasping what appears on the surface of the reality. If this is so, there is nothing to prevent heat, by the fact that it is inherent in fire, from being a form and activity of fire and not its quality, and again being a quality in a different way, when it is taken alone in something else and is no longer a shape of substance but only a trace, a shadow, an image, abandoning its substance, of which it was an activity, to be a quality. All, then, which is incidental and not activities and forms of substance, giving definite shapes, is qualitative. So, for instance, states and other dispositions of the

τῶν ὑποκειμένων λεκτέαι ποιότητες, τὰ δὲ ἀρχέ-
τυπα αὐτῶν, ἐν οἷς πρώτως ἐστίν, ἐνεργείας
ἐκείνων. Καὶ οὐ γίνεται ταὐτὸ ποιότης καὶ οὐ
25 ποιότης, ἀλλὰ τὸ ἀπηρημωμένον οὐσίας ποιόν, τὸ
δὲ σὺν ταύτῃ οὐσίαν ἢ εἶδος ἢ ἐνέργειαν· οὐδὲν
γάρ ἐστι ταὐτὸν ἐν αὐτῷ καὶ ἐν ἄλλῳ μόνον
ἐκπεσὸν τοῦ εἶδος καὶ ἐνέργεια εἶναι. Ὁ μέντοι
μηδέποτε εἶδος ἄλλου, ἀλλὰ συμβεβηκὸς ἀεί,
καθαρῶς ποιότης καὶ μόνον τοῦτο.

underlying realities are to be called qualities, but their archetypal models, in which they exist primarily, are the activities of those intelligible realities. And in this way one and the same thing does not come to be quality and not quality, but that which is isolated from substance is qualitative, and that which is with substance is substance or form or activity; for nothing is the same in itself and when it is alone in something else and has fallen away from being form and activity. That, then, which is never a form of something else but always an incidental attribute, this and only this is pure quality.

ENNEAD II. 7

II. 7. ON COMPLETE TRANSFUSION

Introductory Note

THIS little treatise (No. 37 in Porphyry's chronological order) is devoted to the discussion of the curious Stoic doctrine that two material substances when they are mixed can totally interpenetrate one another. This doctrine aroused a good deal of opposition, especially from the Peripatetics, and Plotinus begins his discussion by stating the Peripatetic objections to it. Here he closely follows the exposition given by Alexander of Aphrodisias in his *De Mixtione* and *Quaestiones et Solutiones* II. 12 (ed. Bruns, p. 57). He often seems to have found that the critical reading of the great Aristotelian expositor and commentator stimulated his own thought. Next he gives the Stoic reply to the Peripatetic arguments, and finally, in ch. 2, his own reflections on the question, which lead him to a criticism of the Peripatetic view that it is the impenetrability of matter which prevents the total interpenetration of bodies. Following up a passing admission of Alexander (cp. Bréhier's excellent introduction to this treatise) he shows that the impenetrability of a body must be due to its qualities, not to any inherent property of the matter.

Ch. 3 is an appendix or footnote on " corporeity," which Plotinus maintains against Alexander of Aphrodisias to be not just an abstract general definition but the formative principle which makes bodies corporeal—a good illustration of the difference between the Platonic and the Aristotelian way of thinking about universals.

ON COMPLETE TRANSFUSION

Synopsis

Summary of the discussion of the question by previous philosophers. The Peripatetic objections to complete transfusion and Stoic answers to them (ch. 1). Plotinus's own discussion, leading to the conclusion that the impenetrability of a body is due to its qualities, not to the matter (ch. 2). Note on the meaning of corporeity (ch. 3).

II. 7. (37) ΠΕΡΙ ΤΗΣ ΔΙ᾽ ΟΛΩΝ ΚΡΑΣΕΩΣ

1. Περὶ τῆς δι᾽ ὅλων λεγομένης τῶν σωμάτων κράσεως ἐπισκεπτέον. Ἆρα ἐνδέχεται ὅλον δι᾽ ὅλου ὑγρὸν ὑγρῷ συμμιχθὲν ἑκάτερον δι᾽ ἑκατέρου ἢ θάτερον διὰ θατέρου χωρεῖν; Διαφέρει γὰρ
5 οὐδὲν ὁποτερωσοῦν, εἰ γίγνοιτο. Οἱ μὲν γὰρ τῇ παραθέσει διδόντες ὡς μιγνύντες μᾶλλον ἢ κιρνάντες ἐατέοι, εἴπερ δεῖ τὴν κρᾶσιν ὁμοιομερὲς τὸ πᾶν ποιεῖν, καὶ ἕκαστον μέρος τὸ σμικρότατον ἐκ τῶν κεκρᾶσθαι λεγομένων εἶναι. Οἱ μὲν οὖν τὰς ποιότητας μόνας κιρνάντες, τὴν δὲ ὕλην παρατιθέν-
10 τες ἑκατέρου τοῦ σώματος καὶ ἐπ᾽ αὐτῶν ἐπάγοντες τὰς παρ᾽ ἑκατέρου [1] ποιότητας, πιθανοὶ ἂν εἶεν τῷ διαβάλλειν τὴν δι᾽ ὅλων κρᾶσιν τῷ τε εἰς τομὰς τὰ μεγέθη συμβαίνειν τῶν ὄγκων ἰέναι, εἰ μηδὲν διάλειμμα μηδετέρῳ τῶν σωμάτων γίνοιτο, εἰ συνεχὴς ἔσται ἡ διαίρεσις τῷ κατὰ πᾶν τὴν
15 διάδυσιν γίνεσθαι θατέρῳ εἰς θάτερον, καὶ δή,

---

[1] ἑκατέρου Kirchhoff, H-S: ἑκατέρας codd.

---

[1] This is a reference to Anaxagoras (cp. Diels 59A54) and Democritus (referred to by Alexander in the passage on which

II. 7. ON COMPLETE TRANSFUSION

1. We must consider the question of what is called the complete transfusion of bodies. Is it possible that when one fluid body is mixed with another both penetrate each other whole through whole, or that one of them penetrates the other totally? For it makes no difference which way it happens, if it happens at all. We can leave out of account those who allow that it happens by simple juxtaposition of particles [1] because they make a mechanical mixture rather than a coalescence, if we grant that a coalescence must make the total a whole of like parts, and each smallest part must be composed of the things which are said to have coalesced. Those, then, who make the qualities only coalesce,[2] juxtaposing the matter of each body and imposing upon these matters the qualities of each, would seem to deserve belief because they disprove complete transfusion by the fact that the magnitudes of the masses will be completely cut away, if there is no interval between the divisions in either of the bodies—on the assumption that the division will be continuous because each of the bodies penetrates the other completely; and

---

this account is based, *De Mixtione* 2 (II. 214, 18 Bruns–Diels 68A64).

[2] The Peripatetics. Cp. Galen's account of the Peripatetic and Stoic positions, *Stoicorum Veterum Fragmenta* II. 463.

ὅταν τὰ κραθέντα μείζω τόπον κατέχῃ ἢ θάτερον
καὶ τοσοῦτον, ὅσον συνελθόντα τὸν ἑκατέρου
τόπον. Καίτοι, εἰ δι' ὅλου ὅλον ἦν διεληλυθός,
τὸν τοῦ ἑτέρου ἔδει, φασί, μένειν τὸν αὐτόν, εἰς ὃ
θάτερον ἐνεβλήθη. Οὗ δὲ μὴ μείζων ὁ τόπος
20 γίνεται, ἀέρος τινὰς ἐξόδους αἰτιῶνται, ἀνθ' ὧν
εἰσέδυ θάτερον. Καὶ τὸ σμικρὸν δὲ ἐν τῷ μείζονι
πῶς ἂν ἐκταθὲν δι' ὅλου χωρήσειε; Καὶ πολλὰ
ἄλλα λέγουσιν. Οἱ δ' αὖ—οἱ τὴν δι' ὅλων κρᾶσιν
εἰσάγοντες—τέμνεσθαι μὲν καὶ μὴ εἰς τομὰς
ἀναλίσκεσθαι λέγειν ἂν δύναιντο καὶ δι' ὅλων τῆς
25 κράσεως γιγνομένης, ἐπεὶ καὶ τοὺς ἱδρῶτας οὐ τοῦ
σώματος τομὰς ποιεῖν οὐδ' αὖ κατατετρῆσθαι
φήσουσι. Καὶ γὰρ εἴ τις λέγοι μηδὲν κωλύειν τὴν
φύσιν οὕτω πεποιηκέναι τοῦ διέναι τοὺς ἱδρῶτας
χάριν, ἀλλ' ἐπὶ τῶν τεχνητῶν, ὅταν λεπτὰ ᾖ καὶ
συνεχῇ, ὁρᾶσθαι τὸ ὑγρὸν δι' ὅλου δεῦον[1] αὐτὰ
30 καὶ διαρρεῖν ἐπὶ θάτερα τὸ ὑγρόν. Ἀλλὰ σωμάτων
ὄντων πῶς οἷόν τε τοῦτο γίγνεσθαι; Ὡς διέναι
μὴ τέμνοντα ἐπινοῆσαι οὐ ῥᾴδιον· τέμνοντα δὲ
κατὰ πᾶν ἀναιρήσει ἄλληλα δηλονότι. Τὰς δὲ
αὔξας ὅταν λέγωσι μὴ γίνεσθαι πολλαχοῦ, διδόασι

---

[1] δεῦον Creuzer: δενοντα codd.

then, too, there is the case when the bodies which have coalesced occupy a larger space than either of them, as much, in fact, as the spaces occupied by each of them put together. And yet, they say, if one had completely penetrated the other, the space of the one would have had to remain the same and the other would have been put into it. But in the case where the space occupied by the mixture does not become greater, they allege as the cause some sort of exit of air, whose place within the one body is taken by the other. And then, when a small body is mixed with a larger one, how could it be extended so as to penetrate the whole? And they have many other arguments. But then, on the other side, those who introduce the idea of complete transfusion could say that it was possible for a body to be divided without being completely used up in the cutting, even when complete transfusion occurs, since they will assert that drops of sweat do not make cuts in the body or even fill it full of holes. For even if someone were to argue that there was no objection to nature having arranged it that way so as to enable the drops of sweat to get through, yet, they could reply, in the case of artificial products, when they are of fine continuous texture, moisture is observed wetting them right through, and it flows through to the other side. But, if they are bodies, how can this happen? So it is not easy to conceive how there can be interpenetration without division; but if the bodies divide each other at every point they will obviously destroy each other. And when they say that in many cases there are no increases in size [when there is coalescence], they give the other party

τοῖς ἑτέροις ἀέρων ἐξόδους αἰτιᾶσθαι. Πρός τε
35 τὴν τῶν τόπων αὔξην χαλεπῶς μέν, ὅμως δὲ τί
κωλύει λέγειν συνεισφερομένου ἑκατέρου σώματος
καὶ τὸ μέγεθος μετὰ τῶν ἄλλων ποιοτήτων ἐξ
ἀνάγκης τὴν αὔξην γίνεσθαι; Μὴ γὰρ μηδὲ τοῦτο
ἀπόλλυσθαι, ὥσπερ οὐδὲ τὰς ἄλλας ποιότητας, καὶ
40 ὥσπερ ἐκεῖ ποιότητος ἄλλο εἶδος μικτὸν ἐξ ἀμφοῖν,
οὕτω καὶ μέγεθος ἄλλο, οὗ δὴ τὸ μῖγμα ποιεῖ τὸ
ἐξ ἀμφοῖν μέγεθος. Ἀλλ᾽ εἰ ἐνταῦθ᾽ ἂν πρὸς
αὐτοὺς οἱ ἕτεροι λέγοιεν, ὡς, εἰ μὲν ἡ ὕλη τῇ ὕλῃ
παράκειται, καὶ ὁ ὄγκος τῷ ὄγκῳ, ᾧ σύνεστι τὸ
μέγεθος, τὸ ἡμέτερον ἂν λέγοιτε· εἰ δὲ δι᾽ ὅλου
45 καὶ ἡ ὕλη μετὰ τοῦ ἐπ᾽ αὐτῇ πρώτως μεγέθους,
οὕτως ἂν γένοιτο οὐχ ὡς γραμμὴ γραμμῇ ἐφεξῆς ἂν
κέοιτο ⟨τῷ⟩[1] κατὰ τὰ πέρατα τοῖς σημείοις ἑαυτῶν
συνάψαι, οὗ δὴ αὔξη ἂν γίνοιτο, ἀλλ᾽ ἐκείνως ὡς
ἂν γραμμὴ γραμμῇ ἐφαρμοσθείη, ὥστε αὔξην μὴ
γίνεσθαι. Τὸ δ᾽ ἔλαττον διὰ παντὸς τοῦ μείζονος
50 καὶ μεγίστου τὸ μικρότατον καὶ ἐφ᾽ ὧν φανερὸν
ὅτι κίρναται. Ἐπὶ γὰρ τῶν ἀδήλων ἔξεστι λέγειν
μὴ εἰς πᾶν φθάνειν, ἀλλ᾽ ἐφ᾽ ὧν γε φανερῶς
συμβαίνει, λέγοιτο ἄν. Καὶ λέγοιεν ἐκτάσεις τῶν
ὄγκων, οὐ σφόδρα πιθανὰ λέγοντες εἰς τοσοῦτον
τὸν σμικρότατον ὄγκον ἐκτείνοντες· οὐδὲ γὰρ μετα-

---

[1] ⟨τῷ⟩ Theiler et nunc Henry et Schwyzer.

the opportunity of alleging exits of air as the cause. And, though it is difficult to refute the argument from the increase of the spaces occupied, yet, all the same, what is the objection to saying that, as each of the two bodies brings its size along with it as well as all the other qualities, an increase must necessarily occur? For certainly size is not destroyed in the coalescence any more than the rest of the qualities, and just as in the case of the others there is another quality compounded of both, so there is another size, where the compounding [of the two sizes] produces the size which results from both. But suppose that at this point the other party replied to them, " If the matter of one body lies alongside the matter of the other, and the mass alongside the mass, with which the size goes, then you would be saying what we say; but if there is complete transfusion of the matter with the size which is primarily imposed upon it, it would come about not as when a line lies end to end with another line in that their terminal points coincide, where there certainly would be increase, but as in that arrangement where one line is made to coincide with another line, so that there is no increase in length." But as for a smaller body penetrating the whole of a larger one, and even the very smallest the very largest, this occurs in things which have manifestly coalesced. In the cases where it is not obvious it is possible to say that the smaller body does not reach every part of the larger one but in the cases where it manifestly occurs it ought to be admitted. They might allege extensions of the masses, but this is not a very plausible explanation when they extend the smallest mass so enormously; for they do not

55 βάλλοντες τὸ σῶμα μέγεθος αὐτῷ πλέον διδόασιν,
ὥσπερ εἰ ἐξ ὕδατος ἀὴρ γίγνοιτο.

2. Τοῦτο δὲ αὐτὸ ἐφ' ἑαυτοῦ ζητητέον, τί
συμβαίνει, ὅταν ὅσπερ ἦν ὄγκος ὕδατος ἀὴρ
γίγνηται, πῶς τὸ μεῖζον ἐν τῷ γενομένῳ· νῦν δὲ
τὰ μὲν εἰρήσθω πολλῶν καὶ ἄλλων παρ' ἑκατέρων
5 λεγομένων. Ἡμεῖς δὲ ἐφ' ἑαυτῶν σκοπῶμεν τί
χρὴ λέγειν περὶ τούτου, τίς δόξα σύμφωνος τοῖς
λεγομένοις ἢ καὶ τίς ἄλλη παρὰ τὰς νῦν λεγομένας
φανεῖται. Ὅταν τοίνυν διὰ τοῦ ἐρίου ῥέῃ τὸ
ὕδωρ ἢ βίβλος ἐκστάζῃ τὸ ἐν αὐτῇ ὕδωρ, πῶς οὐ
τὸ πᾶν ὑδάτινον σῶμα δίεισι δι' αὐτῆς; Ἢ καὶ
10 ὅταν μὴ ῥέῃ, πῶς συνάψομεν τὴν ὕλην τῇ ὕλῃ καὶ
τὸν ὄγκον τῷ ὄγκῳ, τὰς δὲ ποιότητας μόνας ἐν
συγκράσει ποιησόμεθα; Οὐ γὰρ δὴ ἔξω τῆς
βίβλου ἡ τοῦ ὕδατος ὕλη παρακείσεται οὐδ' αὖ ἔν
τισι διαστήμασιν αὐτῆς· πᾶσα γὰρ ὑγρά ἐστι καὶ
οὐδαμοῦ ὕλη κενὴ ποιότητος. Εἰ δὲ πανταχοῦ ἡ
15 ὕλη μετὰ τῆς ποιότητος, πανταχοῦ τῆς βίβλου τὸ
ὕδωρ. Ἢ οὐ τὸ ὕδωρ, ἀλλ' ἡ τοῦ ὕδατος ποιότης.
Ἀλλὰ ποῦ ὄντος [1] τοῦ ὕδατος; Πῶς οὖν οὐχ ὁ
αὐτὸς ὄγκος; Ἢ ἐξέτεινε τὴν βίβλον τὸ προστεθέν·
ἔλαβε γὰρ μέγεθος παρὰ τοῦ εἰσελθόντος. Ἀλλ'
εἰ ἔλαβε, προσετέθη τις ὄγκος· εἰ δὲ προσετέθη,
20 οὐ κατεπόθη ἐν τῷ ἑτέρῳ, δεῖ οὖν ἐν ἄλλῳ καὶ

---

[1] ὄντος F³ᵐᵍ (Ficinus:) ὄντα codd: † ὄντα H-S.

---

[1] I print and translate ὄντος (Ficino's suggestion in the
margin of F). The corruption may have arisen through an
abbreviation of ὄντος (Warmington's suggestion).

even allow a larger size to a body when it changes, as, for instance, if air comes into being out of water.

2. But this is a subject which requires separate investigation, what happens when what was a mass of water becomes air, and how the increase of volume in the air which has come into being is to be explained. Now, however, let us content ourselves with what has been said, although there is a great deal else which is said on both sides. But let us consider independently what we ought to say about this problem, what view will be in accordance with the arguments stated, or what new one will appear going beyond the present arguments. Well, then, when water runs through a fleece, or papyrus exudes the water which is in it, how can we deny that the whole body of the water goes right through the papyrus? Or even when it does not run through, how can we put matter in contact with matter and mass with mass and make the qualities alone coalesce? For surely the matter of the water will not lie outside the papyrus, nor, again, in any interstices of it; for the whole papyrus is wet and its matter is nowhere destitute of the quality [of wetness]. But if the matter is everywhere accompanied by the quality of wetness, the water is everywhere in the papyrus. But perhaps it is not the water but the quality of the water. But where is the water?[1] Why, then, does the mass not remain the same? What was added to the papyrus has extended it: for it took size from the water which entered into it. But if it took size, a mass was added to it; but if it was added, it was not absorbed in the other, and so the matter of the water and the matter of the papyrus must be in two

ἄλλῳ τὴν ὕλην εἶναι. Ἢ τί κωλύει, ὥσπερ δίδωσι
τῆς ποιότητος καὶ λαμβάνει σῶμα θάτερον παρὰ
θατέρου, οὕτω καὶ ἐπὶ τοῦ μεγέθους; Ποιότης
μὲν γὰρ ποιότητι συνελθοῦσα οὐκ ἐκείνη οὖσα,
ἀλλὰ μετ᾽ ἄλλης, ἐν τῷ μετ᾽ ἄλλης εἶναι οὐ καθαρὰ
25 οὖσα οὐκ ἔστι παντελῶς ἐκείνη, ἀλλὰ ἠμαύρωται·
μέγεθος δὲ συνελθὸν ἄλλῳ μεγέθει οὐκ ἀφανίζεται.
Τὸ δὲ σῶμα χωροῦν διὰ σώματος πάντως τομὰς
ποιεῖν πῶς λέγεται, ἐπιστήσειεν ἄν τις· ἐπεὶ καὶ
αὐτοὶ τὰς ποιότητας [τὰς] διὰ τῶν σωμάτων χωρεῖν
λέγομεν καὶ οὐ τομὰς ποιεῖν. Ἢ ὅτι ἀσώματοι.
30 Ἀλλ᾽ εἰ ἡ ὕλη καὶ αὐτὴ ἀσώματος, διὰ τί τῆς ὕλης
ἀσωμάτου οὔσης καὶ τῶν ποιοτήτων, εἰ τοιαῦται
εἶεν ὡς ὀλίγαι εἶναι, οὐ μετὰ τῆς ὕλης τὸν αὐτὸν
τρόπον διίασι; Μὴ διέναι δὲ τὰ στερεά, ὅτι
τοιαύτας ἔχει τὰς ποιότητας ὡς κωλυθῆναι διέναι.
35 Ἢ πολλὰς ὁμοῦ ἀδυνατεῖν μετὰ τῆς ὕλης ποιεῖν
τοῦτο; Εἰ μὲν οὖν τὸ πλῆθος τῶν ποιοτήτων τὸ
πυκνὸν λεγόμενον σῶμα ποιεῖ, τὸ πλῆθος ἂν εἴη
αἴτιον· εἰ δὲ πυκνότης ἰδία ποιότης ἐστίν, ὥσπερ
καὶ ἥν λέγουσι σωματότητα, ἰδία ποιότης· ὥστε
οὐχ ᾗ ποιότητες τὴν μῖξιν ποιήσονται, ἀλλ᾽ ᾗ
40 τοιαίδε, οὐδ᾽ αὖ ἡ ὕλη ᾗ ὕλη οὐ μιχθήσεται, ἀλλ᾽
ᾗ μετὰ τοιᾶσδε ποιότητος, καὶ μάλιστα, εἰ μέγεθος

different places. But what is the objection, just as one body gives and takes a share of quality from the other, to the same thing happening with the size? The objection is that when quality comes together with quality it is not that quality which it was before, but is associated with another, and, because in that association it is not pure, it is no longer perfectly what it was, but is dimmed: but when size comes together with another size it does not disappear. But one should consider carefully the sense of the assertion that when a body passes through a body it cuts it up completely: since we ourselves say that the qualities go through bodies without cutting them. The reason is that they are incorporeal. But if matter itself is incorporeal too, why then, since matter and its qualities are incorporeal, should not the qualities, if they are of such a kind that there are few of them, penetrate with the matter in the same way? We should say that they do not penetrate solid bodies because these have qualities of such a kind as to prevent their penetration. Or perhaps we might say that many qualities all together cannot penetrate with the matter? If, then, the multiplicity of qualities makes what is called a dense body, the multiplicity would be the cause of its impenetrability; but if density is a distinct quality, as is the quality they call corporeity, then this distinct quality is the cause: so that it is not in so far as they are qualities that they will blend but in so far as they are qualities of a certain kind, and it is not matter as matter that will not blend but matter in so far as it is associated with a certain quality: and particularly, if it has no size

οἰκεῖον οὐκ ἔχει, ἀλλ᾽ ἢ[1] μή ἀποβαλοῦσα τὸ
μέγεθος. Ταῦτα μὲν οὖν ἔστω καὶ οὕτω διηπορη-
μένα.

3. Ἐπεὶ δὲ ἐμνήσθημεν σωματότητος, ἐπισκεπτέον πότερα ἡ σωματότης ἐστὶ τὸ ἐκ πάντων
συγκείμενον ἢ εἶδός τι ἡ σωματότης καὶ λόγος τις,
ὃς ἐγγενόμενος τῇ ὕλῃ σῶμα ποιεῖ. Εἰ μὲν οὖν
5 τοῦτό ἐστι τὸ σῶμα τὸ ἐκ πασῶν τῶν ποιοτήτων
σὺν ὕλῃ, τοῦτο ἂν εἴη ἡ σωματότης. Καὶ εἰ λόγος
δὲ εἴη ὃς προσελθὼν ποιεῖ τὸ σῶμα, δηλονότι ὁ
λόγος ἐμπεριλαβὼν ἔχει τὰς ποιότητας ἁπάσας.
Δεῖ δὲ τὸν λόγον τοῦτον, εἰ μή ἐστιν ἄλλως ὥσπερ
ὁρισμὸς δηλωτικὸς τοῦ τί ἐστι τὸ πρᾶγμα, ἀλλὰ
10 λόγος ποιῶν πρᾶγμα, μὴ τὴν ὕλην συμπεριειληφέ-
ναι, ἀλλὰ περὶ ὕλην λόγον εἶναι καὶ ἐγγενόμενον
ἀποτελεῖν τὸ σῶμα, καὶ εἶναι μὲν τὸ σῶμα ὕλην
καὶ λόγον ἐνόντα, αὐτὸν δὲ εἶδος ὄντα ἄνευ ὕλης
ψιλὸν θεωρεῖσθαι, κἂν ὅτι μάλιστα ἀχώριστος
15 αὐτὸς ᾖ. Ὁ γὰρ χωριστὸς ἄλλος, ὁ ἐν νῷ· ἐν νῷ
δέ, ὅτι καὶ αὐτὸς νοῦς. Ἀλλὰ ταῦτα ἄλλοθι.

---

[1] ἢ Kirchhoff, H-S²: εἰ codd.

of its own, except in so far as it has not rejected size. So much, then for the discussion of these difficult questions.

3. But since we have mentioned corporeity, we should enquire whether corporeity is that which is composed of all a body's constituents, or whether corporeity is a form and rational formative principle which enters matter and makes it body. If, then, this is what body is, that which is composed of all the qualities with matter, this is what corporeity would be. And if corporeity was a formative principle which by its coming to matter makes body, obviously the formative principle includes and contains all the qualities. But this rational principle, on the assumption that it is not a sort of definition which declares the nature of the thing but a rational principle which makes a thing, cannot include the matter but must be a principle in relation with matter which enters matter and brings the body to perfection, and the body must be matter and a rational principle present in it, but the rational principle itself, since it is a form, must be contemplated bare, without matter, even if it is itself as inseparable as it can be from matter. For the separated form is a different one, that which is in intellect: and it is in intellect because it is intellect itself. But this we discuss elsewhere.

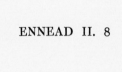

ENNEAD II. 8

II. 8. ON SIGHT, OR HOW DISTANT OBJECTS APPEAR SMALL

Introductory Note

THIS very short treatise (No. 35 in Porphyry's chronological order) is the only surviving evidence of Plotinus's study of optics, mentioned by Porphyry in ch. 14 of the *Life*. It is a school discussion, based probably on the reading of Peripatetic προβλήματα (on this, and for evidence of the origin of the views put forward, see Bréhier's introduction). The question why distant objects appear smaller than they are was much discussed in the philosophical schools, and Plotinus puts forward five different views. The first is Stoic (the light is contracted in proportion to the size of the eye); the second, apparently, bad Aristotelian (we perceive the form without the matter, and so without the size—but, as Plotinus remarks in passing, size is a form); the third (necessity of seeing each part to perceive the size) is Epicurean; the fourth is Aristotelian (we perceive colour primarily, and size only incidentally). This is the solution which Plotinus prefers; he develops it at some length, with an excursus on sounds. The fifth is the mathematical explanation by the lesser angle of vision, which Plotinus seems to find more interesting than any of the first three, but which he none the less rejects.

Synopsis

Why do distant objects appear small? Four different explanations, the first three stated shortly, the fourth developed at length, with some remarks on sound (ch. 1). Rejection of a fifth explanation, from the lesser angle of vision (ch. 2).

II. 8. (35) ΠΕΡΙ ΟΡΑΣΕΩΣ Η ΠΩΣ ΤΑ ΠΟΡΡΩ ΜΙΚΡΑ ΦΑΙΝΕΤΑΙ

1. Ἆρα τὰ πόρρω φαίνεται ἐλάττω καὶ τὰ πολὺ
ἀφεστηκότα ὀλίγον δοκεῖ ἔχειν τὸ μεταξύ, τὰ δ'
ἐγγύθεν ἡλίκα ἐστὶ φαίνεται, καὶ ὅσην ἔχει τὴν
ἀπόστασιν; Ἐλάττω μὲν δοκεῖ τοῖς ὁρῶσι τὰ
5 πόρρω, ὅτι συναιρεῖσθαι πρὸς τὴν ὄψιν ἐθέλει καὶ
πρὸς τὸ μέγεθος τῆς κόρης τὸ φῶς· καὶ ὅσῳ ἂν
πόρρω ἡ ὕλη ᾖ τοῦ ὁρωμένου, τόσῳ τὸ εἶδος οἷον
μεμονωμένον ἀφικνεῖται γινομένου καὶ τοῦ πηλίκου
εἴδους καὶ αὐτοῦ καὶ ποιοῦ, ὡς τὸν λόγον αὐτοῦ
ἀφικνεῖσθαι μόνον. Ἢ καί, ὅτι τὸ μὲν μέγεθος ἐν
10 διεξόδῳ καὶ ἐπελεύσει καθ' ἕκαστον μέρος ὅσον
ἐστὶν αἰσθανόμεθα· παρεῖναι οὖν δεῖ αὐτὸ καὶ πλησίον εἶναι, ἵνα γνωσθῇ ὅσον. Ἢ καί, ὅτι κατὰ συμβεβηκὸς ὁρᾶται τὸ μέγεθος τοῦ χρώματος πρώτως
θεωρουμένου· πλησίον μὲν οὖν ὅσον κέχρωσται
γινώσκεται, πόρρω δὲ ὅτι κέχρωσται, τὰ δὲ μέρη
15 κατὰ ποσὸν συναιρούμενα[1] οὐκ ἀκριβῆ δίδωσι
τὴν τοῦ ποσοῦ διάγνωσιν· ἐπεὶ καὶ τὰ χρώματα
αὐτὰ ἀμυδρὰ προσέρχεται. Τί οὖν θαυμαστόν, εἰ
καὶ τὰ μεγέθη, ὥσπερ καὶ αἱ φωναὶ ἐλάττους,
ὅσῳ ἂν τὸ εἶδος αὐτῶν ἀμυδρὸν ἴῃ; Εἶδος γὰρ

---

[1] συναιρούμενα Harder: συνδιαιρούμενα codd.

II. 8. ON SIGHT, OR HOW DISTANT
OBJECTS APPEAR SMALL

1. Do distant objects appear smaller, and things far apart seem to have only a small space between them, but objects which are near appear the size they are and the distance apart which they are? Distant objects seem smaller to those who look at them because the light tends to be contracted in proportion to the sight and the size of the pupil: and the farther the material of the seen object is away, the more the form comes, so to speak, bare of its matter (though size, too, itself, as well as quality, is a form), so that its rational formative principle comes alone. Or another explanation is that we perceive the size in the process of going over and surveying the thing part by part, each in its actual extent; so it must be on the spot and near at hand in order that its extent may be known. Or another explanation is that the size is seen incidentally, the primary object of contemplation being the colour: so when it is near we know how large a space is coloured, but when it is far off we know that it is coloured, but the parts being quantitatively contracted do not give an accurate determination of the extent: then, too, the colours themselves come to us blurred. Then why is it remarkable if magnitudes too, as well as sounds, are smaller in proportion as their form comes to us

κἀκεῖ ἡ ἀκοὴ ζητεῖ, τὸ δὲ μέγεθος κατὰ συμβε-
20 βηκὸς αἰσθάνεται. ᾽Αλλὰ περὶ τῆς ἀκοῆς, εἰ τὸ
μέγεθος κατὰ συμβεβηκός· τίνι γὰρ πρώτως τὸ
ἐν τῇ φωνῇ μέγεθος, ὥσπερ δοκεῖ τῇ ἁφῇ τὸ
ὁρώμενον; ῍Η τὸ δοκοῦν μέγεθος ἡ ἀκοὴ οὐ κατὰ
τὸ ποσόν, ἀλλὰ κατὰ τὸ μᾶλλον καὶ ἧττον, οὐ
κατὰ συμβεβηκός, οἷον τὸ σφόδρα, ὡς καὶ ἡ
25 γεῦσις τὸ σφόδρα τοῦ γλυκέος οὐ κατὰ συμβεβηκός·
τὸ δὲ κυρίως μέγεθος φωνῆς τὸ ἐφ᾽ ὅσον· τοῦτο δὲ
κατὰ συμβεβηκὸς ἐκ τοῦ σφόδρα σημήνειεν ἄν,
οὐκ ἀκριβῶς δέ. Τὸ μὲν γὰρ σφόδρα ἑκάστῳ τὸ
αὐτό, τὸ δὲ εἰς πλῆθος εἰς ἅπαντα τὸν τόπον, ὃν
ἐπέσχεν. ᾽Αλλ᾽ οὐ σμικρὰ τὰ χρώματα, ἀλλ᾽
30 ἀμυδρά, τὰ δὲ μεγέθη σμικρά. ῍Η ἐν ἀμφοτέροις
κοινὸν τὸ ἧττον ὅ ἐστι· χρῶμα μὲν οὖν τὸ ἧττον
ἀμυδρόν, μέγεθος δὲ τὸ ἧττον σμικρόν, καὶ
ἑπόμενον τῷ χρώματι τὸ μέγεθος ἀνάλογον
ἠλάττωται. Σαφέστερον δὲ ἐπὶ τῶν ποικίλων
γίνεται τὸ πάθος, οἷον ὁρῶν ἐχόντων πολλὰς
35 οἰκήσεις καὶ δένδρων πλῆθος καὶ ἄλλα πολλά, ὧν
ἕκαστον, εἰ μὲν ὁρῷτο, δίδωσιν ἐκ τῶν ὁρωμένων
ἑκάστων μετρεῖν τὸ ὅλον· τοῦ δὲ εἴδους καθ᾽
ἕκαστον οὐκ ἰόντος ἀπεστέρηται τοῦ καθ᾽ ἕκαστον
εἶδος μετροῦσα τὸ ὑποκείμενον μέγεθος τὸ πᾶν
ὅσον ἐστὶ γινώσκειν. ᾽Επεὶ καὶ τὰ πλησίον, ὅταν

blurred? For in the case of sounds, too, it is form that the hearing seeks, and the size is incidentally perceived. (But as regards hearing, it is questionable whether size is perceived incidentally; for to what sense does the size in sound appear as its primary object, as visible size appears as the primary object to touch? The hearing perceives what seems to it the size of the sound not according to an actual quantity but according to a scale of more and less, like intensity, and not incidentally, just as taste perceives the intensity of sweetness not incidentally; but the proper size of sound is the size of the area over which it can be heard; and this would be incidentally perceptible from the intensity, but not accurately. For, on the one hand, each sound has its own intensity which remains the same, on the other, it multiplies itself by extending to the whole space which the sound occupies.) But colours are not small but blurred; it is sizes which are small. Both have in common the " less than they are ": as regards colour the " less " is blurredness, as regards size the " less " is smallness, and, following the colour, the size is lessened proportionately. What happens to them becomes clearer in things of many and varied parts, for instance, hills with many houses on them and a quantity of trees and a great many other things, of which each individual one, if it is seen, enables us to measure the whole from the individual parts which we observe. But if the form does not reach us in individual detail, the possibility of knowing the dimensions of the whole by measuring its basic size according to the forms of individual parts is taken away. For this applies to things near

40 ποικίλα ᾖ, ἀθρόως δὲ γίνηται ἡ ἐπιβολὴ πρὸς αὐτὰ
καὶ μὴ πάντα τὰ εἴδη ὁρῷτο, ἐλάττω ἂν φανείη
κατὰ λόγον, ὅσον ἂν ἕκαστον κλαπῇ ἐν τῇ θέᾳ·
ὅταν δὲ πάντα ὀφθῇ, ἀκριβῶς μετρηθέντα ὅσα
ἐστὶ γινώσκεται. Ὅσα δὲ τῶν μεγεθῶν ὁμοειδῆ
ὁμοιόχροα ὄντα, ψεύδεται καὶ ταῦτα τὸ ποσὸν
45 αὐτῆς οὐ κατὰ μέρος πάνυ τι μετρεῖν δυναμένης
τῆς ὄψεως, ὅτι ἀπολισθάνει κατὰ μέρος μετροῦσα,
ὅτι μὴ ἔχει ἵστασθαι καθ᾿ ἕκαστον μέρος τῇ
διαφορᾷ. Ἐγγύθεν δὲ τὸ πόρρω, ὅτι ⟨τὸ⟩[1]
μεταξὺ συναιρεῖται ὅσον ἐστὶ κατὰ τὴν αὐτὴν
αἰτίαν. Τὸ μὲν γὰρ πλησίον αὐτοῦ, ὅσον οὐ
50 λανθάνει, διὰ τὰ αὐτά· οὐ διεξοδεύουσα δὲ τὸ
πόρρω τοῦ διαστήματος, οἷόν ἐστι κατ᾿ εἶδος,
οὐκ ἂν δύναιτο οὐδ᾿ ὅσον ἐστὶ κατὰ μέγεθος
εἰπεῖν.

2. Τὸ δὲ κατὰ τὰς τῆς ὄψεως γωνίας ἐλάττους
εἴρηται μὲν καὶ ἐν ἄλλοις ὡς οὐκ ἔστι, καὶ νῦν δὲ
ἐκεῖνο λεκτέον, ὡς ὁ λέγων ἔλαττον φαίνεσθαι
ἐλάττονι γωνίᾳ καταλείπει τὴν λοιπὴν ἔξωθέν τι
5 ὁρῶσαν ἢ ἄλλο τι ἢ ὄν τι ἔξωθεν ὅλως, οἷον ἀέρα.
Ὅταν οὖν μηδὲν καταλείπῃ τῷ πολὺ εἶναι τὸ ὄρος,
ἀλλ᾿ ἢ ἰσάζῃ καὶ μηκέτι ἄλλο οἷόν τε ᾖ αὐτῇ ὁρᾶν,
ἅτε τοῦ διαστήματος αὐτῆς συναρμόσαντος τῷ
ὁρωμένῳ, ἢ καὶ ὑπερτείνῃ τὸ ὁρώμενον ἐφ᾿
ἑκάτερα τὴν τῆς ὄψεως προσβολήν, τί ἄν τις
10 ἐνταῦθα λέγοι ἐλάττονος μὲν ἢ ἔστι πολλῷ

[1] ⟨τὸ⟩ Kirchhoff, H-S².

214

at hand too; when they have many parts, but we only take a quick glance at them as a whole and do not observe all the forms of the parts, they seem smaller in proportion as the individual details evade our observation; but when all the details are seen, we measure the objects accurately and know how large they are. And those magnitudes that are of one form and like colour throughout cheat our sight, too, because it is not very well able to measure them part by part, since it slips off them as it measures by parts because it has no firm resting-place given it in each individual part by its distinction from others. And things far off appear near because the real extent of the distance between is contracted for the same reason. The near part of the distance appears in its true extent, from the same causes; but the sight cannot go through the far part of the distance and see its forms as they really are, and so it is not able to say how great in magnitude it really is.

2. It has been said elsewhere that the explanation by lesser angle of vision does not apply; but we should now add this, that the man who says that something appears smaller because of the lesser angle of vision leaves the rest of the sight seeing something outside, either another object or something that is completely out of the angle of vision, air for instance. When, therefore, he leaves nothing outside the angle of vision because the mountain [for instance] is large, but either the eye's range is equal to the object and can see nothing beyond it, in that the dimensions of the field of vision correspond with those of the seen object, or the seen object even extends beyond the field of vision on both sides,

φαινομένου τοῦ ὑποκειμένου, πάσῃ δὲ τῇ ὄψει
ὁρωμένου; Εἰ δὲ δὴ καὶ ἐπὶ τοῦ οὐρανοῦ θεωροῖ,
ἀναμφισβητήτως μάθοι ἄν τις. Πᾶν μὲν γὰρ τὸ
ἡμισφαίριον οὐκ ἄν τις ὁρᾶν μιᾷ προσβολῇ δύναιτο,
οὐδ' ἐπὶ τοσοῦτον χυθῆναι ἡ ὄψις μέχρις αὐτοῦ
15 ἐκτεινομένη. 'Αλλ' εἴ τις βούλεται, δεδόσθω.
Εἰ οὖν πᾶσα μὲν περιέλαβε πᾶν, πολλαπλάσιον δὲ
τὸ μέγεθος τοῦ φαινομένου ὑπάρχει ἐν τῷ οὐρανῷ
τοῦ ἔλαττον πολλῷ ἤ ἐστι φαίνεσθαι, πῶς ἂν
ἐλάττωσιν γωνίας τοῦ ἐλάττω φαίνεσθαι τὰ πόρρω
αἰτιῷτο;

what will anyone say then, when the object appears far smaller than it is but is seen with the whole sight? But certainly, if one looked at the sky one could discover the truth of this without any possibility of doubt. One could not, of course, see the whole hemisphere with one look, nor could the sight be spread out so widely, extending over the whole of it. But if anyone likes, let it be granted that this is possible. If, then, the whole sight includes the whole hemisphere, and the size of what is seen is in the actual sky many times greater than the appearance, far less than it really is, how could one make the lessening of the angle of vision responsible for distant objects appearing small?

ENNEAD II. 9

II. 9. AGAINST THE GNOSTICS

Introductory Note

THIS treatise (No. 33 in Porphyry's chronological order) is in fact the concluding section of a single long treatise which Porphyry, in order to carry out his design of grouping his master's works, more or less according to subject, into six sets of nine treatises, hacked roughly into four parts which he put into different Enneads, the other three being III. 8 (30) V. 8 (31) and V. 5 (32). Porphyry says (*Life* ch. 16. 11) that he gave the treatise the title *Against the Gnostics* (he is presumably also responsible for the titles of the other sections of the cut-up treatise). There is an alternative title in *Life*, ch. 24. 56–57 which runs *Against those who say that the maker of the universe is evil and the universe is evil.*

The treatise as it stands in the Enneads is a most powerful protest on behalf of Hellenic philosophy against the un-Hellenic heresy (as it was from the Platonist as well as the orthodox Christian point of view) of Gnosticism. There were Gnostics among Plotinus's own friends, whom he had not succeeded in converting (ch. 10 of this treatise) and he and his pupils devoted considerable time and energy to anti-Gnostic controversy (*Life* ch. 16). He obviously considered Gnosticism an extremely dangerous influence, likely to pervert the minds even of members of his own circle. It is impossible to attempt to give an account of Gnosticism here. By far the best discussion of what the particular group of Gnostics Plotinus knew believed is M. Puech's admirable contribution to *Entretiens Hardt* V

AGAINST THE GNOSTICS

(*Les Sources de Plotin*) [1]. But it is important for the understanding of this treatise to be clear about the reasons why
Plotinus disliked them so intensely and thought their
influence so harmful. The teaching of the Gnostics seems
to him untraditional, irrational and immoral. They
despise and revile the ancient Platonic teaching and claim
to have a new and superior wisdom of their own: but in
fact anything that is true in their teaching comes from
Plato, and all they have done themselves is to add senseless
complications and pervert the true traditional doctrine
into a melodramatic, superstitious fantasy designed to
feed their own delusions of grandeur. They reject the
only true way of salvation through wisdom and virtue,
the slow patient study of truth and pursuit of perfection
by men who respect the wisdom of the ancients and know
their place in the universe. They claim to be a privileged
caste of beings, in whom alone God is interested, and
who are saved not by their own efforts but by some dra-
matic and arbitrary divine proceeding; and this, Plotinus
says, leads to immorality. Worst of all, they despise
and hate the material universe and deny its goodness and
the goodness of its maker. This for a Platonist is utter
blasphemy, and all the worse because it obviously derives
to some extent from the sharply other-worldly side of
Plato's own teaching (e.g. in the *Phaedo*). At this point
in his attack Plotinus comes very close in some ways to
the orthodox Christian opponents of Gnosticism, who also
insist that this world is the good work of God in his goodness. But, here as on the question of salvation, the
doctrine which Plotinus is defending is as sharply opposed
in other ways to orthodox Christianity as to Gnosticism:
for he maintains not only the goodness of the material universe but also its eternity and its divinity. The idea that
the universe could have a beginning and end is inseparably
connected in his mind with the idea that the divine action

[1] Vandoeuvres 1960, pp. 161–190.

in making it is arbitrary and irrational. And to deny the divinity (though a subordinate and dependent divinity) of the World-Soul, and of those noblest of embodied living beings the heavenly bodies, seems to him both blasphemous and unreasonable.

Synopsis

Short statement of the doctrine of the three hypostases, the One, Intellect and Soul; there cannot be more or fewer than these three. Criticism of attempts to multiply the hypostases, and especially of the idea of two intellects, one which thinks and the other which thinks that it thinks. (ch. 1). The true doctrine of Soul (ch. 2). The law of necessary procession and the eternity of the universe (ch. 3). Attack on the Gnostic doctrine of the making of the universe by a fallen soul, and on their despising of the universe and the heavenly bodies (chs. 4–5). The senseless jargon of the Gnostics, their plagiarism from and perversion of Plato, and their insolent arrogance (ch. 6). The true doctrine about Universal Soul and the goodness of the universe which it forms and rules (chs. 7–8). Refutation of objections from the inequalities and injustices of human life (ch. 9). Ridiculous arrogance of the Gnostics who refuse to acknowledge the hierarchy of created gods and spirits and say that they alone are sons of God and superior to the heavens (ch. 9). The absurdities of the Gnostic doctrine of the fall of " Wisdom " (Sophia) and of the generation and activities of the Demiurge, maker of the visible universe (chs. 10–12). False and melodramatic Gnostic teaching about the cosmic spheres and their influence (ch. 13). The blasphemous falsity of the Gnostic claim to control the higher powers by magic and the absurdity of their claim to cure diseases by casting out demons (ch. 14). The false other-worldliness of the Gnostics leads to immorality (ch. 15). The true Platonic other-worldliness, which loves and venerates the material universe in all its goodness and beauty as the most perfect possible image of the intelligible, contrasted at length with the false, Gnostic, other-worldliness which hates and despises the material universe and its beauties (chs. 16–18).

II. 9. (33) ΠΡΟΣ ΤΟΥΣ ΓΝΩΣΤΙΚΟΥΣ

1. Ἐπειδὴ τοίνυν ἐφάνη ἡμῖν ἡ τοῦ ἀγαθοῦ
ἁπλῆ φύσις καὶ πρώτη—πᾶν γὰρ τὸ οὐ πρῶτον
οὐχ ἁπλοῦν—καὶ οὐδὲν ἔχον ἐν ἑαυτῷ, ἀλλὰ ἕν τι,
καὶ τοῦ ἑνὸς λεγομένου ἡ φύσις ἡ αὐτή—καὶ γὰρ
5 αὕτη οὐκ ἄλλο, εἶτα ἕν, οὐδὲ τοῦτο ἄλλο, εἶτα
ἀγαθόν—ὅταν· λέγωμεν τὸ ἕν, καὶ ὅταν λέγωμεν
τἀγαθόν, τὴν αὐτὴν¹ δεῖ νομίζειν τὴν φύσιν καὶ
μίαν λέγειν οὐ κατηγοροῦντας ἐκείνης οὐδέν,
δηλοῦντας δὲ ἡμῖν αὐτοῖς ὡς οἷόν τε. Καὶ τὸ
πρῶτον δὲ οὕτως, ὅτι ἁπλούστατον, καὶ τὸ αὔταρκες,
ὅτι οὐκ ἐκ πλειόνων· οὕτω γὰρ ἀναρτηθήσεται
10 εἰς τὰ ἐξ ὧν· καὶ οὐκ ἐν ἄλλῳ, ὅτι πᾶν τὸ ἐν
ἄλλῳ καὶ παρ᾽ ἄλλου. Εἰ οὖν μηδὲ παρ᾽ ἄλλου
μηδὲ ἐν ἄλλῳ μηδὲ σύνθεσις μηδεμία, ἀνάγκη
μηδὲν ὑπὲρ αὐτὸ εἶναι. Οὐ τοίνυν δεῖ ἐφ᾽ ἑτέρας
ἀρχὰς ἰέναι, ἀλλὰ τοῦτο προστησαμένους, εἶτα
15 νοῦν μετ᾽ αὐτὸ καὶ τὸ νοοῦν πρώτως, εἶτα ψυχὴν
μετὰ νοῦν—αὕτη γὰρ τάξις κατὰ φύσιν—μήτε
πλείω τούτων τίθεσθαι ἐν τῷ νοητῷ μήτε ἐλάττω.

¹ τὴν αὐτὴν Heigl, H-S²: ταύτην codd.

¹ This is a reference back to the conclusion of what, as
Plotinus wrote it, was the preceding section of the same treatise,
which appears in the *Enneads* as V. 5; cp. V. 5. 13. 33–36.

II. 9. AGAINST THE GNOSTICS

1. Since, then, the simple nature of the Good appeared to us as also primal (for all that is not primal is not simple), and as something which has nothing in itself, but is some one thing;[1] and since the nature of what is called the One is the same (for this is not some other thing first and then one, nor is the Good something else first, and then good), whenever we say "the One" and whenever we say "the Good," we must think that the nature we are speaking of is the same nature, and call it "one" not as predicating anything of it but as making it clear to ourselves as far as we can. And we call it the First in the sense that it is simplest, and the Self-Sufficient, because it is not composed of a number of parts; for if it were, it would be dependent upon the things of which it was composed; and we say that it is not in something else, because everything which is in something else also comes from something else. If, then, it is not from something else or in something else or any kind of compound, it is necessary that there should be nothing above it. So we must not go after other first principles but put this first, and then after it Intellect, that which primally thinks, and then Soul after Intellect (for this is the order which corresponds to the nature of things): and we must not posit more principles than these in the intelligible world, or

Εἴτε γὰρ ἐλάττω, ἢ ψυχὴν καὶ νοῦν ταὐτὸν
φήσουσιν, ἢ νοῦν καὶ τὸ πρῶτον· ἀλλ' ὅτι ἕτερα
ἀλλήλων, ἐδείχθη πολλαχῇ. Λοιπὸν δὲ ἐπισκέ-
20 ψασθαι ἐν τῷ παρόντι, εἰ πλείω τῶν τριῶν τούτων,
τίνες ἂν οὖν εἶεν φύσεις παρ' αὐτάς. Τῆς τε γὰρ
λεχθείσης οὕτως ἔχειν ἀρχῆς τῆς πάντων οὐδεὶς
ἂν εὕροι ἁπλουστέραν οὐδ' ἐπαναβεβηκυῖαν ἡντινοῦν. Οὐ γὰρ δὴ τὴν μὲν δυνάμει, τὴν δὲ ἐνεργείᾳ
25 φήσουσι· γελοῖον γὰρ ἐν τοῖς ἐνεργείᾳ οὖσι καὶ
ἀύλοις τὸ δυνάμει καὶ ἐνεργείᾳ διαιρουμένους
φύσεις ποιεῖσθαι πλείους. Ἀλλ' οὐδὲ ἐν τοῖς
μετὰ ταῦτα· οὐδ' ἐπινοεῖν τὸν μέν τινα νοῦν ἐν
ἡσυχίᾳ τινί, τὸν δὲ οἷον κινούμενον. Τίς γὰρ ἂν

---

¹ Here, and in what follows in the rest of the chapter,
Plotinus is probably not only, or even primarily, concerned
with explicitly Gnostic doctrines. He is attacking views
which were held in the Platonic school and to which he had
himself at one time been prepared to make some concessions.
The idea that there were two or more Intellects seems to have
arisen in the course of discussions about the meaning of Plato,
Timaeus 39E, and the relationship of the intellect of the
Demiurge to the intelligible model of the universe, which
had long been discussed in the Platonic school (as it still is
by modern scholars). Amelius, according to Proclus, (*In
Timaeum* III. 268A, p. 103. 18 ff., Diehl), came to the conclusion
that there were three Intellects, the " existing," the " possess-
ing " and the " seeing," a view which had a considerable influence on the later developments of Neoplatonic doctrine (cp.
Dodds's commentary on Proclus, *Elements of Theology* prop.
167). And in the first of the early notes collected by Porphyry
in III. 9, Plotinus puts forward a distinction between an
Intellect " in repose," and another which is an " activity
proceeding from it " and " sees " it, very similar to the

AGAINST THE GNOSTICS

fewer. For if people posit fewer, they will either assert that Soul and Intellect are the same, or Intellect and the First; but it has been shown in many places that they are different from each other. It remains to investigate in our present discussion, if we are to posit more than these three, whatever other natures there could be beside them. No one could find any principle simpler than the principle of all things which we have said to be as above described, or transcending it. For they will not assert that there is one principle which exists potentially and another which exists actually; for it would be ridiculous to distinguish things existing actually and potentially, and so multiply natures, in things which exist actually and are without matter. It is not even possible to do this in the things which come after these. One cannot conceive one intellect of some sort in a sort of repose and another in a kind of way in motion.[1] What would the repose of Intellect be,

distinction criticised here. This distinction seems to go back to Numenius, whose thought had affinities with Gnosticism (cp. Dodds on Proclus *El. Th.* prop. 168). Dodds also thinks that Numenius may be the author of the other distinction criticised here between the Intellect that thinks and the other which thinks that it thinks. But the passage describing Numenius's doctrine about the thinking of his three Intellects (Proclus *In Tim.* III. 268A–B, p. 103, 28 ff.; Diehl = Numenius test. 25 Leemans) is too obscure for any certainty. Similar ideas were, of course current among the Gnostics, but it is important to remember that they were seriously put forward in Plotinus's own circle, by others than professed Gnostics. The Gnostics themselves, especially Valentinus, derived some of their ideas from Platonism and Neopythagoreanism, which makes it easier to understand the reciprocal influence they exercised on some Platonists and Neopythagoreans.

ἡσυχία νοῦ καὶ τίς κίνησις καὶ προφορὰ ἂν εἴη ἢ
τίς ἀργία καὶ τοῦ ἑτέρου τί ἔργον; Ἔστι γὰρ ὡς
30 ἔστι νοῦς ἀεὶ ὡσαύτως ἐνεργείᾳ κείμενος ἑστώσῃ·
κίνησις δὲ πρὸς αὐτὸν καὶ περὶ αὐτὸν ψυχῆς ἤδη
ἔργον καὶ λόγος ἀπ᾽ αὐτοῦ εἰς ψυχὴν ψυχὴν
νοερὰν ποιῶν, οὐκ ἄλλην τινὰ μεταξὺ νοῦ καὶ
ψυχῆς φύσιν. Οὐ μὴν οὐδὲ διὰ τοῦτο πλείους
νοῦς ποιεῖν, εἰ ὁ μὲν νοεῖ, ὁ δὲ νοεῖ ὅτι νοεῖ. Καὶ
35 γὰρ εἰ ἄλλο τὸ ἐν τούτοις νοεῖν, ἄλλο δὲ τὸ νοεῖν
ὅτι νοεῖ, ἀλλ᾽ οὖν μία προσβολὴ οὐκ ἀναίσθητος
τῶν ἐνεργημάτων ἑαυτῆς· γελοῖον δὲ [1] ἐπὶ τοῦ
ἀληθινοῦ νοῦ τοῦτο ὑπολαμβάνειν, ἀλλὰ πάντως γε
ὁ αὐτὸς ἔσται ὅσπερ ἐνόει ὁ νοῶν ὅτι νοεῖ. Εἰ δὲ
μή, ὁ μὲν ἔσται νοῶν μόνον, ὁ δὲ ὅτι νοεῖ νοῶν
40 ἄλλου ὄντος, ἀλλ᾽ οὐκ αὐτοῦ τοῦ νενοηκότος.
Ἀλλ᾽ εἰ ἐπινοίᾳ φήσουσι, πρῶτον μὲν τῶν πλειόνων
ὑποστάσεων ἀποστήσονται· ἔπειτα δεῖ σκοπεῖν, εἰ
καὶ αἱ ἐπίνοιαι χώραν ἔχουσι λαβεῖν νοῦν νοοῦντα
μόνον, μὴ παρακολουθοῦντα δὲ ἑαυτῷ ὅτι νοεῖ· ὃ
καὶ ἐφ᾽ ἡμῶν αὐτῶν εἰ γίγνοιτο τῶν ἀεὶ ἐπιστα-
45 τούντων ταῖς ὁρμαῖς καὶ ταῖς διανοήσεσιν, εἰ καὶ
μετρίως σπουδαῖοι εἶεν, αἰτίαν ἂν ἀφροσύνης
ἔχοιεν. Ὅταν δὲ δὴ ὁ νοῦς ὁ ἀληθινὸς ἐν ταῖς
νοήσεσιν αὐτὸν νοῇ καὶ μὴ ἔξωθεν ᾖ τὸ νοητὸν

---

[1] δὲ Harder: γὰρ codd. H-S.

and what its motion and " going forth," or what
would be its inactivity, and what the work of the
other intellect? Intellect is as it is, always the same,
resting in a static activity. Movement towards it
and around it is already the work of Soul, and a
rational principle proceeding from Intellect to Soul
and making Soul intellectual, not making another
nature between Intellect and Soul. Again, the
supposition that one intellect thinks and the other
thinks that it thinks, is certainly not a reason for
making several intellects. For even if on our level
it is one thing for an intellect to think and another
for it to think that it thinks, yet all the same its
thinking is a single application of the mind not un-
aware of its own activities; but it would be absurd to
suppose this duality to exist in the case of the true
Intellect, but the intellect which thinks that it thinks
will be altogether the same as the intellect which
did the thinking. Otherwise one intellect will be
only thinking, and the other will be thinking that
it thinks, but the thinking subject will be another, and
not itself. But if they are going to assert that the
distinction is only in our thought, first of all they will
be abandoning the idea of a plurality of hypostases.
Then we must consider if we can make distinctions
in thought which leave room for the assumption of an
intellect which only thinks, but is not conscious of its
thinking. If this happened to ourselves, who always
watch over our impulses and thought processes, if
we are even moderately serious people, we should be
blamed for witlessness. But certainly when the
true Intellect thinks itself in its thoughts and its object of thought is not outside but it is itself also its

αὐτοῦ, ἀλλ᾽ αὐτὸς ᾖ καὶ τὸ νοητόν, ἐξ ἀνάγκης ἐν
τῷ νοεῖν ἔχει ἑαυτὸν καὶ ὁρᾷ ἑαυτόν· ὁρῶν δ᾽
50 ἑαυτὸν οὐκ ἀνοηταίνοντα, ἀλλὰ νοοῦντα ὁρᾷ.
Ὥστε ἐν τῷ πρώτως νοεῖν ἔχοι ἂν καὶ τὸ νοεῖν
ὅτι νοεῖ ὡς ἓν ὄν· καὶ οὐδὲ τῇ ἐπινοίᾳ ἐκεῖ διπλοῦν.
Εἰ δὲ καὶ ἀεὶ νοῶν εἴη, ὅπερ ἔστι, τίς χώρα τῇ
ἐπινοίᾳ τῇ χωριζούσῃ τὸ νοεῖν ἀπὸ τοῦ νοεῖν ὅτι
νοεῖ; Εἰ δὲ δὴ καὶ ἑτέραν ἐπίνοιάν τις τρίτην
55 ἐπεισάγοι τὴν ἐπὶ τῇ δευτέρᾳ τῇ λεγούσῃ νοεῖν
ὅτι νοεῖ, τὴν λέγουσαν ὅτι νοεῖ ὅτι νοεῖ ὅτι νοεῖ,
ἔτι μᾶλλον καταφανὲς τὸ ἄτοπον. Καὶ διὰ τί οὐκ
εἰς ἄπειρον οὕτω; Τὸν δὲ λόγον ὅταν τις ἀπὸ τοῦ
νοῦ ποιῇ, εἶτα ἀπὸ τούτου γίνεσθαι ἐν ψυχῇ ἄλλον
60 ἀπ᾽ αὐτοῦ τοῦ λόγου, ἵνα μεταξὺ ψυχῆς καὶ νοῦ ᾖ
οὗτος, ἀποστερήσει τὴν ψυχὴν τοῦ νοεῖν, εἰ μὴ
παρὰ τοῦ νοῦ κομιεῖται, ἀλλὰ παρὰ ἄλλου τοῦ
μεταξύ, τὸν λόγον· καὶ εἴδωλον λόγου, ἀλλ᾽ οὐ
λόγον ἕξει, καὶ ὅλως οὐκ εἰδήσει νοῦν οὐδὲ ὅλως
νοήσει.

2. Οὐ τοίνυν οὔτε πλείω τούτων οὔτε ἐπινοίας
περιττὰς ἐν ἐκείνοις, ἃς οὐ δέχονται, θετέον, ἀλλ᾽
ἕνα νοῦν τὸν αὐτὸν ὡσαύτως ἔχοντα, ἀκλινῆ
πανταχῇ, μιμούμενον τὸν πατέρα καθ᾽ ὅσον οἷόν
5 τε αὐτῷ. Ψυχῆς δὲ ἡμῶν τὸ μὲν ἀεὶ πρὸς

object of thought, it necessarily in its thinking possesses itself and sees itself: and when it sees itself it does so not as without intelligence but as thinking. So that in its primary thinking it would have also the thinking that it thinks, as an existent unity; and it is not double, even in thought, there in the intelligible world. And further, if it is always thinking what it is, what room is there for the distinction in thought which separates thinking from thinking that it thinks? But if one even introduced another, third, distinction in addition to the second one which said that it thinks that it thinks, one which says that it thinks that it thinks that it thinks, the absurdity would become even clearer. And why should one not go on introducing distinctions in this way to infinity? But when someone makes the rational principle proceed from Intellect, and then makes another principle come to be in the soul from the first rational principle itself, in order to make this first principle an intermediary between soul and Intellect, he will deprive soul of thinking, if it does not get its principle of thinking from Intellect but from another principle, the intermediary: and it will have an image of a rational principle, but not a principle, and it will not know Intellect at all or think at all.

2. One must not, then, posit more beings than these, nor make superfluous distinctions in the realities of the intelligible world which the nature of these realities does not admit: we must lay down that there is one intellect, unchangeably the same, without any sort of decline, imitating the Father as far as is possible to it: and that one part of our soul is

ἐκείνοις, τὸ δὲ πρὸς ταῦτα ἔχειν, τὸ δ' ἐν μέσῳ
τούτων· φύσεως γὰρ οὔσης μιᾶς ἐν δυνάμεσι
πλείοσιν ὁτὲ μὲν τὴν πᾶσαν συμφέρεσθαι τῷ
ἀρίστῳ αὐτῆς καὶ τοῦ ὄντος, ὁτὲ δὲ τὸ χεῖρον
αὐτῆς καθελκυσθὲν συνεφελκύσασθαι τὸ μέσον·
10 τὸ γὰρ πᾶν αὐτῆς οὐκ ἦν θέμις καθελκύσαι. Καὶ
τοῦτο συμβαίνει αὐτῇ τὸ πάθος, ὅτι μὴ ἔμεινεν
ἐν τῷ καλλίστῳ, ὅπου ψυχὴ μείνασα ἡ μὴ μέρος,
μηδὲ ἧς ἡμεῖς ἔτι μέρος, ἔδωκε τῷ παντὶ σώματι
αὐτῷ τε ἔχειν ὅσον δύναται παρ' αὐτῆς ἔχειν,
μένει τε ἀπραγμόνως αὐτὴ οὐκ ἐκ διανοίας
15 διοικοῦσα οὐδέ τι διορθουμένη, ἀλλὰ τῇ εἰς τὸ
πρὸ αὐτῆς θέᾳ κατακοσμοῦσα δυνάμει θαυμαστῇ.
Ὅσον γὰρ πρὸς αὐτῇ ἐστι, τόσῳ καλλίων καὶ
δυνατωτέρα· κἀκεῖθεν ἔχουσα δίδωσι τῷ μετ'
αὐτὴν καὶ ὥσπερ ἐλλάμπουσα ἀεὶ ἐλλάμπεται.

3. Ἀεὶ οὖν ἐλλαμπομένη καὶ διηνεκὲς ἔχουσα
τὸ φῶς δίδωσιν εἰς τὰ ἐφεξῆς, τὰ δ' ἀεὶ συνέχεται
καὶ ἄρδεται τούτῳ τῷ φωτὶ καὶ ἀπολαύει τοῦ
ζῆν καθ' ὅσον δύναται· ὥσπερ εἰ πυρὸς ἐν μέσῳ
5 που κειμένου ἀλαίνοιντο οἷς οἷόν τε. Καίτοι τὸ
πῦρ ἐστιν ἐν μέτρῳ· ὅταν δὲ δυνάμεις μὴ μετρηθεῖ-
σαι μὴ ἐκ τῶν ὄντων ὦσιν ἀνηρημέναι, πῶς οἷόν
τε εἶναι μέν, μηδὲν δὲ αὐτῶν μεταλαμβάνειν;
Ἀλλ' ἀνάγκη ἕκαστον τὸ αὑτοῦ διδόναι καὶ ἄλλῳ,
ἢ τὸ ἀγαθὸν οὐκ ἀγαθὸν ἔσται, ἢ ὁ νοῦς οὐ νοῦς,
10 ἢ ψυχὴ μὴ τοῦτο, εἰ μή τι μετὰ τοῦ πρώτως ζῆν

always directed to the intelligible realities, one to the things of this world, and one is in the middle between these; for since the soul is one nature in many powers, sometimes the whole of it is carried along with the best of itself and of real being, sometimes the worse part is dragged down and drags the middle with it; for it is not lawful for it to drag down the whole. This misfortune befalls it because it does not remain in the noblest, where the soul remains which is not a part—and at that stage we, too, are not a part of it—and grants to the whole of body to hold whatever it can hold from it, but remains itself untroubled, not managing body as a result of discursive thinking, nor setting anything right, but ordering it with a wonderful power by its contemplation of that which is before it. The more it is directed to that contemplation, the fairer and more powerful it is. It receives from there and gives to what comes after it, and is always illuminated as it illuminates.

3. Since, therefore, it is always illuminated and continually holds the light, it gives it to what comes next after it, and this is held together and fertilised by this light and enjoys its share of life as far as it can; as if there was a fire placed somewhere in the middle and those who were capable of it were warmed. Yet fire has its limited dimensions; but when powers which are not limited to precise dimensions are not separated from real being, how can they exist without anything participating in them? But each of necessity must give of its own to something else as well, or the Good will not be the Good, or Intellect Intellect, or the soul this that it is, unless with the

ζωή¹ καὶ δευτέρως ἕως ἔστι τὸ πρώτως. Ἀνάγκη
τοίνυν ἐφεξῆς εἶναι πάντα ἀλλήλοις καὶ ἀεί,
γενητὰ δὲ τὰ ἕτερα τῷ παρ᾽ ἄλλων εἶναι. Οὐ
τοίνυν ἐγένετο, ἀλλ᾽ ἐγίνετο καὶ γενήσεται, ὅσα
γενητὰ λέγεται· οὐδὲ φθαρήσεται, ἀλλ᾽ ἢ ὅσα
15 ἔχει εἰς ἅ· ὃ δὲ μὴ ἔχει εἰς ὅ, οὐδὲ φθαρήσεται.
Εἰ δέ τις εἰς ὕλην λέγοι, διὰ τί οὐ καὶ τὴν ὕλην;
Εἰ δὲ καὶ τὴν ὕλην φήσει, τίς ἦν ἀνάγκη, φήσομεν,
γενέσθαι; Εἰ δὲ ἀναγκαῖον εἶναι φήσουσι παρα-
κολουθεῖν, καὶ νῦν ἀνάγκη. Εἰ δὲ μόνη καταλει-
φθήσεται, οὐ πανταχοῦ, ἀλλ᾽ ἔν τινι τόπῳ
20 ἀφωρισμένῳ τὰ θεῖα ἔσται καὶ οἷον ἀποτετειχισ-
μένα· εἰ δὲ οὐχ οἷόν τε, ἐλλαμφθήσεται.

4. Εἰ δὲ οἷον πτερορρυήσασαν τὴν ψυχὴν
φήσουσι πεποιηκέναι, οὐχ ἡ τοῦ παντὸς τοῦτο
πάσχει· εἰ δὲ σφαλεῖσαν αὐτοὶ φήσουσι, τοῦ
σφάλματος λεγέτωσαν τὴν αἰτίαν. Πότε δὲ
5 ἐσφάλη; Εἰ μὲν γὰρ ἐξ ἀιδίου, μένει κατὰ τὸν
αὐτῶν λόγον ἐσφαλμένη· εἰ δὲ ἤρξατο, διὰ τί οὐ
πρὸ τοῦ; Ἡμεῖς δὲ οὐ νεῦσίν φαμεν τὴν ποιοῦσαν,

---

¹ ζωή Perna et nunc Henry et Schwyzer: ζωὴ wxy, H-S:
ζωῇ Q.

---

¹ The phrase is taken from Plato, *Phaedrus* 246C. It is
clear from what follows in Plato that the reference is only to
the fall of *human* souls. But a reading of the passage will
show how the Gnostics might have misinterpreted it to fit in
with their own doctrines.

primal living some secondary life lives as long as the primal exists. Of necessity, then, all things must exist for ever in ordered dependence upon each other: those other than the First have come into being in the sense that they are derived from other, higher, principles. Things that are said to have come into being did not just come into being [at a particular moment] but always were and always will be in process of becoming: nor will anything be dissolved except those things which have something to be dissolved into; that which has nothing into which it can be dissolved will not perish. If anyone says that it will be dissolved into matter, why should he not also say that matter will be dissolved? But if he is going to say that, what necessity was there, we shall reply, for it to come into being? But if they are going to assert that it was necessary for it to come into being as a consequence of the existence of higher principles, the necessity is there *now* as well. But if matter is going to remain alone, the divine principles will not be everywhere but in a particular limited place; they will be, so to speak, walled off from matter; but if this is impossible, matter will be illuminated by them.

4. But if they are going to assert that the soul made the world when it had, so to speak, " shed its wings," [1] this does not happen to the Soul of the All; but if they are going to say that it made the world as the result of a moral failure, let them tell us the cause of the failure. But when did it fail? If it was from eternity, it abides in a state of failure according to their own account. If it began to fail, why did it not begin before? But we say that the making act of the

ἀλλὰ μᾶλλον μὴ νεῦσιν. Εἰ δὲ ἔνευσε, τῷ
ἐπιλελῆσθαι δηλονότι τῶν ἐκεῖ· εἰ δὲ ἐπελάθετο,
πῶς δημιουργεῖ; Πόθεν γὰρ ποιεῖ ἢ ἐξ ὧν εἶδεν
10 ἐκεῖ; Εἰ δὲ ἐκείνων μεμνημένη ποιεῖ, οὐδὲ ὅλως
ἔνευσεν, οὐδὲ γὰρ εἰ ἀμυδρῶς ἔχει. Οὐ μᾶλλον
νεύει ἐκεῖ, ἵνα μὴ ἀμυδρῶς ἴδῃ; Διὰ τί γὰρ ἂν
οὐκ ἠθέλησεν ἔχουσα ἡντινοῦν μνήμην ἐπανελθεῖν;
Τί γὰρ ἂν ἑαυτῇ καὶ ἐλογίζετο γενέσθαι ἐκ τοῦ
κοσμοποιῆσαι; Γελοῖον γὰρ τὸ ἵνα τιμῷτο, καὶ
μεταφερόντων ἀπὸ τῶν ἀγαλματοποιῶν τῶν
15 ἐνταῦθα. Ἐπεὶ καὶ εἰ διανοίᾳ ἐποίει καὶ μὴ ἐν τῇ
φύσει ἦν τὸ ποιεῖν καὶ ἡ δύναμις ἡ ποιοῦσα ἦν,
πῶς ἂν κόσμον τόνδε ἐποίησε; Πότε δὲ καὶ
φθερεῖ αὐτόν; εἰ γὰρ μετέγνω, τί ἀναμένει; Εἰ
δὲ οὔπω, οὐδ᾽ ἂν μεταγνοίη ἔτι ἤδη εἰθισμένη καὶ
τῷ χρόνῳ προσφιλεστέρα γενομένη. Εἰ δὲ τὰς
20 καθ᾽ ἕκαστον ψυχὰς ἀναμένει, ἤδη ἔδει μηκέτι
ἐλθεῖν εἰς γένεσιν πάλιν πειραθείσας ἐν τῇ προτέρᾳ
γενέσει τῶν τῇδε κακῶν· ὥστε ἤδη ἂν ἐπέλιπον
ἰοῦσαι. Οὐδὲ τὸ κακῶς γεγονέναι τόνδε τὸν
κόσμον δοτέον τῷ πολλὰ εἶναι ἐν αὐτῷ δυσχερῆ·
τοῦτο γὰρ ἀξίωμα μεῖζόν ἐστι περιτιθέντων αὐτῷ,
25 εἰ ἀξιοῦσι τὸν αὐτὸν εἶναι τῷ νοητῷ, ἀλλὰ μὴ

soul is not a declination but rather a non-declination. But if it declined, it was obviously because it had forgotten the intelligible realities; but if it forgot them, how is it the craftsman of the world? For what is the source of its making, if not what it saw in the intelligible world? But if it makes in re-membrance of those intelligible realities, it has not declined at all, not even if it only has them dimly present in it. Does it not rather incline to the intelligible world, in order not to see dimly? For why, if it had any memory at all, did it not want to ascend there? For whatever advantage did it think was going to result for it from making the universe? It is ridiculous to suppose that it did so in order to be honoured; the people who suppose so are transferring to it what is true of the sculptors here below. Then again, if it made the world by discursive reasoning and its making was not in its nature, and its power was not a productive power, how could it have made this particular universe? And when, too, is it going to destroy it? For if it was sorry it had made it, what is it waiting for? But if it is not sorry yet, it is not likely to be, since it has got used to the universe by now and grown more kindly disposed to it with the passage of time. But if it is waiting for the individual souls, they ought by now to have stopped coming again to birth, since they have made trial in their former birth of the evils in this world; so that they would have left off coming here by now. We cannot grant, either, that this universe had an evil origin because there are many unpleasant things in it: this is a judgement of people who rate it too highly, if they claim that it ought to be the same as

237

εἰκόνα ἐκείνου. Ἢ τίς ἂν ἐγένετο ἄλλη καλλίων
εἰκὼν ἐκείνου; Τί γὰρ ἄλλο πῦρ βελτίων[1] τοῦ
ἐκεῖ πυρὸς παρὰ τὸ ἐνταῦθα πῦρ; Ἢ τίς γῆ ἄλλη
παρὰ ταύτην μετὰ τὴν ἐκεῖ γῆν; Τίς δὲ σφαῖρα
ἀκριβεστέρα καὶ σεμνοτέρα ἢ εὐτακτοτέρα τῇ
30 φορᾷ μετὰ τὴν ἐκεῖ τοῦ κόσμου τοῦ νοητοῦ
περιοχὴν ἐν αὑτῷ; Ἄλλος δὲ ἥλιος μετ᾽ ἐκεῖνον
πρὸ τούτου τοῦ ὁρωμένου τίς;

5. Ἀλλ᾽ αὐτοὺς μὲν σῶμα ἔχοντας, οἷον ἔχουσιν
ἄνθρωποι, καὶ ἐπιθυμίαν καὶ λύπας καὶ ὀργὰς τὴν
παρ᾽ αὐτοῖς δύναμιν μὴ ἀτιμάζειν, ἀλλ᾽ ἐφάπτεσθαι
τοῦ νοητοῦ λέγειν ἐξεῖναι, μὴ εἶναι δὲ ἐν ἡλίῳ
5 ταύτης ἀπαθεστέραν ἐν τάξει μᾶλλον καὶ οὐκ ἐν
ἀλλοιώσει μᾶλλον οὖσαν, οὐδὲ φρόνησιν ἔχειν
ἀμείνονα ἡμῶν τῶν ἄρτι γενομένων καὶ διὰ
τοσούτων κωλυομένων τῶν ἀπατώντων ἐπὶ τὴν
ἀλήθειαν ἐλθεῖν· οὐδὲ τὴν μὲν αὐτῶν ψυχὴν
ἀθάνατον καὶ θείαν λέγειν καὶ τὴν τῶν φαυλοτάτων
10 ἀνθρώπων, τὸν δὲ οὐρανὸν πάντα καὶ τὰ ἐκεῖ
ἄστρα μὴ τῆς ἀθανάτου κεκοινωνηκέναι ἐκ πολλῷ
καλλιόνων καὶ καθαρωτέρων ὄντα, ὁρῶντας ἐκεῖ
μὲν τὸ τεταγμένον καὶ εὔσχημον καὶ εὔτακτον καὶ
μάλιστα τὴν ἐνταῦθα περὶ γῆν ἀταξίαν αὐτοὺς
αἰτιωμένους· ὥσπερ τῆς ἀθανάτου ψυχῆς τὸν
15 χείρω τόπον ἐπίτηδες ἑλομένης, παραχωρῆσαι δὲ
τοῦ βελτίονος τῇ θνητῇ ψυχῇ ἑλομένης. Ἄλογος
δὲ καὶ ἡ παρεισαγωγὴ αὐτοῖς τῆς ἑτέρας ψυχῆς

[1] βελτίων Heigl, H-S²: βέλτιον codd.

the intelligible world and not only an image of it. Surely, what other fairer image of the intelligible world could there be ? For what other fire could be a better image of the intelligible fire than the fire here ? Or what other earth could be better than this, after the intelligible earth ? And what sphere could be more exact or more dignified or better ordered in its circuit [than the sphere of this universe] after the self-enclosed circle there of the intelligible universe ? And what other sun could there be which ranked after the intelligible sun and before this visible sun here ?

5. But really ! For these people who have a body like men have, and desire and griefs and passions, by no means to despise their own power but to say that *they* can grasp the intelligible, but that there is no power in the sun which is freer than this power of ours from affections and more ordered and more unchangeable, and that the sun has not a better understanding than we have, who have only just come to birth and are hindered by so many things that cheat us from coming to the truth ! And to say that *their* soul, and the soul of the meanest of men, is immortal and divine, but that the whole heaven and the stars there have no share given them in the immortal soul, though they are made of much fairer and purer material, though these people see the order there and the excellence of form and arrangement, and are particularly addicted to complaining about the disorder here around the earth ! As if the immortal soul had taken care to choose the worse place, and chosen to retire from the better in favour of the mortal soul ! Unreasonable, too, is their slipping in of this

ταύτης, ἣν ἐκ τῶν στοιχείων συνιστᾶσι· πῶς γὰρ
ἂν ζωὴν ἡντινοῦν ἔχοι ἡ ἐκ τῶν στοιχείων σύστασις;
20 Ἡ γὰρ τούτων κρᾶσις ἢ θερμὸν ἢ ψυχρὸν ἢ
μικτὸν ποιεῖ, ἢ ξηρὸν ἢ ὑγρὸν ἢ μῖγμα ἐκ τούτων.
Πῶς δὲ συνοχὴ τῶν τεσσάρων ὑστέρα γενομένη ἐξ
αὐτῶν; Ὅταν δὲ προστιθῶσι καὶ ἀντίληψιν αὐτῇ
καὶ βούλευσιν καὶ ἄλλα μυρία, τί ἄν τις εἴποι;
25 Ἀλλὰ οὐ τιμῶντες ταύτην τὴν δημιουργίαν οὐδὲ
τήνδε τὴν γῆν καινὴν αὐτοῖς γῆν φασι γεγονέναι,
εἰς ἣν δὴ ἐντεῦθεν ἀπελεύσονται· τοῦτο δὲ λόγον
εἶναι κόσμου. Καίτοι τί δεῖ αὐτοῖς ἐκεῖ γενέσθαι
ἐν παραδείγματι κόσμου, ὃν μισοῦσι; Πόθεν δὲ
τὸ παράδειγμα τοῦτο; Τοῦτο γὰρ κατ' αὐτοὺς
νενευκότος ἤδη πρὸς τὰ τῇδε τοῦ τὸ παράδειγμα
30 πεποιηκότος. Εἰ μὲν οὖν ἐν αὐτῷ τῷ ποιήσαντι
πολλὴ φροντὶς τοῦ κόσμου[1] μετὰ τὸν κόσμον τὸν
νοητὸν ὂν ἔχει ἄλλον ποιῆσαι—καὶ τί ἔδει;—καὶ
εἰ μὲν πρὸ τοῦ κόσμου, ἵνα τί; Ἵνα φυλάξωνται αἱ
ψυχαί. Πῶς οὖν; οὐκ ἐφυλάξαντο, ὥστε μάτην
ἐγένετο. Εἰ δὲ μετὰ τὸν κόσμον ἐκ τοῦ κόσμου
35 λαβὼν ἀποσυλήσας τῆς ὕλης τὸ εἶδος, ἦρκει ἡ

---

[1] κόσμον Kirchhoff, H-S: κόσμου codd.

---

[1] Cp. the Coptic Gnostic work edited by C. Schmidt (in
Koptisch-Gnostische Schriften I, Leipzig, 1905: ed. altera ed.
W. Till, Berlin 1954) and by C. A. Baynes (*A Coptic Gnostic
Treatise contained in the Codex Brucianus*, Cambridge, 1933).

other soul of theirs, which they compose of the elements. For how could the composition of the elements have any sort of life? For the mixture of the
elements makes hot or cold or a mixture of the two,
or dry or wet or a mixture of these. And how can the
soul be the principle which holds the four elements
together when it has come into being out of them
afterwards? But what can one say when they attribute to the soul compounded of the elements perception and deliberation and innumerable other
things as well? But they do not honour this creation or this earth, but say that a new earth [1] has come
into existence for them, to which, say they, they will
go away from this one: and that this is the rational
form of the universe. And yet why do they feel the
need to be there in the archetype of the universe
which they hate? And where did this archetype
come from? It came into existence according to
them, when its maker had already inclined towards
this world. Well, then, if there was in the maker
himself a great concern to make a universe after the
intelligible universe which he possesses—and what
need was there to do so?—and if it existed before
our universe, what did he make it for? To put the
souls on their guard. How could that be? They
were not on their guard, so there was no point in its
existence. But if he made it after this universe,
taking the form out of the universe and stripping it
off the matter, then their testing in this world would

The new earth is spoken of at p. 352, 6–12 Schmidt, p. 136
Baynes: Nicotheos, one of the alleged authors of spurious
Gnostic revelations mentioned by Porphyry in the *Life* (ch. 16)
appears in this Coptic Treatise.

πεῖρα ταῖς πειραθείσαις ψυχαῖς πρὸς τὸ φυλάξασθαι.
Εἰ δ᾽ ἐν ταῖς ψυχαῖς λαβεῖν ἀξιοῦσι τοῦ κόσμου
τὸ εἶδος, τί τὸ καινὸν τοῦ λόγου;

6. Τὰς δὲ ἄλλας ὑποστάσεις τί χρὴ λέγειν ἃς
εἰσάγουσι, παροικήσεις καὶ ἀντιτύπους καὶ μετα-
νοίας; Εἰ μὲν γὰρ ψυχῆς ταῦτα λέγουσι πάθη,
ὅταν ἐν μετανοίᾳ ᾖ, καὶ ἀντιτύπους, ὅταν οἷον
5 εἰκόνας τῶν ὄντων ὄντων, ἀλλὰ μὴ αὐτά πω τὰ ὄντα
θεωρῇ, καινολογούντων ἐστὶν εἰς σύστασιν τῆς
ἰδίας αἱρέσεως· ὡς γὰρ τῆς ἀρχαίας Ἑλληνικῆς
οὐχ ἁπτόμενοι ταῦτα σκευωροῦνται εἰδότων καὶ
σαφῶς τῶν Ἑλλήνων ἀτύφως λεγόντων ἀναβάσεις
ἐκ τοῦ σπηλαίου καὶ κατὰ βραχὺ εἰς θέαν ἀληθεσ-
10 τέραν μᾶλλον καὶ μᾶλλον προιούσας. Ὅλως γὰρ
τὰ μὲν αὐτοῖς παρὰ τοῦ Πλάτωνος εἴληπται, τὰ
δέ, ὅσα καινοτομοῦσιν, ἵνα ἰδίαν φιλοσοφίαν
θῶνται, ταῦτα ἔξω τῆς ἀληθείας εὕρηται. Ἐπεὶ
καὶ αἱ δίκαι καὶ οἱ ποταμοὶ οἱ ἐν Ἅιδου καὶ αἱ
μετενσωματώσεις ἐκεῖθεν. Καὶ ἐπὶ τῶν νοητῶν
15 δὲ πλῆθος ποιῆσαι, τὸ ὂν καὶ τὸν νοῦν καὶ τὸν
δημιουργὸν ἄλλον καὶ τὴν ψυχήν, ἐκ τῶν ἐν τῷ
Τιμαίῳ λεχθέντων εἴληπται· εἰπόντος γὰρ αὐτοῦ
"ᾗπερ οὖν νοῦς ἐνούσας ἰδέας ἐν τῷ ὅ ἐστι

---

[1] παροίκησις, μετάνοια, and ἀντίτυποι appear in the Coptic
Gnostic treatise referred to in the note on ch. 5. p. 361, 35–
p. 362, 3 Schmidt: p. 180 Baynes: on the extremely vague
and fluctuating Gnostic meaning of these terms see the discussion in Entretiens Hardt V p. 181–2 (ἀντίτυποι) and p.
189–90 (μετάνοια and παροίκησις).

suffice to put on their guard the souls which had been
tested in it. But if they claim to have received the
form of the universe in their souls, what does this
new way of speaking mean?

6. And what ought one to say of the other beings
they introduce, their " Exiles " and " Impressions "
and " Repentings "? [1] For if they say that these
are affections of the soul, when it has changed its
purpose, and " Impressions " when it is contemplat-
ing, in a way, images of realities and not the realities
themselves, then these are the terms of people in-
venting a new jargon to recommend their own school:
they contrive this meretricious language as if they
had no connection with the ancient Hellenic school,
though the Hellenes knew all this and knew it clearly,
and spoke without delusive pomposity of ascents from
the cave and advancing gradually closer and closer
to a truer vision. [2] Generally speaking, some of these
peoples' doctrines have been taken from Plato, but
others, all the new ideas they have brought in to
establish a philosophy of their own, are things they
have found outside the truth. For the judgements
too, and the rivers in Hades and the reincarnations
come from Plato. [3] And the making a plurality in
the intelligible world, Being, and Intellect, and the
Maker different from Intellect, and Soul, is taken
from the words in the *Timaeus*: for Plato says,
" The maker of this universe thought that it should

[2] This, of course, refers to the simile of the Cave in Plato
Republic VII. 514A ff.

[3] Cp. *Phaedo* 111D ff.; the mention of the "rivers in Hades"
suggests that this is the one of Plato's myths of the after-life
which Plotinus had particularly in mind here.

ζῷον καθορᾷ, τοσαύτας καὶ ὁ τόδε ποιῶν τὸ
πᾶν διενοήθη σχεῖν." Οἱ δὲ οὐ συνέντες τὸν
20 μὲν ἔλαβον ἐν ἡσυχίᾳ ἔχοντα ἐν αὑτῷ πάντα τὰ
ὄντα, τὸν δὲ νοῦν ἕτερον παρ' αὐτὸν θεωροῦντα,
τὸν δὲ διανοούμενον—πολλάκις δὲ αὐτοῖς ἀντὶ τοῦ
διανοουμένου ψυχή ἐστιν ἡ δημιουργοῦσα—καὶ κατὰ
Πλάτωνα τοῦτον οἴονται εἶναι τὸν δημιουργὸν
ἀφεστηκότες τοῦ εἰδέναι τίς ὁ δημιουργός. Καὶ
25 ὅλως τὸν τρόπον τῆς δημιουργίας καὶ ἄλλα πολλὰ
καταψεύδονται αὐτοῦ καὶ πρὸς τὸ χεῖρον ἕλκουσι
τὰς δόξας τοῦ ἀνδρὸς ὡς αὐτοὶ μὲν τὴν νοητὴν
φύσιν κατανενοηκότες, ἐκείνου δὲ καὶ τῶν ἄλλων
τῶν μακαρίων ἀνδρῶν μή. Καὶ πλῆθος νοητῶν
ὀνομάζοντες τὸ ἀκριβὲς ἐξευρηκέναι δόξειν οἴονται
30 αὐτῷ τῷ πλήθει τὴν νοητὴν φύσιν τῇ αἰσθητικῇ
καὶ ἐλάττονι εἰς ὁμοιότητα ἄγοντες, δέον ἐκεῖ τὸ
ὡς ὅτι μάλιστα ὀλίγον εἰς ἀριθμὸν διώκειν καὶ
τῷ μετὰ τὸ πρῶτον τὰ πάντα ἀποδιδόντας ἀπηλ-
λάχθαι, ἐκείνου τῶν πάντων ὄντος καὶ νοῦ τοῦ
πρώτου καὶ οὐσίας καὶ ὅσα ἄλλα καλὰ μετὰ τὴν
35 πρώτην φύσιν. Ψυχῆς δὲ εἶδος τρίτον· διαφορὰς
δὲ ψυχῶν ἐν πάθεσιν ἢ ἐν φύσει ἰχνεύειν μηδὲν
τοὺς θείους ἄνδρας διασύροντας, ἀλλ' εὐμενῶς
δεχομένους τὰ ἐκείνων ὡς παλαιοτέρων καὶ ἃ
καλῶς λέγουσι παρ' ἐκείνων λαβόντας, ψυχῆς

---

[1] *Timaeus* 39E 7–9.

[2] Again, it looks as if Plotinus was thinking of " Gnosticis-
ing " Platonists, who derived their ideas to some extent from
Numenius, at least as much as of Gnostics properly so called;
cp. the second note on ch. 1.

contain all the forms that intelligence discerns contained in the Living Being that truly is." [1]   But they did not understand, and took it to mean that there is one mind which contains in it in repose all realities, and another mind different from it which contemplates them, and another which plans—but often they have soul as the maker instead of the planning mind—and they think that this is the maker according to Plato, being a long way from knowing who the maker is.[2]   And in general they falsify Plato's account of the manner of the making, and a great deal else, and degrade the great man's teachings as if they had understood the intelligible nature, but he and the other blessed philosophers had not.[3] And by giving names to a multitude of intelligible realities they think they will appear to have discovered the exact truth, though by this very multiplicity they bring the intelligible nature into the likeness of the sense-world, the inferior world, when one ought there in the intelligible to aim at the smallest possible number, and attribute everything to the reality which comes after the First and so be quit of multiplicity, since it is all things and the first intellect and substance and all the other excellences that come after the first nature.   The form of soul should come third; and they should trace the differences of souls in affections or in nature, without in any way disparaging those godlike men, but receiving their teaching with a good grace since it is the teaching of more ancient authorities and they themselves have received what is good in what they

[3] Cp. what Porphyry says about the Gnostics in *Life* ch. 16, 8–9.

ἀθανασίαν, νοητὸν κόσμον, θεὸν τὸν πρῶτον, τὸ
40 τὴν ψυχὴν δεῖν φεύγειν τὴν πρὸς τὸ σῶμα ὁμιλίαν,
τὸν χωρισμὸν τὸν ἀπ' αὐτοῦ, τὸ ἐκ γενέσεως
φεύγειν εἰς οὐσίαν· ταῦτα γὰρ κείμενα παρὰ τῷ
Πλάτωνι σαφῶς οὑτωσὶ λέγοντες καλῶς ποιοῦσιν.
Οἷς θέλουσι διαφωνεῖν φθόνος οὐδεὶς λεγόντων
οὐδ' ἐν τῷ τοὺς Ἕλληνας διασύρειν καὶ ὑβρίζειν
45 τὰ αὑτῶν ἐν συστάσει παρὰ τοῖς ἀκούουσι ποιεῖν,
ἀλλ' αὐτὰ παρ' αὑτῶν δεικνύναι ὀρθῶς ἔχοντα,
ὅσα ἴδια αὐτοῖς ἔδοξε παρὰ τὴν ἐκείνων δόξαν
λέγειν, εὐμενῶς καὶ φιλοσόφως αὐτὰς τὰς δόξας
τιθέντας αὑτῶν καὶ οἷς ἐναντιοῦνται δικαίως, πρὸς
50 τὸ ἀληθὲς βλέποντας, οὐ τὴν εὐδοκίμησιν θηρωμέ-
νους ἐκ τοῦ [πρὸς] ἄνδρας κεκριμένους ἐκ παλαιοῦ
οὐ παρὰ φαύλων ἀνδρῶν ἀγαθοὺς εἶναι ψέγειν,
λέγοντας ἑαυτοὺς ἐκείνων ἀμείνους εἶναι. Ἐπεὶ
τά γε εἰρημένα τοῖς παλαιοῖς περὶ τῶν νοητῶν
55 πολλῷ ἀμείνω καὶ πεπαιδευμένως εἴρηται καὶ
τοῖς μὴ ἐξαπατωμένοις τὴν ἐπιθέουσαν εἰς ἀνθρώπους ἀπάτην ῥᾳδίως γνωσθήσεται τάδ' [1] ὕστερον
τούτοις παρ' ἐκείνων ληφθέντα, προσθήκας δέ
τινας οὐδὲν προσηκούσας εἰληφότα, ἔν γε [2] οἷς
ἐναντιοῦσθαι θέλουσι γενέσεις καὶ φθορὰς εἰσάγοντες παντελεῖς καὶ μεμφόμενοι τῷδε τῷ παντὶ καὶ
60 τὴν πρὸς τὸ σῶμα κοινωνίαν τῇ ψυχῇ αἰτιώμενοι
καὶ τὸν διοικοῦντα τόδε τὸ πᾶν ψέγοντες καὶ εἰς

[1] γνωσθήσεται τάδ' nunc Henry et Schwyzer: γνωσθήσεται· τὰ
δ' H-S.
[2] ἔν γε Müller et nunc Henry et Schwyzer: ἔν τε wxQ:
ὥστε y.

say from them, the immortality of the soul, the intelligible universe, the first god, the necessity for the soul to shun fellowship with the body, the separation from the body, the escape from becoming to being. For these doctrines are there in Plato, and when they state them clearly in this way they do well. If they wish to disagree on these points, there is no unfair hostility in saying to them that they should not recommend their own opinions to their audience by ridiculing and insulting the Greeks but that they should show the correctness on their own merits of all the points of doctrine which are peculiar to them and differ from the views of the Greeks, stating their real opinions courteously, as befits philosophers, and fairly on the points where they are opposed, looking to the truth and not hunting fame by censuring men who have been judged good from ancient times by men of worth and saying that they themselves are better than the Greeks. For what was said by the ancients about the intelligible world is far better, and is put in a way appropriate to educated men, and it will be easily recognised by those who are not utterly deceived by the delusion that is rushing upon men that these teachings have been taken by the Gnostics later from the ancients, but have acquired some in no way appropriate additions; on the points, at any rate, on which they wish to oppose the ancient teachings they introduce all sorts of comings into being and passings away, and disapprove of this universe, and blame the soul for its association with the body, and censure the director of this universe, and identify its maker with the soul, and attribute to this universal soul the same

247

ταὐτὸν ἄγοντες τὸν δημιουργὸν τῇ ψυχῇ καὶ τὰ
αὐτὰ πάθη διδόντες, ἅπερ καὶ τοῖς ἐν μέρει.

7. Ὅτι μὲν οὖν οὔτε ἤρξατο οὔτε παύσεται,
ἀλλ᾽ ἔστιν ἀεὶ καὶ ὅδε ὁ κόσμος, ἕως ἂν ἐκεῖνα ᾖ,
εἴρηται. Τὴν δὲ πρὸς τὸ σῶμα τῇ ψυχῇ κοινωνίαν
τῇ ἡμετέρᾳ πρὸ αὐτῶν εἴρηται ὡς οὐκ ἄμεινον τῇ
5 ψυχῇ· τὸ δὲ ἀπὸ τῆς ἡμετέρας καὶ τὴν τοῦ παντὸς
λαμβάνειν ὅμοιον, ὡς εἴ τις τὸ τῶν χυτρέων ἢ
χαλκέων λαβὼν γένος ἐν πόλει εὖ οἰκουμένῃ τὴν
ἅπασαν ψέγοι. Δεῖ δὲ τὰς διαφορὰς λαμβάνειν
τὰς τῆς ὅλης ὅπως διοικεῖ, ὅτι μὴ ὁ αὐτὸς τρόπος
μηδ᾽ ἐνδεδεμένη. Πρὸς γὰρ αὖ ταῖς ἄλλαις
10 διαφοραῖς, αἳ μυρίαι εἴρηνται ἐν ἄλλοις, κἀκεῖνο
ἐνθυμεῖσθαι ἔδει ὅτι ἡμεῖς μὲν ὑπὸ τοῦ σώματος
δεδέμεθα ἤδη δεσμοῦ γεγενημένου. Ἐν γὰρ τῇ
πάσῃ ψυχῇ ἡ τοῦ σώματος φύσις δεδεμένη ἤδη
συνδεῖ ὃ ἂν περιλάβῃ· αὐτὴ δὲ ἡ τοῦ παντὸς
ψυχὴ οὐκ ἂν δέοιτο ὑπὸ τῶν ὑπ᾽ αὐτῆς δεδεμένων·
15 ἄρχει γὰρ ἐκείνη. Διὸ καὶ ἀπαθὴς πρὸς αὐτῶν,
ἡμεῖς δὲ τούτων οὐ κύριοι· τὸ δ᾽ ὅσον αὐτῆς πρὸς
τὸ θεῖον τὸ ὑπεράνω ἀκέραιον μένει καὶ οὐκ
ἐμποδίζεται, ὅσον δὲ αὐτῆς δίδωσι τῷ σώματι
ζωὴν οὐδὲν παρ᾽ αὐτοῦ προσλαμβάνει. Ὅλως γὰρ
τὸ μὲν ἄλλου πάθημα τὸ ἐν αὐτῷ ἐξ ἀνάγκης
20 δέχεται, ὃ δ᾽ αὐτὸ ἐκείνῳ οὐκέτι τὸ αὐτοῦ δίδωσιν
οἰκείαν ζωὴν ἔχοντι· οἷον εἰ ἐγκεντρισθέν τι εἴη
ἐν ἄλλῳ, παθόντος μὲν τοῦ ἐν ᾧ συμπέπονθεν,
αὐτὸ δὲ ξηρανθὲν εἴασεν ἐκεῖνο τὴν αὐτοῦ ζωὴν

affections as those which the souls in parts of the universe have.

7. It has been said already that this universe did not begin and will not come to an end but exists always as long as the intelligible realities exist. And it has been said before the Gnostics that the association of our soul with body is not to the advantage of the soul. But to apply conclusions drawn from our soul to the Soul of the All is as if somebody were to take the tribe of potters or smiths in a well-ordered city and make them a reason for blaming the whole. But one must take into account the differences between the universal soul and ours, in its management of body; it does not direct it in the same way, and is not bound to it. For, as well as all the other differences (of which we have mentioned a vast number elsewhere) this ought to have been taken into consideration, that we are bound by a body which has already become a bond. For the nature of body is already bound in the universal soul and binds whatever it grasps; but the Soul of the All could not be bound by the things it binds itself: for it is the ruler. Therefore it is unaffected by them, but we are not their masters; but that part of the universal which is directed to the divine above it remains pure, and is not hindered, but that part which gives life to the body takes no addition from it. For in general anything which is in something else is affected by what happens to it, but it does not itself give of its own to that other which has its own life. For instance, if a shoot of one tree is grafted on another, when anything happens to the stock the shoot is affected with it, but if the shoot is withered

ἔχειν. Ἐπεὶ οὐδ' ἀποσβεννυμένου τοῦ ἐν σοὶ
πυρὸς τὸ ὅλον πῦρ ἀπέσβη· ἐπεὶ οὐδ' εἰ τὸ πᾶν
25 πῦρ ἀπόλοιτο, πάθοι ἄν τι ἡ ψυχὴ ἡ ἐκεῖ, ἀλλ' ἡ τοῦ
σώματος σύστασις, καὶ εἰ οἷόν τε εἴη διὰ τῶν
λοιπῶν κόσμον τινὰ εἶναι, οὐδὲν ἂν μέλοι τῇ
ψυχῇ τῇ ἐκεῖ. Ἐπεὶ οὐδὲ ἡ σύστασις ὁμοίως τῷ
παντὶ καὶ ζῴῳ ἑκάστῳ· ἀλλ' ἐκεῖ οἷον ἐπιθεῖ
κελεύσασα μένειν, ἐνταῦθα δὲ ὡς ὑπεκφεύγοντα
30 εἰς τὴν τάξιν τὴν ἑαυτῶν δέδεται δεσμῷ δευτέρῳ·
ἐκεῖ δὲ οὐκ ἔχει ὅπου φύγῃ. Οὔτε οὖν ἐντὸς δεῖ
κατέχειν οὔτε ἔξωθεν πιέζουσαν εἰς τὸ εἴσω ὠθεῖν,
ἀλλ' ὅπου ἠθέλησεν ἐξ ἀρχῆς αὐτῆς ἡ φύσις μένει.
Ἐὰν δέ πού τι αὐτῶν κατὰ φύσιν κινηθῇ, οἷς οὐκ
ἔστι κατὰ φύσιν, ταῦτα πάσχει, αὐτὰ δὲ καλῶς
35 φέρεται ὡς τοῦ ὅλου· τὰ δὲ φθείρεται οὐ δυνάμενα
τὴν τοῦ ὅλου τάξιν φέρειν, οἷον εἰ χοροῦ μεγάλου
ἐν τάξει φερομένου ἐν μέσῃ τῇ πορείᾳ αὐτοῦ
χελώνη ληφθεῖσα πατοῖτο οὐ δυνηθεῖσα φυγεῖν τὴν
τάξιν τοῦ χοροῦ· εἰ μέντοι μετ' ἐκείνης τάξειεν
ἑαυτήν, οὐδὲν ἂν ὑπὸ τούτων οὐδ' αὐτὴ πάθοι.

8. Τὸ δὲ διὰ τί ἐποίησε κόσμον ταὐτὸν τῷ διὰ
τί ἔστι ψυχὴ καὶ διὰ τί ὁ δημιουργὸς ἐποίησεν.
Ὃ πρῶτον μὲν ἀρχὴν λαμβανόντων ἐστὶ τοῦ ἀεί·

up it leaves the stock to live its own life. So also, if the fire in you is quenched, the universal fire is not quenched as well: since even if the universal fire were destroyed, the soul there in the universe would not be in any way affected, but only the structure of its body, and, provided that the other elements made it possible for some sort of universe to exist, it would not in any way concern the soul there. For the structure is not the same in the All and in each living creature; but in the All soul, so to speak, runs over the surface ordering things to stay in their places, but in the individual the parts, as if they were trying to escape, are bound into their proper places by a second bond; but in the universe there is nowhere for them to escape to. Therefore soul does not have to hold them together within, or press upon them from outside and push them inwards, but its nature remains where it wished to be from the beginning. But if any of the parts of the universe is moved according to its nature, the parts with whose nature the movement is not in accord suffer, but those which are moved go on well, as parts of the whole; but the others are destroyed because they are not able to endure the order of the whole; as if when a great company of dancers was moving in order a tortoise was caught in the middle of its advance and trampled because it was not able to get out of the way of the ordered movement of the dancers: yet if it had ranged itself with that movement, even it would have taken no harm from them.

8. To ask why Soul made the universe is like asking why there is a soul and why the Maker makes. First, it is the question of people who assume a

ἔπειτα οἴονται τραπέντα ἔκ τινος εἴς τι καὶ
5 μεταβάλλοντα αἴτιον τῆς δημιουργίας γεγονέναι.
Διδακτέον οὖν αὐτούς, εἰ εὐγνωμόνως ἀνέχοιντο,
τίς ἡ φύσις τούτων, ὡς αὐτοὺς παύσασθαι τῆς εἰς
τὰ τίμια λοιδορίας ἣν εὐχερῶς ποιοῦνται ἀντὶ
πολλῆς προσηκόντως ἂν γενομένης εὐλαβείας.
Ἐπεὶ οὐδὲ τοῦ παντὸς τὴν διοίκησιν ὀρθῶς ἄν
10 τις μέμψαιτο πρῶτον μὲν ἐνδεικνυμένην τῆς νοητῆς
φύσεως τὸ μέγεθος. Εἰ γὰρ οὕτως εἰς τὸ ζῆν
παρελήλυθεν, ὡς μὴ ζωὴν ἀδιάρθρωτον ἔχειν—
ὁποῖα τὰ σμικρότερα τῶν ἐν αὐτῷ, ἃ τῇ πολλῇ
ζωῇ τῇ ἐν αὐτῷ ἀεὶ νύκτωρ καὶ μεθ' ἡμέραν
γεννᾶται—ἀλλ' ἔστι συνεχὴς καὶ ἐναργὴς καὶ
15 πολλὴ καὶ πανταχοῦ ζωὴ σοφίαν ἀμήχανον
ἐνδεικνυμένη, πῶς οὐκ ἄν τις ἄγαλμα ἐναργὲς
καὶ καλὸν τῶν νοητῶν θεῶν εἴποι; Εἰ δὲ
μιμούμενον μή ἐστιν ἐκεῖνο, αὐτὸ τοῦτο κατὰ
φύσιν ἔχει· οὐ γὰρ ἦν ἔτι μιμούμενον. Τὸ δὲ
ἀνομοίως μεμιμῆσθαι ψεῦδος· οὐδὲν γὰρ παραλέ-
20 λειπται ὧν οἷόν τε ἦν καλὴν εἰκόνα φυσικὴν ἔχειν.
Ἀναγκαῖον μὲν γὰρ ἦν εἶναι οὐκ ἐκ διανοίας καὶ
ἐπιτεχνήσεως τὸ μίμημα· οὐ γὰρ οἷόν τε ἦν
ἔσχατον τὸ νοητὸν εἶναι. Εἶναι γὰρ αὐτοῦ
ἐνέργειαν ἔδει διττήν, τὴν μὲν ἐν ἑαυτῷ, τὴν δὲ εἰς
ἄλλο. Ἔδει οὖν εἶναί τι μετ' αὐτό· ἐκείνου γὰρ
25 μόνου οὐδέν ἐστιν ἔτι πρὸς τὸ κάτω, ὃ τῶν πάντων
ἀδυνατώτατόν ἐστι. Δύναμις δὲ θαυμαστὴ ἐκεῖ

---

[1] Cp. Plato *Timaeus* 37C6–7.
[2] Cp. ch. 3 for this law of necessary procession. Plotinus

252

beginning of that which always is: then they think that the cause of the making was a being who turned from one thing to another and changed. So they must be taught, if only they would endure the teaching with a good will, what is the nature of these beings, so as to stop them from abusing what are worthy of all honour, which they frivolously do instead of showing the reverent care which would be becoming. For it is not right to disapprove of the management of the All, first of all because it manifests the greatness of the intelligible nature. For if it has come into life in such a way that its life is not a disjointed one—like the smaller things in it which in its fullness of life it produces continually night and day—but coherent and clear and great and everywhere life, manifesting infinite wisdom, how should one not call it a clear and noble image of the intelligible gods?[1] If, being an image, it is not that intelligible world, this is precisely what is natural to it; if it was the intelligible world, it would not be an image of it. But it is false to say that the image is unlike the original; for nothing has been left out which it was possible for a fine natural image to have. The image has to exist, necessarily, not as the result of thought and contrivance;[2] the intelligible could not be the last, for it had to have a double activity, one in itself and one directed to something else. There had, then, to be something after it, for only that which is the most powerless of all things has nothing below it. But There a

always insists that the eternal production of the universe is a unitary spontaneous act without any previous planning: cp. V. 8. 7.

θεῖ· ὥστε καὶ εἰργάσατο. Εἰ μὲν δὴ ἄλλος
κόσμος ἔστι τούτου ἀμείνων, τίς οὗτος; Εἰ δὲ
ἀνάγκη εἶναι, ἄλλος δὲ οὐκ ἔστιν, οὗτός ἐστιν ὁ
τὸ μίμημα ἀποσῴζων ἐκείνου. Γῆ μὲν δὴ πᾶσα
30 ζῴων ποικίλων πλήρης καὶ ἀθανάτων καὶ μέχρις
οὐρανοῦ μεστὰ πάντα· ἄστρα δὲ τά τε ἐν ταῖς
ὑποκάτω σφαίραις τά τε ἐν τῷ ἀνωτάτω διὰ τί
οὐ θεοὶ ἐν τάξει φερόμενα καὶ κόσμῳ περιόντα;
Διὰ τί γὰρ οὐκ ἀρετὴν ἕξουσιν ἢ τί κώλυμα πρὸς
κτῆσιν ἀρετῆς αὐτοῖς; Οὐ γὰρ δὴ ταῦτά ἐστιν
35 ἐκεῖ, ἅπερ τοὺς ἐνταῦθα ποιεῖ κακούς, οὐδ' ἡ τοῦ
σώματος κακία ἐνοχλουμένη καὶ ἐνοχλοῦσα. Διὰ
τί δὲ οὐ συνιᾶσιν ἐπὶ σχολῆς ἀεὶ καὶ ἐν νῷ λαμβά-
νουσι τὸν θεὸν καὶ τοὺς ἄλλους τοὺς νοητοὺς θεούς,
ἀλλ' ἡμῖν σοφία βελτίων ἔσται τῶν ἐκεῖ; Ταῦτα
τίς ἂν μὴ ἔκφρων γεγενημένος ἀνάσχοιτο; Ἐπεὶ
40 καὶ αἱ ψυχαὶ εἰ μὲν βιασθεῖσαι ὑπὸ τῆς τοῦ παντὸς
ψυχῆς ἦλθον, πῶς βελτίους αἱ βιασθεῖσαι; Ἐν
γὰρ ψυχαῖς τὸ κρατῆσαν κρεῖττον. Εἰ δ' ἑκοῦσαι,
τί μέμφεσθε εἰς ὃν ἑκόντες ἤλθετε διδόντος καὶ
ἀπαλλάττεσθαι, εἴ τις μὴ ἀρέσκοιτο; Εἰ δὲ δὴ
καὶ τοιοῦτόν ἐστι τόδε τὸ πᾶν, ὡς ἐξεῖναι ἐν αὐτῷ
45 καὶ σοφίαν ἔχειν καὶ ἐνταῦθα ὄντας βιοῦν κατ'
ἐκεῖνα, πῶς οὐ μαρτυρεῖ ἐξηρτῆσθαι τῶν ἐκεῖ;

---

[1] Plotinus maintains that the celestial bodies of the astral
gods (the visible heavenly bodies), though material, are altogether superior to our earthly bodies, being everlasting,

wonderful power runs, and so besides its inward activity it produces. If there is another universe better than this one, then what is this one? But if there must be a universe which preserves the image of the intelligible world, and there is no other, then this is that universe. Now certainly the whole earth is full of living creatures and immortal beings, and everything up to the sky is full of them: why, then are not the stars, both those in the lower spheres and those in the highest, gods moving in order, circling in well-arranged beauty? Why should they not possess virtue? What hindrance prevents them from acquiring it? The causes are not present there which make people bad here below, and there is no badness of body, disturbed and disturbing.[1] And why should they not have understanding, in their everlasting peace, and grasp in their intellect God and the intelligible gods? Shall our wisdom be greater than that of the gods there in the sky? Who, if he has not gone out of his mind, could tolerate the idea? Since, again, if the souls here came under compulsion by the Soul of the All, how are the souls under compulsion better? For among souls the dominant is the better. But if the souls came willingly, why do you blame the universe into which you came of your own free will, when it gives you leave, too, to get out of it, if any of you dislike it? But if this All is of such a kind that it is possible to have wisdom in it and to live according to that higher world when we are here, how does it not bear witness that it depends on the realities There?

impassible and no obstacles to the activity of soul: cp. II. 1 and IV. 4. 42. 24–30.

9. Πλούτους δὲ καὶ πενίας εἴ τις μέμφοιτο καὶ
τὸ οὐκ ἴσον ἐν τοῖς τοιούτοις ἅπασι, πρῶτον μὲν
ἀγνοεῖ, ὡς ὁ σπουδαῖος ἐν τούτοις τὸ ἴσον οὐ
ζητεῖ, οὐδέ τι νομίζει τοὺς πολλὰ κεκτημένους
5 πλέον ἔχειν, οὐδὲ τοὺς δυναστεύοντας τῶν ἰδιωτῶν,
ἀλλὰ τὴν τοιαύτην σπουδὴν ἄλλους ἐᾷ ἔχειν, καὶ
καταμεμάθηκεν ὡς διττὸς ὁ ἐνθάδε βίος, ὁ μὲν
τοῖς σπουδαίοις, ὁ δὲ τοῖς πολλοῖς τῶν ἀνθρώπων,
τοῖς μὲν σπουδαίοις πρὸς τὸ ἀκρότατον καὶ τὸ
ἄνω, τοῖς δὲ ἀνθρωπικωτέροις διττὸς αὖ ὢν ὁ μὲν
10 μεμνημένος ἀρετῆς μετίσχει ἀγαθοῦ τινος, ὁ δὲ
φαῦλος ὄχλος οἷον χειροτέχνης τῶν πρὸς ἀνάγκην
τοῖς ἐπιεικεστέροις. Εἰ δὲ φονεύει τις ἢ ἥττᾶται
τῶν ἡδονῶν ὑπὸ ἀδυναμίας, τί θαυμαστὸν καὶ
ἁμαρτίας εἶναι οὐ νῷ, ἀλλὰ ψυχαῖς ὥσπερ παισὶν
ἀνήβοις; Εἰ δὲ γυμνάσιον εἴη νικώντων καὶ
15 ἡττωμένων, πῶς οὐ καὶ ταύτῃ καλῶς ἔχει; Εἰ
δ᾽ ἀδικεῖ, τί δεινὸν τῷ ἀθανάτῳ; Καὶ εἰ φονεύει,
ἔχεις ὃ θέλεις. Εἰ δὲ ἤδη μέμφῃ, πολιτεύεσθαι
ἀνάγκην οὐκ ἔχεις. Ὁμολογεῖται δὲ καὶ δίκας
εἶναι ἐνθάδε καὶ κολάσεις. Πῶς οὖν ὀρθῶς ἔχει
μέμφεσθαι πόλει διδούσῃ ἑκάστῳ τὴν ἀξίαν; Οὗ
20 καὶ ἀρετὴ τετίμηται, καὶ κακία τὴν προσήκουσαν
ἀτιμίαν ἔχει, καὶ θεῶν οὐ μόνον ἀγάλματα, ἀλλὰ

---

[1] Cp. III. 2, [47] 8 and 15.

9. But if anyone objects to wealth and poverty and the fact that all have not an equal share in things of this kind, first, he is ignorant that the good and wise man does not look for equality in these things, and does not think that people who have acquired a great deal of them have any kind of advantage, or that those who hold power have the advantage over private persons; he leaves concern of this kind to others. He has learnt that there are two kinds of life here below, one for the good and wise and one for the mass of men, that for the good and wise being directed to the highest point and the upper region, and that for the more human sort being of two kinds again; one is mindful of virtue and has a share in some sort of good, but the common crowd is there, so to speak, to do manual work to provide for the necessities of the better sort. But if anyone commits murder, or is worsted by his passions because of his incapacity, why is it surprising that there should be sins, not in intellect but in souls that are like children which have not grown up? And if the world is like a sports-ground, where some win and others lose, what is there wrong with that?[1] If you are wronged, what is there dreadful in that to an immortal? And even if you are murdered, you have what you want. But if you have come by now to dislike the world, you are not compelled to remain a citizen of it. It is agreed that there are judgements and punishments here. How, then, is it possible rightly to disapprove of a city which gives each man his deserts? In this city [of the world] virtue is honoured and vice has its appropriate dishonour, and not merely the images of gods but gods

257

καὶ αὐτοὶ ἄνωθεν ἐφορῶντες, οἳ ῥῃδίως αἰτίας,
φησίν, ἀποφεύξονται πρὸς ἀνθρώπων, πάντα
ἄγοντες τάξει ἐξ ἀρχῆς εἰς τέλος μοῖραν ἑκάστῳ
τὴν προσήκουσαν διδόντες κατὰ ἀμοιβὰς βίων τοῖς
25 προϋπηργμένοις ἀκόλουθον· ἦν ὁ ἀγνοῶν προπετέ-
στερος ἀνθρώπων περὶ πραγμάτων θείων ἀγροικι-
ζόμενος. Ἀλλὰ χρὴ ὡς ἄριστον μὲν αὐτὸν
πειρᾶσθαι γίνεσθαι, μὴ μόνον δὲ αὐτὸν νομίζειν
ἄριστον δύνασθαι γενέσθαι—οὕτω γὰρ οὔπω ἄριστος
30 —ἀλλὰ καὶ ἀνθρώπους ἄλλους ἀρίστους, ἔτι καὶ
δαίμονας ἀγαθοὺς εἶναι, πολὺ δὲ μᾶλλον θεοὺς
τούς τε ἐν τῷδε ὄντας κἀκεῖ βλέποντας, πάντων
δὲ μάλιστα τὸν ἡγεμόνα τοῦδε τοῦ παντός, ψυχὴν
μακαριωτάτην· ἐντεῦθεν δὲ ἤδη καὶ τοὺς νοητοὺς
35 ὑμνεῖν θεούς, ἐφ' ἅπασι δὲ ἤδη τὸν μέγαν τὸν
ἐκεῖ βασιλέα καὶ ἐν τῷ πλήθει μάλιστα τῶν θεῶν
τὸ μέγα αὐτοῦ ἐνδεικνυμένους· οὐ γὰρ τὸ συστεῖλαι
εἰς ἕν, ἀλλὰ τὸ δεῖξαι πολὺ τὸ θεῖον, ὅσον ἔδειξεν
αὐτός, τοῦτό ἐστι δύναμιν θεοῦ εἰδότων, ὅταν
μένων ὅς ἐστι πολλοὺς ποιῇ πάντας εἰς αὐτὸν
ἀνηρτημένους καὶ δι' ἐκεῖνον καὶ παρ' ἐκείνου
40 ὄντας. Καὶ ὁ κόσμος δὲ ὅδε δι' ἐκεῖνόν ἐστι
κἀκεῖ βλέπει, καὶ πᾶς καὶ θεῶν ἕκαστος καὶ τὰ
ἐκείνου προφητεύει ἀνθρώποις καὶ χρῶσιν ἃ
ἐκείνοις φίλα. Εἰ δὲ μὴ τοῦτό εἰσιν, ὃ ἐκεῖνός
ἐστιν, αὐτὸ τοῦτο κατὰ φύσιν ἔχει. Εἰ δ' ὑπερορᾶν

---

[1] Plotinus may be thinking here of *Epinomis* 983E6–984A2,
where the heavenly bodies are said to be either gods themselves
or images made by the gods themselves.

themselves look down upon us from above,[1] who, as
the saying goes, will easily acquit themselves of
men's blame, leading all things in order from beginning to end, giving to each his fitting portion in
changes of lives as a consequence of the deeds he
did in previous existences; he who ignores this is one
of the rasher sort of humans who deals boorishly with
divine things.

But one ought to try to become as good as possible oneself, but not to think that only oneself can
become perfectly good—for if one thinks this one is
not yet perfectly good. One must rather think that
there are other perfectly good men, and good spirits
as well, and, still more, the gods who are in this
world and look to the other, and, most of all, the
ruler of this universe, the most blessed Soul. Then
at this point one should go on to praise the intelligible gods, and then, above all, the great king of
that other world, most especially by displaying his
greatness in the multitude of the gods. It is not
contracting the divine into one but showing it in that
multiplicity in which God himself has shown it,
which is proper to those who know the power of God,
inasmuch as, abiding who he is, he makes many
gods, all depending upon himself and existing
through him and from him. And this universe
exists through him and looks to him, the whole of it
and each and every one of the gods in it, and it
reveals what is his to men, and it and the gods in it
declare in their oracles what is pleasing to the intelligible gods. But if they are not what that
supreme God is, this in itself is according to the
nature of things. But if you want to despise them,

259

θέλεις καὶ σεμνύνεις σαυτὸν ὡς οὐ χείρων, πρῶτον
45 μέν, ὅσῳ τις ἄριστος, πρὸς πάντας εὐμενῶς ἔχει
καὶ πρὸς ἀνθρώπους· ἔπειτα σεμνὸν δεῖ εἰς μέτρον
μετὰ οὐκ ἀγροικίας, ἐπὶ τοσοῦτον ἰόντα ἐφ' ὅσον
ἡ φύσις δύναται ἡμῶν, ἀνιέναι, τοῖς δ' ἄλλοις
νομίζειν εἶναι χώραν παρὰ τῷ θεῷ καὶ μὴ αὐτὸν
μόνον μετ' ἐκεῖνον τάξαντα ὥσπερ ὀνείρασι
50 πέτεσθαι ἀποστεροῦντα ἑαυτὸν καὶ ὅσον ἐστὶ
δυνατὸν ψυχῇ ἀνθρώπου θεῷ γενέσθαι· δύναται
δὲ εἰς ὅσον νοῦς ἄγει· τὸ δ' ὑπὲρ νοῦν ἤδη ἐστὶν
ἔξω νοῦ πεσεῖν. Πείθονται δὲ ἄνθρωποι ἀνόητοι
τοῖς τοιούτοις τῶν λόγων ἐξαίφνης ἀκούοντες ὡς
σὺ ἔσῃ βελτίων ἁπάντων οὐ μόνον ἀνθρώπων,
55 ἀλλὰ καὶ θεῶν—πολλὴ γὰρ ἐν ἀνθρώποις ἡ
αὐθάδεια—καὶ ὁ πρότερον ταπεινὸς καὶ μέτριος
καὶ ἰδιώτης ἀνήρ, εἰ ἀκούσειε· σὺ εἶ θεοῦ παῖς,
οἱ δ' ἄλλοι, οὓς ἐθαύμαζες, οὐ παῖδες οὐδ' ἃ
τιμῶσιν ἐκ πατέρων λαβόντες, σὺ δὲ κρείττων καὶ
τοῦ οὐρανοῦ οὐδὲν πονήσας—εἶτα καὶ συνεπηχῶσιν
60 ἄλλοι; Οἷον εἰ ἐν πλείστοις ἀριθμεῖν οὐκ εἰδόσιν
ἀριθμεῖν οὐκ εἰδὼς πήχεων χιλίων εἶναι ἀκούοι,
τί ἄν, εἰ χιλιόπηχυς εἶναι νομίζοι, τοὺς ἄλλους
πενταπήχεις εἶναι ἀκούοι; μόνον δὲ φαντάζοιτο
ὡς τὰ χίλια ἀριθμὸς μέγας. Εἶτ' ἐπὶ τούτοις
65 ὑμῶν προνοεῖ ὁ θεός, τοῦ δὲ κόσμου παντὸς ἐν ᾧ
καὶ αὐτοὶ διὰ τί ἀμελεῖ; Εἰ μὲν γάρ, ὅτι οὐ σχολὴ

---

[1] Cp. St. Irenaeus's equally indignant protest against the claim of the Gnostics to be superior to the Creator and his creation in *Adversus Haereses* II. 30.

[2] Cp. Plato, *Republic* IV, 426D8–E1.

and exalt yourself, alleging that you are no worse than they are, then, first of all, in proportion to a man's excellence he is graciously disposed to all, to men too. Then the man of real dignity must ascend in due measure, with an absence of boorish arrogance, going only so far as our nature is able to go, and consider that there is room for the others at God's side, and not set himself alone next after God; this is like flying in our dreams and will deprive him of becoming a god, even as far as the human soul can. It can as far as intellect leads it; but to set oneself above intellect is immediately to fall outside it. But stupid men believe this sort of talk as soon as they hear " you shall be better than all, not only men, but gods "—for there is a great deal of arrogance among men—and the man who was once meek and modest, an ordinary private person, if he hears " you are the son of God, and the others whom you used to admire are not, nor the beings they venerate according to the tradition received from their fathers; but you are better than the heaven without having taken any trouble to become so "—then are other people really going to join in the chorus?[1] It is just as if, in a great crowd of people who did not know how to count, someone who did not know how to count heard that he was a thousand cubits tall; what would happen if he thought he was a thousand cubits, and heard that the others were five cubits? He would only imagine that the " thousand " was a big number.[2] Then besides this, God in his providence cares for you; why does he neglect the whole universe in which you yourselves are? For if it is because he has no time to look at it, and it is not

αὐτῷ πρὸς αὐτὸν βλέπειν, οὐδὲ θέμις αὐτῷ πρὸς
τὸ κάτω· καὶ πρὸς αὐτοὺς βλέπων διὰ τί οὐκ
ἔξω βλέπει καὶ πρὸς τὸν κόσμον δὲ βλέπει ἐν ᾧ
εἰσιν; Εἰ δὲ μὴ ἔξω, ἵνα μὴ τὸν κόσμον ἐφορᾷ,
70 οὐδὲ αὐτοὺς βλέπει. Ἀλλ' οὐδὲν δέονται αὐτοῦ·
ἀλλ' ὁ κόσμος δεῖται καὶ οἶδε τὴν τάξιν αὐτοῦ καὶ
οἱ ἐν αὐτῷ ὅπως ἐν αὐτῷ καὶ ὅπως ἐκεῖ, καὶ
ἀνδρῶν οἳ ἂν θεῷ ὦσι φίλοι, πράως μὲν τὰ παρὰ
τοῦ κόσμου φέροντες, εἴ τι ἐκ τῆς τῶν πάντων
φορᾶς ἀναγκαῖον αὐτοῖς συμβαίνει· οὐ γὰρ πρὸς
75 τὸ ἑκάστῳ καταθύμιον, ἀλλὰ πρὸς τὸ πᾶν δεῖ
βλέπειν· τιμῶν δὲ ἑκάστους κατ' ἀξίαν, σπεύδων δ'
ἀεὶ οὗ πάντα σπεύδει τὰ δυνάμενα—πολλὰ δὲ εἶναι
τὰ σπεύδοντα ἐκεῖ [πάντα],[1] καὶ τὰ μὲν τυγχάνοντα
μακάρια, τὰ δὲ ὡς δυνατὸν ἔχει τὴν προσήκουσαν
αὐτοῖς μοῖραν—οὐχ αὑτῷ μόνῳ διδοὺς τὸ δύνασθαι·
80 οὐ γάρ, ᾗ ἐπαγγέλλει, τὸ ἔχειν, ὃ λέγει τις ἔχειν,
ἀλλὰ πολλὰ καὶ εἰδότες ὅτι μὴ ἔχουσι, λέγουσιν
ἔχειν καὶ οἴονται ἔχειν οὐκ ἔχοντες καὶ μόνοι ἔχειν,
ὃ αὐτοὶ μόνοι οὐκ ἔχουσι.

10. Πολλὰ μὲν οὖν καὶ ἄλλα, μᾶλλον δὲ πάντα
ἄν τις ἐξετάζων ἀφθονίαν ἔχοι ἂν καθ' ἕκαστον
λόγον δεικνὺς ὡς ἔχει. Αἰδὼς γάρ τις ἡμᾶς ἔχει
πρός τινας τῶν φίλων, οἳ τούτῳ τῷ λόγῳ ἐντυχόν-

---

[1] [πάντα] Kirchhoff et nunc Henry et Schwyzer: πάντα codd.
H-S.

lawful for him to regard what is below him: why, when he looks at the Gnostics, does he not look outside himself and at the universe in which they are? But if he does not look outside, in order that he may not supervise the universe, he does not look at them either. But they have no need of him. But the universe does need him, and knows its station, and the beings in it know how they are in it and how they are there in that higher world, and those of men who are dear to God know this, and take kindly what comes to them from the universe, if any unavoidable necessity befalls them from the movement of all things. For one must not look at what is agreeable to the individual but at the All. A man who does this values individuals according to their worth, but presses on always to that goal to which all press on that can—he knows that there are many that press on to the higher world, and those that attain are blessed, others, according to what is possible for them, have the destiny which fits them —and he does not attribute the ability to himself alone. For if someone says he has something, having does not come by claiming it; but the Gnostics say that they have many things, even though they know they have not got them, and think they have them when they have not, and that they alone have what they alone have not.

10. There are many other points, or rather all the points of their doctrine, which if one investigated, one would have ample opportunity of showing the real state of the case in regard to each argument. [But we shall not continue this detailed refutation] for we feel a certain regard for some of our friends

5 τες πρότερον ἢ ἡμῖν φίλοι γενέσθαι οὐκ οἶδ' ὅπως
ἐπ' αὐτοῦ μένουσι. Καίτοι αὐτοὶ οὐκ ὀκνοῦσι—τὰ
αὑτῶν ἐθέλοντες δοκεῖν εἶναι ἀληθῆ ἀξιοπίστως ἢ
καὶ οἰόμενοι τὰ αὑτῶν οὕτως ἔχειν—λέγειν ἃ δὴ
λέγουσιν· ἀλλ' ἡμεῖς πρὸς τοὺς γνωρίμους, οὐ
πρὸς αὐτοὺς λέγοντες—πλέον γὰρ οὐδὲν ἂν γίγνοιτο
10 πρὸς τὸ πείθειν αὐτούς—ἵνα μὴ πρὸς αὐτῶν
ἐνοχλοῖντο οὐκ ἀποδείξεις κομιζόντων—πῶς γάρ;—
ἀλλὰ ἀπαυθαδιζομένων, ταῦτα εἰρήκαμεν, ἄλλου
ὄντος τρόπου, καθ' ὃν ἄν τις γράφων ἠμύνατο τοὺς
διασύρειν τὰ τῶν παλαιῶν καὶ θείων ἀνδρῶν καλῶς
καὶ τῆς ἀληθείας ἐχομένως εἰρημένα τολμῶντας.
15 Ἐκείνως μὲν οὖν ἐατέον ἐξετάζειν· καὶ γὰρ τοῖς
ταῦτα ἀκριβῶς λαβοῦσι τὰ νῦν εἰρημένα ἔσται καὶ
περὶ τῶν ἄλλων ἁπάντων ὅπως ἔχει εἰδέναι·
ἐκεῖνο[1] δὲ εἰπόντα ἐατέον τὸν λόγον, ὃ δὴ καὶ
πάντα ὑπερβέβληκεν ἀτοπίᾳ, εἰ δεῖ ἀτοπίαν τοῦτο
λέγειν. Ψυχὴν γὰρ εἰπόντες νεῦσαι κάτω καὶ
20 σοφίαν τινά, εἴτε τῆς ψυχῆς ἀρξάσης, εἴτε τῆς

---

[1] ἐκεῖνο Kirchhoff, H-S: ἐκεῖνα codd.

---

[1] From this point to the end of ch. 12 Plotinus is attacking
a Gnostic myth known to us best at present in the form it
took in the system of Valentinus. The Mother, Sophia-
Achamoth, produced as a result of the complicated sequence
of events which followed the fall of the higher Sophia, and her
offspring the Demiurge, the inferior and ignorant maker of
the material universe, are Valentinian figures; cp. Irenaeus
Adv. Haer. I.4 and 5. Valentinus had been in Rome, and
there is nothing improbable in the presence of Valentinians
there in the time of Plotinus. But the evidence in the *Life*
ch. 16 suggests that the Gnostics in Plotinus's circle belonged

who happened upon this way of thinking before they
became our friends, and, though I do not know how
they manage it, continue in it. Yet they themselves
do not shrink from saying what they say—either
because they wish their opinions to have a plausible
appearance of truth or because they think that they
really are true. But we have addressed what we
have said so far to our own intimate pupils, not to the
Gnostics (for we could make no further progress
towards convincing them), so that they may not be
troubled by these latter, who do not bring forward
proofs—how could they?—but make arbitrary, arro-
gant assertions. Another style of writing would be
appropriate to repel those who have the insolence to
pull to pieces what godlike men of antiquity have said
nobly and in accordance with the truth. So let us
leave that detailed examination; for those who have
grasped precisely what we have been saying up till
now will be able to know what the real state of the
case is as regards all their other doctrines. But,
before we leave the argument, that one point must be
mentioned which surpasses all the rest of their doctrine in absurdity—if absurdity is what one ought to
call it.[1] For they say that Soul declined to what was
below it, and with it some sort of " Wisdom," whether

rather to the older group called Sethians or Archontics, related
to the Ophites or Barbelognostics: they probably called
themselves simply " Gnostics." Gnostic sects borrowed
freely from each other, and it is likely that Valentinus took
some of his ideas about Sophia from older Gnostic sources,
and that his ideas in turn influenced other Gnostics. The
probably Sethian Gnostic library discovered at Nag Ham-
madi includes Valentinian treatises: cp. Puech, *l.c.* pp. 162–
163 and 179–180.

τοιαύτης αἰτίας γενομένης σοφίας, εἴτε ἄμφω
ταὐτὸν θέλουσιν εἶναι, τὰς μὲν ἄλλας ψυχὰς
συγκαταληλυθέναι λέγοντες καὶ μέλη τῆς σοφίας
ταύτας μὲν ἐνδῦναι λέγουσι σώματα, οἷον τὰ
ἀνθρώπων· ἧς δὲ χάριν καὶ αὐταὶ κατῆλθον,
25 ἐκείνην λέγουσι πάλιν αὖ μὴ κατελθεῖν, οἷον μὴ
νεῦσαι, ἀλλ' ἐλλάμψαι μόνον τῷ σκότῳ, εἶτ'
ἐκεῖθεν εἴδωλον ἐν τῇ ὕλῃ γεγονέναι. Εἶτα τοῦ
εἰδώλου εἴδωλον πλάσαντες ἐνταῦθά που δι' ὕλης
ἢ ὑλότητος ἢ ὅ τι ὀνομάζειν θέλουσι, τὸ μὲν ἄλλο,
τὸ δ' ἄλλο λέγοντες, καὶ πολλὰ ἄλλα ὀνόματα
30 εἰπόντες οὗ λέγουσιν εἰς ἐπισκότησιν, τὸν λεγόμενον
παρ' αὐτοῖς δημιουργὸν γεννῶσι καὶ ἀποστάντα
τῆς μητρὸς ποιήσαντες τὸν κόσμον παρ' αὐτοῦ
ἕλκουσιν [1] ἐπ' ἔσχατα εἰδώλων, ἵνα σφόδρα λοιδο-
ρήσηται ὁ τοῦτο γράψας.

11. Πρῶτον μὲν οὖν, εἰ μὴ κατῆλθεν, ἀλλ'
ἐνέλαμψε τὸ σκότος, πῶς ἂν ὀρθῶς λέγοιτο
νενευκέναι; Οὐ γάρ, εἴ τι παρ' αὐτῆς ἔρρευσεν
οἷον φῶς, ἤδη νενευκέναι αὐτὴν λέγειν προσήκει·
5 εἰ μή που τὸ μὲν ἔκειτό που ἐν τῷ κάτω, ἡ δὲ
ἦλθε τοπικῶς πρὸς αὐτὸ καὶ ἐγγὺς γενομένη
ἐνέλαμψεν. Εἰ δ' ἐφ' αὑτῆς μένουσα ἐνέλαμψε
μηδὲν εἰς τοῦτο ἐργασαμένη, διὰ τί μόνη αὐτὴ
ἐνέλαμψεν, ἀλλ' οὐ τὰ δυνατώτερα αὐτῆς ἐν τοῖς
οὖσιν; Εἰ δὲ τῷ λογισμὸν λαβεῖν αὐτῇ κόσμου
10 ἠδυνήθη ἐλλάμψαι ἐκ τοῦ λογισμοῦ, διὰ τί οὐχ
ἅμα ἐλλάμψασα καὶ κόσμον ἐποίησεν, ἀλλ' ἔμεινε

---

[1] ἕλκουσιν Theiler et nunc Henry et Schwyzer: λέγουσιν
codd. H-S.

Soul started it or whether Wisdom was a cause of
Soul being like this, or whether they mean both
to be the same thing, and then they tell us that
the other souls came down too, and as members of
Wisdom put on bodies, human bodies for instance.
But again they say that very being for the sake of
which these souls came down did not come down
itself, did not decline, so to put it, but only illumined
the darkness, and so an image from it came into
existence in matter. Then they form an image of
the image somewhere here below, through matter
or materiality or whatever they like to call it—they
use now one name and now another, and say many
other names just to make their meaning obscure—
and produce what they call the Maker, and make him
revolt from his mother and drag the universe which
proceeds from him down to the ultimate limit of
images. The man who wrote this just meant to be
blasphemous!

11. First of all then, if it did not come down, but
illumined the darkness, how can it rightly be said to
have declined? For if something like light streamed
from it, it is not proper to say that it declined when
that happened; unless the darkness lay somewhere
below it and it moved spatially towards it and illumined it when it came close to it. But if Soul
remained in itself and illumined matter without
taking any action to this end, why did only it illumine matter, and not the powers greater than it
in the realm of existence? But if it was by forming
a rational conception of the universe that it was able
to illumine as a result of its rational conception, why
did it not make the universe at the same time as it

τὴν τῶν εἰδώλων γένεσιν; Ἔπειτα καὶ ὁ λογισμὸς
ὁ τοῦ κόσμου, ἡ γῆ αὐτοῖς ἡ ξένη λεγομένη
γενομένη ὑπὸ τῶν μειζόνων, ὡς λέγουσιν αὐτοί, οὐ
κατήγαγεν εἰς νεῦσιν τοὺς ποιήσαντας. Ἔπειτα
15 πῶς ἡ ὕλη φωτισθεῖσα εἴδωλα ψυχικὰ ποιεῖ, ἀλλ'
οὐ σωμάτων φύσιν; Ψυχῆς δὲ εἴδωλον οὐδὲν ἂν
δέοιτο σκότους ἢ ὕλης, ἀλλὰ γενόμενον, εἰ γίνεται,
παρακολουθοῖ ἂν τῷ ποιήσαντι καὶ συνηρτημένον
ἔσται. Ἔπειτα πότερον οὐσία τοῦτο ἤ, ὡς φασιν,
ἐννόημα; Εἰ μὲν γὰρ οὐσία, τίς ἡ διαφορὰ πρὸς
20 τὸ ἀφ' οὗ; Εἰ δ' ἄλλο εἶδος ψυχῆς, εἰ ἐκείνη
λογική, τάχ' ἂν φυτικὴ καὶ γεννητικὴ αὕτη· εἰ
δὲ τοῦτο, πῶς ἂν ἔτι, ἵνα τιμῷτο, καὶ πῶς δι'
ἀλαζονείαν καὶ τόλμαν ποιεῖ; Καὶ ὅλως τὸ διὰ
φαντασίας καὶ ἔτι μᾶλλον τοῦ λογίζεσθαι ἀνῄρηται.
Τί δ' ἔτι ἔδει ἐμποιεῖν ἐξ ὕλης καὶ εἰδώλου τὸν
25 ποιήσαντα; Εἰ δ' ἐννόημα, πρῶτον τὸ ὄνομα
ἐπισημαντέον ὅθεν· ἔπειτα πῶς ἐστιν, εἰ μὴ τῷ
ἐννοήματι δώσει τὸ ποιεῖν; Ἀλλὰ πρὸς τῷ
πλάσματι πῶς ἡ ποίησις; Τουτὶ μὲν πρῶτον,
ἄλλο δὲ μετ' ἐκεῖνο, ἀλλ' ὡς ἐπ' ἐξουσίας λέγοντες.
Διὰ τί δὲ πρῶτον πῦρ;

---

[1] This and similar ideas are common to most kinds of
Gnosticism: cp. Irenaeus *Adv. Haer.* I. 29 (a non-Valentinian
system) and Clement of Alexandria, *Strom.* IV ch. 13, 89
(Valentinus).

illumined, instead of waiting for the production of the images? Then, too, the rational conception of the universe, "the strange land," as they call it, which was brought into being by higher powers, as they say themselves, would not have brought its makers down to declination. Then how did matter when it was illumined make images of the soul kind, instead of bodily nature? An image of soul would have no sort of use for darkness or matter, but when it had come into being, if it did come into being, would correspond to its maker and remain in close connection with it. Then is this image a substance or, as they say, a "thought"? If it is a substance, what is the difference between it and its origin? But if it is another kind of soul, then if that higher soul is the rational soul, presumably this latter is the growth-soul which is the principle of generation. But if this is what it is, how will their statements still apply that it created for the sake of being honoured, and how does it create out of arrogance and rash self-assertion?[1] In fact, all possibility of a soul of this kind creating through imagination and, still more, through rational activity, is taken away. And why was there still any need to introduce into their system the maker of the universe derived from matter and image? But if the image is a thought, first of all they must explain whence they derive this name for it; and then how it exists, unless Soul is going to give the thought power to make. But, over and above the fact that this is pure fiction, how does the making work? They say this comes first, and another after that, but they speak quite arbitrarily. And why does fire come first?

12. Καὶ ἄρτι γενόμενον πῶς ἐπιχειρεῖ; Μνήμῃ
ὧν εἶδεν. Ἀλλ᾽ ὅλως οὐκ ἦν, ἵνα ἂν καὶ εἶδεν,
οὔτε αὐτὸς οὔτε ἡ μήτηρ, ἣν διδόασιν αὐτῷ.
Εἶτα πῶς οὐ θαυμαστὸν αὐτοὺς μὲν οὐκ εἴδωλα
5 ψυχῶν ἐνθάδε ἐλθόντας εἰς τὸν κόσμον τόνδε, ἀλλὰ
ἀληθινὰς ψυχάς, μόλις καὶ ἀγαπητῶς ἕνα ἢ δύο
αὐτῶν ἐκ τοῦ κόσμου κινηθῆναι, ⟨καὶ⟩ [1] ἐλθόντας
εἰς ἀνάμνησιν μόλις ἀναπόλησιν λαβεῖν ὧν ποτε
εἶδον, τὸ δὲ εἴδωλον τοῦτο, εἰ καὶ ἀμυδρῶς, ὡς
λέγουσιν, ἀλλ᾽ οὖν ἄρτι γενόμενον ἐνθυμηθῆναι
10 ἐκεῖνα ἢ καὶ τὴν μητέρα αὐτοῦ, εἴδωλον ὑλικόν,
καὶ μὴ μόνον ἐνθυμηθῆναι ἐκεῖνα καὶ κόσμου
λαβεῖν ἔννοιαν καὶ κόσμου ἐκείνου, ἀλλὰ καὶ
μαθεῖν ἐξ ὧν ἂν γένοιτο; Πόθεν δὴ καὶ πρῶτον
πῦρ ποιῆσαι; Οἰηθέντα δεῖν τοῦτο πρῶτον; Διὰ
τί γὰρ οὐκ ἄλλο; Ἀλλ᾽ εἰ ἐδύνατο ποιεῖν ἐνθυμη-
15 θεὶς πῦρ, διὰ τί ἐνθυμηθεὶς κόσμον—πρῶτον μὲν
γὰρ ἔδει ἐνθυμηθῆναι τὸ ὅλον—οὐ κόσμον ἀθρόως
ἐποίει; Ἐμπεριείχετο γὰρ κἀκεῖνα ἐν τῇ ἐνθυμή-
σει. Φυσικώτερον γὰρ πάντως, ἀλλ᾽ οὐχ ὡς αἱ
τέχναι ἐποίει· ὕστεραι γὰρ τῆς φύσεως καὶ τοῦ
κόσμου αἱ τέχναι. Ἐπεὶ καὶ νῦν καὶ τὰ κατὰ
20 μέρος γινόμενα ὑπὸ τῶν φύσεων οὐ πρῶτον πῦρ,
εἶθ᾽ ἕκαστον, εἶτα φύρασις τούτων, ἀλλὰ περιβολὴ
καὶ περιγραφὴ τυποῦσα ἐπὶ τοῖς καταμηνίοις
παντὸς τοῦ ζῴου. Διὰ τί οὖν οὐ κἀκεῖ ἡ ὕλη

---

[1] ⟨καὶ⟩ Heigl, et nunc Henry et Schwyzer.

12. And how does this thought set to its task of making when it has just come into being? By memory of what it saw. But it did not exist at all so as even to see, neither it nor the mother whom they give it. Then is it not surprising that they themselves come here into this world not as images of souls but as real souls, but only one or two of them with difficulty just manage to get out of the world and, when they attain to recollection, with difficulty recapitulate what they once saw; but this image, even if dimly, as they say, yet does manage to form a conception of the intelligible realities when it has just come into being, itself or even its mother, an image in matter, and not only to conceive them and form an idea of a world, and of that world, but to learn the elements from which it could come into being? What could have been the reason why it made fire first? Because it thought that fire must come first? Why not something else? But if it was able to make fire when it conceived it, why when it conceived the world—for it must have conceived the whole first—did it not make the world straight away? For the elements, too, were included in its conception. For it made the world in every way after the manner of nature rather than as the arts make; for the arts are later than nature and the world. Even now the things which are parts of the world when they are brought into being by natural principles do not come into existence like this, first fire, then each individual constituent, and then a mixture of them, but there is an outline and sketch plan of the whole living thing impressing the form on the menstrual fluid. Why then, in the making

271

περιεγράφετο τύπῳ κόσμου, ἐν ᾧ τύπῳ καὶ γῆ
καὶ πῦρ καὶ τὰ ἄλλα; Ἀλλ᾽ ἴσως αὐτοὶ οὕτω
25 κόσμον ἐποίησαν ὡς ἂν ἀληθεστέρᾳ ψυχῇ χρώμενοι,
ἐκεῖνος δὲ οὕτως ἠγνόει ποιῆσαι. Καίτοι προιδεῖν
καὶ μέγεθος οὐρανοῦ, μᾶλλον δὲ τοσοῦτον εἶναι,
καὶ τὴν λόξωσιν τῶν ζῳδίων καὶ τῶν ὑπ᾽ αὐτὸν
τὴν φορὰν καὶ τὴν γῆν οὕτως, ὡς ἔχειν εἰπεῖν
αἰτίας δι᾽ ἃς οὕτως, οὐκ εἰδώλου ἦν, ἀλλὰ πάντως
30 ἀπὸ τῶν ἀρίστων τῆς δυνάμεως ἐλθούσης· ὃ καὶ
αὐτοὶ ἄκοντες ὁμολογοῦσιν. Ἡ γὰρ ἔλλαμψις ἡ
εἰς τὸ σκότος ἐξετασθεῖσα ποιήσει ὁμολογεῖν τὰς
ἀληθεῖς τοῦ κόσμου αἰτίας. Τί γὰρ ἐλλάμπειν
ἔδει, εἰ μὴ πάντως ἔδει; Ἢ γὰρ κατὰ φύσιν ἢ
παρὰ φύσιν ἀνάγκη. Ἀλλ᾽ εἰ μὲν κατὰ φύσιν, ἀεὶ
35 οὕτως· εἰ δὲ παρὰ φύσιν, καὶ ἐν τοῖς ἐκεῖ
ἔσται τὸ παρὰ φύσιν, καὶ τὰ κακὰ πρὸ τοῦ
κόσμου τοῦδε, καὶ οὐχ ὁ κόσμος αἴτιος τῶν κακῶν,
ἀλλὰ τἀκεῖ τούτῳ, καὶ τῇ ψυχῇ οὐκ ἐντεῦθεν, ἀλλὰ
παρ᾽ αὐτῆς ἐνταῦθα· καὶ ἥξει ὁ λόγος ἀναφέρων
τὸν κόσμον ἐπὶ τὰ πρῶτα. Εἰ δὲ δή, καὶ ἡ ὕλη,
40 ὅθεν φανείη. Ἡ γὰρ ψυχὴ ἡ νεύσασα ἤδη ὂν τὸ
σκότος, φασίν, εἶδε καὶ κατέλαμψε. Πόθεν οὖν

of the world, too, was not matter marked in outline with the form of the universe, in which form earth and fire and the rest were contained? But perhaps they would have made the world like this, since they possess a more genuine soul, but that creator of theirs did not know how to. Yet to see, before it existed, the greatness of the heaven—or rather to see its exact size—and the inclination of the zodiac and the circuit of the stars below it, and the earth, in such a way that it is possible to give reasons why all these things are so :—this does not belong to an image, but altogether to a power which comes from the best principles. And this even they themselves unwillingly admit. For their " illumination of the darkness," if it is investigated, will make them admit the true causes of the universe. For why was it necessary for the soul to illuminate, unless the necessity was universal? It was either according to soul's nature or against it. But if it was according to its nature, it must always be so. If, on the other hand, it was against its nature, then there will be a place for what is against nature in the higher world, and evil will exist before this universe, and the universe will not be responsible for evil, but the higher world will be the cause of evil for this world, and evil will not come from the world here to the soul, but from the soul to the world here; and the course of the argument will lead to the attribution of re-sponsibility for the universe to the first principles: and if the universe, then also the matter, from which the universe on this hypothesis would have emerged. For the soul which declined saw, they say, and illuminated the darkness already in existence.

PLOTINUS: ENNEAD II. 9.

τοῦτο; Εἰ δ' αὐτὴν φήσουσι ποιῆσαι νεύσασαν,
οὐκ ἦν δηλονότι ὅπου ἂν ἔνευσεν, οὐδ' αὐτὸ τὸ
σκότος αἴτιον τῆς νεύσεως, ἀλλ' αὐτὴ ἡ ψυχῆς
φύσις. Τοῦτο δὲ ταὐτὸν ταῖς προηγησαμέναις
ἀνάγκαις· ὥστε ἐπὶ τὰ πρῶτα ἡ αἰτία.

13. Ὁ ἄρα μεμφόμενος τῇ τοῦ κόσμου φύσει
οὐκ οἶδεν ὅ τι ποιεῖ, οὐδ' ὅπου τὸ θράσος αὐτοῦ
τοῦτο χωρεῖ. Τοῦτο δέ, ὅτι οὐκ ἴσασι τάξιν τῶν
ἐφεξῆς πρώτων καὶ δευτέρων καὶ τρίτων καὶ ἀεὶ
5 μέχρι τῶν ἐσχάτων, καὶ ὡς οὐ λοιδορητέον τοῖς
χείροσι τῶν πρώτων, ἀλλὰ πράως συγχωρητέον
τῇ πάντων φύσει αὐτὸν θέοντα πρὸς τὰ πρῶτα
παυσάμενον τῆς τραγῳδίας τῶν φοβερῶν, ὡς
οἴονται, ἐν ταῖς τοῦ κόσμου σφαίραις, αἳ δὴ
πάντα μείλιχα τεύχουσιν αὐτοῖς· τί γὰρ
φοβερὸν ἔχουσιν αὗται, ὡς φοβοῦσι τοὺς ἀπείρους
10 λόγων καὶ πεπαιδευμένης ἀνηκόους καὶ ἐμμελοῦς
γνώσεως; Οὐ γάρ, εἰ πύρινα τὰ σώματα αὐτῶν,
φοβεῖσθαι δεῖ συμμέτρως πρὸς τὸ πᾶν καὶ πρὸς
τὴν γῆν ἔχοντα, εἰς δὲ τὰς ψυχὰς αὐτῶν βλέπειν,
αἷς καὶ αὐτοὶ δήπουθεν ἀξιοῦσι τίμιοι εἶναι.
15 Καίτοι καὶ τὰ σώματα αὐτῶν μεγέθει καὶ κάλλει

---

[1] The cosmic spheres and the Archons who ruled them were
for the Gnostics formidable barriers which the soul had to
pass on its journey upwards to its true home. To do so it was
necessary to know the correct formula with which to address

274

Where, then, did the darkness come from? If they are going to say that the soul made it when it declined, there was obviously nowhere for it to decline to, and the darkness itself was not responsible for the decline, but the soul's own nature. But this is the same as attributing the responsibility to pre-existing necessities; so the responsibility goes back to the first principles.

13. The man who censures the nature of the universe does not know what he is doing, and how far this rash criticism of his goes. This is so because the Gnostics do not know that there is an order of firsts, seconds and thirds in regular succession, and so on to the last, and that the things that are worse than the first should not be reviled; one should rather calmly and gently accept the nature of all things, and hurry on oneself to the first, ceasing to concern oneself with the melodrama of the terrors, as they think, in the cosmic spheres,[1] which in reality " make all things sweet and lovely " [2] for them. For what is there terrible about the spheres, which makes them terrify people who are unpractised in reasoning and have never heard anything of a cultured and harmonious " gnosis." For even if their bodies are fiery, there is no need to fear them, since they are duly proportioned to the All and the earth; but one should look at their souls—it is on their souls that the Gnostics themselves, of course, base their claim to honour. Yet their bodies, too, are outstanding in size and beauty and are partners and co-operators in

each Archon: cp. the Ophite spells in Origen *Against Celsus* VI. 31, with H. Chadwick's commentary.

[2] A reminiscence of Pindar *Olympians* I. 48.

διαφέροντα συμπράττοντα καὶ συνεργοῦντα τοῖς
κατὰ φύσιν γιγνομένοις, ἃ οὐκ ἂν οὐ γένοιτό ποτε
ἔστ' ἂν ᾖ τὰ πρῶτα, συμπληροῦντα δὲ τὸ πᾶν καὶ
μεγάλα μέρη ὄντα τοῦ παντός. Εἰ δ' ἄνθρωποι
τίμιόν τι παρ' ἄλλα ζῷα, πολλῷ μᾶλλον ταῦτα οὐ
20 τυραννίδος ἕνεκα ἐν τῷ παντὶ ὄντα, ἀλλὰ κόσμον
καὶ τάξιν παρέχοντα. Ἃ δὲ λέγεται γίνεσθαι παρ'
αὐτῶν, σημεῖα νομίζειν τῶν ἐσομένων εἶναι,
γίνεσθαι δὲ τὰ γινόμενα διάφορα καὶ τύχαις—οὐ
γὰρ οἷόν τε ἦν ταὐτὰ περὶ ἑκάστους συμβαίνειν—
καὶ καιροῖς γενέσεων καὶ τόποις πλεῖστον ἀφεστη-
25 κόσι καὶ διαθέσεσι ψυχῶν. Καὶ οὐκ ἀπαιτητέον
πάλιν ἀγαθοὺς πάντας, οὐδ' ὅτι μὴ τοῦτο δυνατόν,
μέμφεσθαι προχείρως πάλιν ἀξιοῦσι μηδὲν διαφέ-
ρειν ταῦτα ἐκείνων, τό τε κακὸν μὴ νομίζειν ἄλλο
τι ἢ τὸ ἐνδεέστερον εἰς φρόνησιν καὶ ἔλαττον
30 ἀγαθὸν καὶ ἀεὶ πρὸς τὸ μικρότερον· οἷον εἴ τις
τὴν φύσιν κακὸν λέγοι, ὅτι μὴ αἴσθησίς ἐστι, καὶ
τὸ αἰσθητικόν, ὅτι μὴ λόγος. Εἰ δὲ μή, κἀκεῖ τὰ
κακὰ ἀναγκασθήσονται λέγειν εἶναι· καὶ γὰρ ἐκεῖ
ψυχὴ χεῖρον νοῦ καὶ οὗτος ἄλλου ἔλαττον.

14. Μάλιστα δὲ αὐτοὶ καὶ ἄλλως ποιοῦσιν οὐκ
ἀκήρατα τὰ ἐκεῖ. Ὅταν γὰρ ἐπαοιδὰς γράφωσιν

---

[1] For a full exposition of Plotinus's thought about astral
signs and astral influences see II. 3, especially chs. 7–8 and
10–15.
[2] Plotinus himself does sometimes come very near to saying
that all procession, with its necessary falling below the highest,
is an evil: cp. III. 8. 8. 35–6 (of the procession of Intellect

all that happens according to nature, and cannot ever not happen as long as the first principles exist; they are essential to the completeness of the All and are important parts of the All. And if men have a degree of honour in comparison with other living things, these are much more honourable, as they are not in the All to exercise tyrannical rule but as the givers of beauty and order. As for what is said to happen as a result of their influence, one should consider that they give signs of things to come, but that the variety of things that happen is due to chance—it was not possible that the fortune of each individual should be the same—and to reasons of birth, and places far different from each other, and the dispositions of souls.[1] And again, one should not demand that everybody should be good nor, because this is not possible, should they be ready with censure, demanding that this world should differ in no way from that higher one; nor is it right not to consider evil as anything else than a falling short in wisdom, and a lesser good, continually diminishing; as if one were to say that the growth-principle was evil because it is not perception, and the principle of perception, because it is not reason. Otherwise, they will be compelled to say that there are evils in the higher world too: for there soul is worse than intellect and intellect than Something Else.[2]

14. But they themselves most of all impair the inviolate purity of the higher powers in another way too. For when they write magic chants, intending to

from the One) and III. 7. 11. 15 ff. (of the procession of Soul from Intellect). But this cosmic pessimism is not his normal thought.

ὡς πρὸς ἐκεῖνα λέγοντες, οὐ μόνον πρὸς ψυχήν,
ἀλλὰ καὶ τὰ ἐπάνω, τί ποιοῦσιν ἢ γοητείας καὶ
5 θέλξεις καὶ πείσεις λέγουσι καὶ λόγῳ ὑπακούειν
καὶ ἄγεσθαι, εἴ τις ἡμῶν τεχνικώτερος εἰπεῖν ταδὶ
καὶ οὑτωσὶ μέλη καὶ ἤχους καὶ προσπνεύσεις καὶ
σιγμοὺς τῆς φωνῆς καὶ τὰ ἄλλα, ὅσα ἐκεῖ μαγεύειν
γέγραπται. Εἰ δὲ μὴ βούλονται τοῦτο λέγειν, ἀλλὰ
πῶς φωναῖς τὰ ἀσώματα; Ὥστε οἴοις [1] σεμνοτέ-
10 ρους αὐτῶν τοὺς λόγους ποιοῦσι φαίνεσθαι, τούτοις
λελήθασιν αὐτοὺς τὸ σεμνὸν ἐκείνων ἀφαιρούμενοι.
Καθαίρεσθαι δὲ νόσων λέγοντες αὐτούς, λέγοντες
μὲν ἂν σωφροσύνῃ καὶ κοσμίᾳ διαίτῃ, ἔλεγον ἂν
ὀρθῶς, καθάπερ οἱ φιλόσοφοι λέγουσι· νῦν δὲ
ὑποστησάμενοι τὰς νόσους δαιμόνια εἶναι καὶ
15 ταῦτα ἐξαιρεῖν λόγῳ φάσκοντες δύνασθαι καὶ
ἐπαγγελλόμενοι σεμνότεροι μὲν ἂν εἶναι δόξαιεν
παρὰ τοῖς πολλοῖς, οἳ τὰς παρὰ τοῖς μάγοις
δυνάμεις θαυμάζουσι, τοὺς μέντοι εὖ φρονοῦντας
οὐκ ἂν πείθοιεν, ὡς οὐχ αἱ νόσοι τὰς αἰτίας ἔχουσιν
ἢ καμάτοις ἢ πλησμοναῖς ἢ ἐνδείαις ἢ σήψεσι καὶ
20 ὅλως μεταβολαῖς ἢ ἔξωθεν τὴν ἀρχὴν ἢ ἔνδοθεν
λαβούσαις. Δηλοῦσι δὲ καὶ αἱ θεραπεῖαι αὐτῶν.
Γαστρὸς γὰρ ῥυείσης ἢ φαρμάκου δοθέντος
διεχώρησε κάτω εἰς τὸ ἔξω τὸ νόσημα καὶ αἵματος
ἀφηρημένου, καὶ ἔνδεια δὲ ἰάσατο. Ἢ πεινήσαντος
τοῦ δαιμονίου καὶ τοῦ φαρμάκου ποιήσαντος

---

[1] οἴοις Heigl: οἱ A¹ˢExUC H-S: οἷς A (in ras.) Q: εἰ S.

address them to those powers, not only to the soul
but to those above it as well, what are they doing
except making the powers obey the word and follow
the lead of people who say spells and charms and
conjurations, any one of us who is well skilled in the
art of saying precisely the right things in the right
way, songs and cries and aspirated and hissing sounds
and everything else which their writings say has
magic power in the higher world? But even if they
do not want to say this, how are the incorporeal
beings affected by sounds? So by the sort of statements [1] with which they give an appearance of
majesty to their own words, they, without realising
it, take away the majesty of the higher powers.
But when they say they free themselves from diseases,
if they meant that they did so by temperance and
orderly living, they would speak well, just as the philosophers do; but in fact they assume that the diseases
are evil spirits, and claim to be able to drive them
out by their word; by this claim they might make
themselves more impressive in the eyes of the masses,
who wonder at the powers of magicians, but would
not persuade sensible people that diseases do not
have their origin in strain or excess or deficiency or
decay, and in general in changes which have their
origin outside or inside. The cures of diseases make
this clear too. With a vigorous motion of the bowels
or the giving of a drug the illness goes through the
downward passage and out, and it goes out too with
blood-letting; and fasting also heals. Does the evil
spirit starve, and does the drug make it waste away,

[1] I read here οἵοις (Heigl), not οἳ (Henry–Schwyzer with
most MSS).

25 τήκεσθαι, ποτὲ δὲ ἀθρόως ἐξελθόντος, ἢ μένοντος
ἔνδον; Ἀλλ᾽ εἰ μὲν ἔτι μένοντος, πῶς ἔνδον
ὄντος οὐ νοσεῖ ἔτι; Εἰ δὲ ἐξελήλυθε, διὰ τί; Τί
γὰρ αὐτὸ πέπονθεν; Ἢ ὅτι ἐτρέφετο ὑπὸ τῆς
νόσου. Ἦν ἄρα ἡ νόσος ἑτέρα οὖσα τοῦ δαίμονος.
Ἔπειτα, εἰ οὐδενὸς ὄντος αἰτίου εἴσεισι, διὰ τί
30 οὐκ ἀεὶ νοσεῖ; Εἰ δὲ γενομένου αἰτίου, τί δεῖ τοῦ
δαίμονος πρὸς τὸ νοσεῖν; Τὸ γὰρ αἴτιον τὸν πυρε-
τὸν αὔταρκές ἐστιν ἐργάσασθαι. Γελοῖον δὲ τὸ ἅμα
τὸ αἴτιον γενέσθαι καὶ εὐθέως ὥσπερ παρυποστῆναι
τῷ αἰτίῳ τὸ δαιμόνιον ἕτοιμον ὄν. Ἀλλὰ γάρ,
35 ὅπως καὶ ταῦτα εἴρηται αὐτοῖς καὶ ὅτου χάριν,
δῆλον· τούτου γὰρ ἕνεκα οὐχ ἧττον καὶ τούτων
τῶν δαιμονίων ἐμνήσθημεν. Τὰ δ᾽ ἄλλα ὑμῖν
καταλείπω ἀναγινώσκουσιν ἐπισκοπεῖσθαι καὶ θεωρεῖν ἐκεῖνο πανταχοῦ, ὡς τὸ μὲν παρ᾽ ἡμῶν εἶδος
φιλοσοφίας μεταδιωκόμενον πρὸς τοῖς ἄλλοις
40 ἅπασιν ἀγαθοῖς καὶ τὴν ἁπλότητα τοῦ ἤθους μετὰ
τοῦ φρονεῖν καθαρῶς ἐνδείκνυται, τὸ σεμνόν, οὐ
τὸ αὔθαδες μεταδιώκουσα, τὸ θαρραλέον μετὰ
λόγου καὶ μετ᾽ ἀσφαλείας πολλῆς καὶ εὐλαβείας
καὶ πλείστης περιωπῆς ἔχουσα· τὰ δὲ ἄλλα τῷ
τοιούτῳ παραβάλλειν. Τὸ δὲ παρὰ τῶν ἄλλων
ἐναντιώτατα κατεσκεύασται διὰ πάντων· οὐδὲν
45 γὰρ ἂν πλέον· οὕτω γὰρ περὶ αὐτῶν λέγειν ἡμῖν
ἂν πρέποι.

15. Ἐκεῖνο δὲ μάλιστα δεῖ μὴ λανθάνειν ἡμᾶς,
τί ποτε ποιοῦσιν οὗτοι οἱ λόγοι εἰς τὰς ψυχὰς τῶν

and does it sometimes come out all at once, or stay inside? But if it continues to stay, how does the patient not continue to be ill while it is still inside him? But if it went out, why did it go? What happened to it? Presumably because it was fed by the disease. So then the disease was different from the spirit. Then, if it came into the man without any cause of disease, why is he not always ill? But if there was a cause, what need is there of the spirit to produce the illness? For the cause is sufficient by itself to produce the fever. It is ridiculous to suppose that as soon as the cause occurs the evil spirit, all ready and waiting, immediately takes up its position in support of it. But it is clear how they say this and also why they say it; it was for this reason, too, that we mentioned these evil spirits. The rest of their teachings I leave to you to investigate by reading their books, and to observe throughout that the kind of philosophy which we pursue, besides all its other excellences, displays simplicity and straightforwardness of character along with clear thinking, and aims at dignity, not rash arrogance, and combines its confident boldness with reason and much safeguarding and caution and a great deal of circumspection: you are to use philosophy of this kind as a standard of comparison for the rest. But the system of the others [the Gnostics] is in every part constructed on entirely opposed principles—for I would not like to say more; this is the way in which it would be suitable for us to speak about them.

15. But there is one point which we must be particularly careful not to let escape us, and that is what these arguments do to the souls of those who

281

ἀκουόντων καὶ τοῦ κόσμου καὶ τῶν ἐν αὐτῷ
καταφρονεῖν πεισθέντων. Δυοῖν γὰρ οὐσῶν αἱρέ-
5 σεων τοῦ τυχεῖν τοῦ τέλους, μιᾶς μὲν τῆς ἡδονὴν
τὴν τοῦ σώματος τέλος τιθεμένης, ἑτέρας δὲ τῆς τὸ
καλὸν καὶ τὴν ἀρετὴν αἱρουμένης, οἷς καὶ ἐκ θεοῦ
καὶ εἰς θεὸν ἀνήρτηται ἡ ὄρεξις, ὡς δὲ ἐν ἄλλοις [1]
θεωρητέον, ὁ μὲν Ἐπίκουρος τὴν πρόνοιαν ἀνελὼν
τὴν ἡδονὴν καὶ τὸ ἥδεσθαι, ὅπερ ἦν λοιπόν, τοῦτο
10 διώκειν παρακελεύεται· ὁ δὲ λόγος οὗτος ἔτι
νεανικώτερον τὸν τῆς προνοίας κύριον καὶ αὐτὴν
τὴν πρόνοιαν μεμψάμενος καὶ πάντας νόμους τοὺς
ἐνταῦθα ἀτιμάσας καὶ τὴν ἀρετὴν τὴν ἐκ παντὸς
τοῦ χρόνου ἀνηυρημένην τό τε σωφρονεῖν τοῦτο
ἐν γέλωτι θέμενος, ἵνα μηδὲν καλὸν ἐνταῦθα δὴ
15 ὀφθείη ὑπάρχον, ἀνεῖλε τὸ σωφρονεῖν [2] καὶ τὴν
ἐν τοῖς ἤθεσι σύμφυτον δικαιοσύνην τὴν τελειου-
μένην ἐκ λόγου καὶ ἀσκήσεως καὶ ὅλως καθ' ἃ
σπουδαῖος ἄνθρωπος ἂν γένοιτο. Ὥστε αὐτοῖς
καταλείπεσθαι τὴν ἡδονὴν καὶ τὸ περὶ αὐτοὺς καὶ
20 τὸ οὐ κοινὸν πρὸς ἄλλους ἀνθρώπους καὶ τὸ τῆς
χρείας μόνον, εἰ μή τις τῇ φύσει τῇ αὐτοῦ κρείττων
εἴη τῶν λόγων τούτων· τούτων γὰρ οὐδὲν αὐτοῖς
καλόν, ἀλλὰ ἄλλο τι, ὅ ποτε μεταδιώξουσι.
Καίτοι ἐχρῆν τοὺς ἤδη ἐγνωκότας ἐντεῦθεν διώκειν,

---

[1] ὡς δὲ ἐν ἄλλοις nunc Henry et Schwyzer: ὡς δέ, ἐν ἄλλοις
H-S.
[2] τὸ σωφρονεῖν A et nunc Henry et Schwyzer: τε τὸ σωφρονεῖν
Exy: τότε σωφρονεῖν Q.

hear them and are persuaded by them to despise the
universe and the beings in it. For there are two
schools of thought about attaining the end, one which
puts forward the pleasure of the body as the end, and
another which chooses nobility and virtue, for whose
members desire depends on God and leads back to
God (as must be studied elsewhere): Epicurus, who
abolishes providence, exhorts to pursue pleasure
and its enjoyment, which is what is left; but this
doctrine censures the lord of providence and providence itself still more crudely, and despises all the
laws of this world and the virtue whose winning
extends back through all time, and makes self-
control here something to laugh at, that nothing
noble may be seen existing here below, and abolishes
self-control and the righteousness which comes to
birth with men's characters and is perfected by reason and training, and altogether everything by which
a man could become nobly good.[1] So pleasure is
left for them, and what concerns themselves alone,
and what other men have no share in, and what is
nothing but a matter of their needs—unless one of
them is by nature better than these teachings of
theirs: for nothing here is of value for them, but
something else is, which they will go after one day.
Yet those who already have the *gnosis* [2] should start

[1] On the question of how far the charges of immorality
brought against the Gnostics by their opponents were justified,
see the discussion in *Entretiens Hardt* V, pp. 186–189.

[2] I have translated ἐγνωκότας in this way, following Harder
and Cilento, as it seems clear that Plotinus is referring to the
distinctive Gnostic claim to possess a *gnosis*, not, that is,
just ordinary knowledge but a special secret knowledge which
had power to save.

διώκοντας δὲ πρῶτα κατορθοῦν ταῦτα ἐκ θείας
25 φύσεως ἥκοντας· ἐκείνης γὰρ τῆς φύσεως καλοῦ
ἐπαΐειν, τὴν ἡδονὴν τοῦ σώματος ἀτιμαζούσης.
Οἷς δὲ ἀρετῆς μὴ μέτεστιν, οὐκ ἂν εἶεν τὸ παράπαν
κινηθέντες πρὸς ἐκεῖνα. Μαρτυρεῖ δὲ αὐτοῖς καὶ
τόδε τὸ μηδένα λόγον περὶ ἀρετῆς πεποιῆσθαι,
ἐκλελοιπέναι δὲ παντάπασι τὸν περὶ τούτων λόγον,
30 καὶ μήτε τί ἐστιν εἰπεῖν μήτε πόσα μήτε ὅσα
τεθεώρηται πολλὰ καὶ καλὰ τοῖς τῶν παλαιῶν
λόγοις, μήτε ἐξ ὧν περιέσται καὶ κτήσεται, μήτε
ὡς θεραπεύεται ψυχὴ μήτε ὡς καθαίρεται. Οὐ
γὰρ δὴ τὸ εἰπεῖν "βλέπε πρὸς θεόν" προύργου τι
ἐργάζεται, ἐὰν μὴ πῶς καὶ βλέψῃ διδάξῃ. Τί γὰρ
35 κωλύει, εἴποι τις ἄν, βλέπειν καὶ μηδεμιᾶς
ἀπέχεσθαι ἡδονῆς, ἢ ἀκρατῆ θυμοῦ εἶναι μεμνημέ-
νον μὲν ὀνόματος τοῦ "θεός," συνεχόμενον δὲ
ἅπασι πάθεσι, μηδὲν δὲ αὐτῶν πειρώμενον ἐξαιρεῖν; Ἀρετὴ μὲν οὖν εἰς τέλος προιοῦσα καὶ ἐν
ψυχῇ ἐγγενομένη μετὰ φρονήσεως θεὸν δείκνυσιν·
40 ἄνευ δὲ ἀρετῆς ἀληθινῆς θεὸς λεγόμενος ὄνομά ἐστι.

16. Οὐδ' αὖ τὸ καταφρονῆσαι κόσμου καὶ θεῶν
τῶν ἐν αὐτῷ καὶ τῶν ἄλλων καλῶν ἀγαθόν ἐστι
γενέσθαι. Καὶ γὰρ πᾶς κακὸς καὶ πρὸ τοῦ
καταφρονήσειεν ἂν θεῶν, καὶ μὴ πρότερον πάγκακος [1] καταφρονήσας, καὶ εἰ τὰ ἄλλα μὴ πάντα
5 κακὸς εἴη, αὐτῷ τούτῳ ἂν γεγονὼς εἴη. Καὶ γὰρ

---

[1] πάγκακος Heigl, H-S² (sed nunc protulerint Henry et
Schwyzer [πᾶς κακὸς] Kirchhoff): πᾶς κακὸς codd.

going after it here and now, and in their pursuit should first of all set right their conduct here below, as they come from a divine nature; for that nature is aware of nobility and despises the pleasure of the body. But those who have no share of virtue would not be moved at all towards that higher world. This, too, is evidence of their indifference to virtue, that they have never made any treatise about virtue, but have altogether left out the treatment of these subjects; they do not tell us what kind of thing virtue is, nor how many parts it has, nor about all the many noble studies of the subject to be found in the treatises of the ancients, nor from what virtue results and how it is to be attained, nor how the soul is tended, nor how it is purified. For it does no good at all to say " Look to God," unless one also teaches how one is to look. For someone could say, " What prevents me from looking and refraining from no pleasure, or from having no control over my emotions and from re-membering the name ' God ' and at the same time being in the grip of all the passions and making no attempt to get rid of any of them." In reality it is virtue which goes before us to the goal and, when it comes to exist in the soul along with wisdom, shows God; but God, if you talk about him without true virtue, is only a name.

16. Again, despising the universe and the gods in it and the other noble things is certainly not becoming good. Every wicked man, in former times too, was capable of despising the gods, and even if he was not altogether wicked before, when he despised them he became so by this very fact, even if he was not wicked in everything else. Then again the honour which

ἂν καὶ ἡ πρὸς τοὺς νοητοὺς θεοὺς λεγομένη αὐτοῖς
τιμὴ ἀσυμπαθὴς ἂν γένοιτο· ὁ γὰρ τὸ φιλεῖν πρὸς
ὁτιοῦν ἔχων καὶ τὸ συγγενὲς πᾶν οὗ φιλεῖ ἀσπάζε-
ται καὶ τοὺς παῖδας ὧν τὸν πατέρα ἀγαπᾷ· ψυχὴ
10 δὲ πᾶσα πατρὸς ἐκείνου. Ψυχαὶ δὲ καὶ ἐν τούτοις
καὶ νοεραὶ καὶ ἀγαθαὶ καὶ συναφεῖς τοῖς ἐκεῖ πολὺ
μᾶλλον ἢ αἱ ἡμῶν. Πῶς γὰρ ἂν ἀποτμηθεὶς ὅδε
ὁ κόσμος ἐκείνου ἦν; πῶς δὲ οἱ ἐν αὐτῷ θεοί;
Ἀλλὰ ταῦτα μὲν καὶ πρότερον· νῦν δέ, ὅτι καὶ
τῶν συγγενῶν ἐκείνοις καταφρονοῦντες, [ὅτι]¹ μηδὲ
15 ἐκεῖνα ἴσασιν, ἀλλ' ἢ λόγῳ. Ἐπεὶ καὶ τὸ πρόνοιαν
μὴ διικνεῖσθαι εἰς τὰ τῇδε ἢ εἰς ὁτιοῦν, πῶς
εὐσεβές; Πῶς δὲ σύμφωνον ἑαυτοῖς; Λέγουσι
γὰρ αὐτῶν προνοεῖν αὖ μόνων. Πότερα δὲ ἐκεῖ
γενομένων ἢ καὶ ἐνθάδε ὄντων; Εἰ μὲν γὰρ ἐκεῖ,
πῶς ἦλθον; Εἰ δὲ ἐνθάδε, πῶς ἔτι εἰσὶν ἐνθάδε
20 Πῶς δὲ οὐ καὶ αὐτός ἐστιν ἐνθάδε; Πόθεν γὰρ
γνώσεται, ὅτι εἰσὶν ἐνθάδε; Πῶς δέ, ὅτι ἐνθάδε
ὄντες οὐκ ἐπελάθοντο αὐτοῦ καὶ ἐγένοντο κακοί;
Εἰ δὲ γινώσκει τοὺς μὴ γενομένους κακούς, καὶ
τοὺς γενομένους γινώσκει, ἵνα διακρίνῃ ἀπ'
ἐκείνων αὐτούς. Πᾶσιν οὖν παρέσται καὶ ἔσται
25 ἐν τῷ κόσμῳ τῷδε, ὅστις ὁ τρόπος· ὥστε καὶ

¹ [ὅτι] Kirchhoff et nunc Henry et Schwyzer: ὅτι codd. H-S.

these people say they give to the intelligible gods
would be of a very unfeeling sort. For anyone who
feels affection for anything at all shows kindness to
all that is akin to the object of his affection, and to the
children of the father he loves. But every soul is a
child of That Father. And there are souls in these
[the heavenly bodies] too, and intelligent and good
ones, much more closely in touch with the beings of
the higher world than our souls are. How could this
universe exist if it was cut off from that other world?
How could the gods in it? But we spoke of this before,
too: our point now is that because they despise the
kindred of those higher realities, also, they do not
know the higher beings either but only talk as if they
did. Then, another point, what piety is there in deny-
ing that providence extends to this world and to anything and everything? And how are they consistent
with themselves in this denial? For they say that
God does care providentially for them, and them
alone. Did he care for them only when they were in
the higher world, or does he care for them when they
are here, too? If he cared for them when they were
there, how did they come here? But if he cares for
them here, why are they here still? And how is it
possible that God is not here, too? For from what
source does he know that they are here? And how
does he know that while they have been here they have
not forgotton him and become wicked? But if he
knows those who have not become wicked, he knows
those who have become wicked too, in order to be
able to separate the good from them. So he will be
present to all and will be in this universe, whatever
the manner of his presence; so that the universe

287

μεθέξει αὐτοῦ ὁ κόσμος. Εἰ δ᾽ ἄπεστι τοῦ κόσμου,
καὶ ὑμῶν ἀπέσται, καὶ οὐδ᾽ ἂν ἔχοιτέ τι λέγειν
περὶ αὐτοῦ οὐδὲ τῶν μετ᾽ αὐτόν. Ἀλλ᾽ εἴτε ὑμῖν
πρόνοιά τις ἔρχεται ἐκεῖθεν, εἴτε ὅ τι βούλεσθε,
ἀλλ᾽ ὅ γε κόσμος ἐκεῖθεν ἔχει καὶ οὐκ ἀπολέλειπται
30 οὐδ᾽ ἀπολειφθήσεται. Πολὺ γὰρ μᾶλλον τῶν
ὅλων ἢ τῶν μερῶν ἡ πρόνοια καὶ ἡ μέθεξις
κἀκείνης τῆς ψυχῆς πολὺ μᾶλλον· δηλοῖ δὲ καὶ
τὸ εἶναι καὶ τὸ ἐμφρόνως εἶναι. Τίς γὰρ οὕτω
τεταγμένος ἢ ἔμφρων τῶν ὑπερφρονούντων ἀφρό-
35 νως, ὡς τὸ πᾶν; Ἡ παραβάλλειν καὶ γελοῖον
καὶ πολλὴν τὴν ἀτοπίαν ἔχει, καὶ ὅ γε μὴ τοῦ
λόγου ἕνεκα παραβάλλων οὐκ ἔξω ἂν τοῦ ἀσεβεῖν
γένοιτο· οὐδὲ τὸ ζητεῖν περὶ τούτων ἔμφρονος,
ἀλλὰ τυφλοῦ τινος καὶ παντάπασιν οὔτε αἴσθησιν
οὔτε νοῦν ἔχοντος καὶ πόρρω τοῦ νοητὸν κόσμον
ἰδεῖν ὄντος, ὃς τοῦτον οὐ βλέπει. Τίς γὰρ ἂν
40 μουσικὸς ἀνὴρ εἴη, ὃς τὴν ἐν νοητῷ ἁρμονίαν ἰδὼν
οὐ κινήσεται τῆς ἐν φθόγγοις αἰσθητοῖς ἀκούων;
Ἡ τίς γεωμετρίας καὶ ἀριθμῶν ἔμπειρος, ὃς τὸ
σύμμετρον καὶ ἀνάλογον καὶ τεταγμένον ἰδὼν δι᾽
ὀμμάτων οὐχ ἡσθήσεται; Εἴπερ οὐχ ὁμοίως τὰ
45 αὐτὰ βλέπουσιν οὐδ᾽ ἐν ταῖς γραφαῖς οἱ δι᾽ ὀμμάτων
τὰ [1] τῆς τέχνης βλέποντες, ἀλλ᾽ ἐπιγινώσκοντες
μίμημα ἐν τῷ αἰσθητῷ τοῦ ἐν νοήσει κειμένου
οἷον θορυβοῦνται καὶ εἰς ἀνάμνησιν ἔρχονται τοῦ

---

[1] τὰ Kirchhoff H-S: τῶν codd.

will participate in him. But if he is absent from the universe, he will be absent from you, and then you would have nothing to say about him or the beings which come after him. But whether a providence comes to you from the higher world or—whatever you like, the universe anyhow has providential care from that world; it has not been abandoned and it will not be abandoned. For providential care is much more of wholes than of parts, and the participation in God of that universal soul, too, is much greater. Its existence, and its intelligent existence, make this clear. For who of those who are so mindlessly high-minded in looking down on it is as well ordered or has as intelligent a mind as the All? The comparison is ridiculous and very much out of place; anyone who made it except for the sake of argument would not be able to avoid impiety. It is not the part of an intelligent man even to enquire about this but of someone who is blind, utterly without perception or intelligence, and far from seeing the intelligible universe, since he does not even see this one here. For how could there be a musician who sees the melody in the intelligible world and will not be stirred when he hears the melody in sensible sounds? Or how could there be anyone skilled in geometry and numbers who will not be pleased when he sees right relation, proportion and order with his eyes? For, indeed, even in pictures those who look at the works of art with their eyes do not see the same things in the same way, but when they recognise an imitation on the level of sense of someone who has a place in their thought they feel a kind of disturbance and come to a recollection of the truth; this is the

ἀληθοῦς· ἐξ οὗ δὴ πάθους καὶ κινοῦνται οἱ ἔρωτες.
Ἀλλ' ὁ μὲν ἰδὼν κάλλος ἐν προσώπῳ εὖ μεμιμημέ-
50 νον[1] φέρεται ἐκεῖ, ἀργὸς δὲ τίς οὕτως ἔσται τὴν
γνώμην καὶ εἰς οὐδὲν ἄλλο κινήσεται, ὥστε ὁρῶν
σύμπαντα μὲν τὰ ἐν αἰσθητῷ κάλλη, σύμπασαν δὲ
συμμετρίαν καὶ τὴν μεγάλην εὐταξίαν ταύτην καὶ
τὸ ἐμφαινόμενον ἐν τοῖς ἄστροις εἶδος καὶ πόρρωθεν
οὖσιν οὐκ ἐντεῦθεν ἐνθυμεῖται, καὶ σέβας αὐτὸν
55 λαμβάνει, οἷα ἀφ' οἵων; Οὐκ ἄρα οὔτε ταῦτα
κατενόησεν, οὔτε ἐκεῖνα εἶδεν.

17. Καίτοι, εἰ καὶ μισεῖν αὐτοῖς ἐπήει τὴν τοῦ
σώματος φύσιν, διότι ἀκηκόασι Πλάτωνος πολλὰ
μεμψαμένου τῷ σώματι οἷα ἐμπόδια παρέχει τῇ
ψυχῇ—καὶ πᾶσαν τὴν σωματικὴν φύσιν εἶπε
5 χείρονα—ἐχρῆν ταύτην περιελόντας τῇ διανοίᾳ
ἰδεῖν τὸ λοιπόν, σφαῖραν νοητὴν τὸ ἐπὶ τῷ κόσμῳ
εἶδος ἐμπεριέχουσαν, ψυχὰς ἐν τάξει, ἄνευ τῶν
σωμάτων μέγεθος δούσας κατὰ τὸ νοητὸν εἰς
διάστασιν προαγαγούσας, ὡς τῷ μεγέθει τὸ
γενόμενον τῷ ἀμερεῖ τῷ[2] τοῦ παραδείγματος εἰς
10 δύναμιν ἐξισωθῆναι· τὸ γὰρ ἐκεῖ μέγα ἐν δυνάμει
ἐνταῦθα ἐν ὄγκῳ. Καὶ εἴτε κινουμένην ταύτην

---

[1] μεμμημένον Creuzer, H-S: μεμιγμένον codd.
[2] τὸ γενόμενον τῷ ἀμερεῖ τῷ Kirchhoff: τοῦ γενομένου τω
ἀμερεῖ τὸ (τῷΑ) codd: † τοῦ γενομένου τῷ ἀμερεῖ τὸ † H-S².

---

[1] Cp. Plato *Phaedrus* 251A2–3.
[2] E.g. *Phaedo* 66B.

experience from which passionate loves arise. But if someone who sees beauty excellently represented in a face is carried to that higher world,[1] will anyone be so sluggish in mind and so immovable that, when he sees all the beauties in the world of sense, all its good proportion and the mighty excellence of its order, and the splendour of form which is manifested in the stars, for all their remoteness, he will not thereupon think, seized with reverence, " What wonders, and from what a source ? " If he did not, he would neither have understood this world here nor seen that higher world.

17. And yet, even if it occurred to them to hate the nature of body because they have heard Plato often reproaching the body for the kind of hindrances it puts in the way of the soul [2]—and he said that all bodily nature was inferior—they should have stripped off this bodily nature in their thought and seen what remained, an intelligible sphere embracing the form imposed upon the universe, souls in their order which without bodies give magnitude and advance to dimension according to the intelligible pattern, so that what has come into being may become equal, to the extent of its power, by its magnitude to the partlessness of its archetype:[3] for greatness in the intelligible world is in power, here below in bulk. And, whether they wish to think of this sphere as moved,

---

[3] It seems impossible (as Henry and Schwyzer now agree) to extract any tolerable sense from the MSS readings here. I read τὸ γενόμενον (Kirchhoff) for τοῦ γενομένου and τῷ τοῦ παραδείγματος for τὸ τοῦ παραδείγματος (this τῷ has no real MS authority, the τω of A being a manifest error, but is required by the sense).

τὴν σφαῖραν ἐβούλοντο νοεῖν περιαγομένην ὑπὸ
θεοῦ δυνάμεως ἀρχὴν καὶ μέσα καὶ τέλος τῆς
πάσης ἔχοντος, εἴτε ἑστῶσαν ὡς οὔπω καὶ ἄλλο τι
διοικούσης, καλῶς ἂν εἶχεν εἰς ἔννοιαν τῆς τόδε
15 τὸ πᾶν ψυχῆς διοικούσης. Ἐνθέντας δὲ ἤδη καὶ
τὸ σῶμα αὐτῇ, ὡς οὐδὲν ἂν παθούσης, δούσης δὲ
ἑτέρῳ, ὅτι μὴ θέμις φθόνον ἐν τοῖς θεοῖς εἶναι,
ἔχειν, εἴ τι δύναται λαμβάνειν ἕκαστα, οὕτως
αὐτοὺς διανοεῖσθαι κατὰ κόσμον, τοσούτῳ διδόντας
τῇ τοῦ κόσμου ψυχῇ δυνάμεως, ὅσῳ τὴν σώματος
20 φύσιν οὐ καλὴν οὖσαν ἐποίησεν, ὅσον ἦν αὐτῇ
καλλύνεσθαι, μετέχειν κάλλους· ὃ καὶ αὐτὸ τὰς
ψυχὰς θείας οὔσας κινεῖ. Εἰ μὴ ἄρα αὐτοὶ φαῖεν
μὴ κινεῖσθαι, μηδὲ διαφόρως αἰσχρὰ καὶ καλὰ
ὁρᾶν σώματα· ἀλλ᾽ οὕτως οὐδὲ διαφόρως αἰσχρὰ
καὶ καλὰ ἐπιτηδεύματα οὐδὲ καλὰ μαθήματα
25 οὐδὲ θεωρίας τοίνυν· οὐδὲ θεὸν τοίνυν. Καὶ γὰρ
διὰ τὰ πρῶτα ταῦτα. Εἰ οὖν μὴ ταῦτα, οὐδὲ
ἐκεῖνα· μετ᾽ ἐκεῖνα τοίνυν ταῦτα καλά. Ἀλλ᾽
ὅταν λέγωσι καταφρονεῖν τοῦ τῇδε κάλλους,
καλῶς ἂν ποιοῖεν τοῦ ἐν παισὶ καὶ γυναιξὶ καταφρονοῦντες, ὡς μὴ εἰς ἀκολασίαν ἡττᾶσθαι. Ἀλλ᾽
30 εἰδέναι δεῖ, ὅτι οὐκ ἂν σεμνύνοιντο, εἰ αἰσχροῦ
καταφρονοῖεν, ἀλλ᾽ ὅτι καταφρονοῦσι πρότερον
εἰπόντες καλόν· καὶ πῶς διατιθέντες; Ἔπειτα,
ὅτι οὐ ταὐτὸν κάλλος ἐπὶ μέρει καὶ ὅλῳ καὶ πᾶσι

---

[1] Cp. Plato, *Phaedrus* 247A7, and *Timaeus* 29E1–2.
[2] Cp. Plato, *Symposium* 211C4–8.

carried round by the power of God who holds the
beginning and the middle and the end of the whole
of its power, or standing still because it is not yet also
directing something else, it would be well adapted
to give an idea of the soul which directs this universe.
And if they already put a body into it, they should
think about the universe in this way, that soul would
not be affected by body but would give to something
else (since it is not lawful for there to be envy among
the gods) [1] to possess whatever each and every thing
can take; they should grant to the soul of the universe that amount of power with which it made the
nature of body, not beautiful in itself, to share in
beauty as far as it was possible for it to be beautified:
it is this very beauty which moves souls, which are
godlike. But perhaps they may say that they are
not moved, and do not look any differently at ugly
or beautiful bodies; but if this is so, they do not look
any differently at ugly or beautiful ways of life, or
beautiful subjects of study; [2] they have no contemplation, then, and hence no God. For the beauties
here exist because of the first beauties. If, then,
these here do not exist, neither do those; so these are
beautiful in their order after those. But when they
say they despise the beauty here, they would do well
if they despised the beauty in boys and women, to
avoid being overcome by it to the point of abandoned
wickedness. But one should notice that they would
not give themselves airs if they despised something
ugly; they do so because they despise something
which they begin by calling beautiful: and what sort
of a way of managing is that? Then one should be
aware that there is not the same beauty in part and

PLOTINUS: ENNEAD II. 9.

καὶ παντί· εἶθ' ὅτι ἐστὶ τοιαῦτα κάλλη καὶ ἐν
αἰσθητοῖς καὶ τοῖς ἐν μέρει, οἷα δαιμόνων, ὡς
35 θαυμάσαι τὸν πεποιηκότα καὶ πιστεῦσαι, ὡς
ἐκεῖθεν, καὶ ἐντεῦθεν ἀμήχανον τὸ ἐκεῖ κάλλος
εἰπεῖν, οὐκ ἐχόμενον τούτων, ἀλλ' ἀπὸ τούτων ἐπ'
ἐκεῖνα ἰόντα, μὴ λοιδορούμενον δὲ τούτοις· καὶ εἰ
μὲν καὶ τὰ ἔνδον καλά, σύμφωνα ἀλλήλοις εἶναι
λέγειν· εἰ δὲ τἄνδον φαῦλα, τοῖς βελτίοσιν ἠλατ-
40 τῶσθαι. Μήποτε δὲ οὐδὲ ἔστιν ὄντως τι καλὸν
ὂν τὰ ἔξω αἰσχρὸν εἶναι τἄνδον· οὗ γὰρ τὸ ἔξω
πᾶν καλόν, κρατήσαντός ἐστι τοῦ ἔνδον. Οἱ δὲ
λεγόμενοι καλοὶ τἄνδον αἰσχροὶ ψεῦδος καὶ τὸ ἔξω
κάλλος ἔχουσιν. Εἰ δέ τις φήσει ἑωρακέναι
καλοὺς ὄντως ὄντας, αἰσχροὺς δὲ τἄνδον, οἶμαι
45 μὲν αὐτὸν μὴ ἑωρακέναι, ἀλλ' ἄλλους εἶναι νομίζειν
τοὺς καλούς· εἰ δ' ἄρα, τὸ αἰσχρὸν αὐτοῖς ἐπίκτη-
τον εἶναι καλοῖς τὴν φύσιν οὖσι· πολλὰ γὰρ ἐνθάδε
τὰ κωλύματα εἶναι ἐλθεῖν εἰς τέλος. Τῷ δὲ παντὶ
καλῷ ὄντι τί ἐμπόδιον ἦν εἶναι καλῷ καὶ τἄνδον;
50 Καὶ μὴν οἷς μὴ τὸ τέλειον ἀπέδωκεν ἐξ ἀρχῆς ἡ
φύσις, τούτοις τάχ' ἂν οὐκ ἐλθεῖν εἰς τέλος γένοιτο,
ὥστε καὶ φαύλοις ἐνδέχεσθαι γενέσθαι, τῷ δὲ
παντὶ οὐκ ἦν ποτε παιδὶ ὡς ἀτελεῖ εἶναι οὐδὲ

---

[1] Plotinus is probably thinking of Plato, *Republic* VI. 509A6,
where the word is used, though half-jokingly, of τὸ ἀγαθόν,
rather than of *Symposium* 218E2, where it is used in a much
less serious context of the beauty Alcibiades sees in Socrates.

whole and in all individual things and the All: and
then that there are such beauties in things perceived
by the senses and in partial things (the beauties of
spirits, for instance) that one admires their maker,
and believes that they come from the higher world,
and, judging from them, says that the beauty there is
overwhelming; [1] one does not cling to them, but
goes on from them to the beauties of the higher
world, but without insulting these beauties here;
and if their inward parts are beautiful, one acknow-
ledges the harmony of inward and outward; but if
their inward parts are bad, they are deficient in the
better part. But perhaps it is not really possible for
anything to be beautiful outwardly but ugly in-
wardly; for if the outside of anything is wholly
beautiful, it is so by the domination of what is within.
Those who are called beautiful and are ugly within
have an outward beauty, too, which is not genuine.
But if anyone is going to say that he has seen people
who are really beautiful but are ugly within, I think
that he has not really seen them, but thinks that
beautiful people are other than who they are. But
if he has really seen them, then their ugliness was
something superadded, not really belonging to people
who were beautiful by nature: for there are many
hindrances here below to arriving at perfection.
But what was there to hinder the All, which is
beautiful, from being also beautiful within? It
might, perhaps, happen to beings to whom nature
has not given perfection from the beginning not to
arrive at their completion, so that it is possible for
them even to become bad; but it never happened
to the All to be incomplete like a child, nor does any

προσεγίνετο αὐτῷ προσιόν[1] τι καὶ προσετίθετο
εἰς σῶμα. Πόθεν γάρ; Πάντα γὰρ εἶχεν. Ἀλλ᾽
55 οὐδὲ εἰς ψυχὴν πλάσειεν ἄν τις. Εἰ δ᾽ ἄρα τοῦτό
τις αὐτοῖς χαρίσαιτο, ἀλλ᾽ οὐ κακόν τι.

18. Ἀλλ᾽ ἴσως φήσουσιν ἐκείνους μὲν τοὺς
λόγους φεύγειν τὸ σῶμα ποιεῖν πόρρωθεν μισοῦντας,
τοὺς δὲ ἡμετέρους κατέχειν τὴν ψυχὴν πρὸς αὐτῷ.
Τοῦτο δὲ ὅμοιον ἂν εἴη, ὥσπερ ἂν εἰ δύο οἶκον
5 καλὸν τὸν αὐτὸν οἰκούντων, τοῦ μὲν ψέγοντος τὴν
κατασκευὴν καὶ τὸν ποιήσαντα καὶ μένοντος οὐχ
ἧττον ἐν αὐτῷ, τοῦ δὲ μὴ ψέγοντος, ἀλλὰ τὸν
ποιήσαντα τεχνικώτατα πεποιηκέναι λέγοντος,
τὸν δὲ χρόνον ἀναμένοντος ἕως ἂν ἥκῃ, ἐν ᾧ
ἀπαλλάξεται, οὗ μηκέτι οἴκου δεήσοιτο, ὁ δὲ
10 σοφώτερος οἴοιτο εἶναι καὶ ἑτοιμότερος ἐξελθεῖν,
ὅτι οἶδε λέγειν ἐκ λίθων ἀψύχων τοὺς τοίχους καὶ
ξύλων συνεστάναι καὶ πολλοῦ δεῖν τῆς ἀληθινῆς
οἰκήσεως, ἀγνοῶν ὅτι τῷ μὴ φέρειν τὰ ἀναγκαῖα
διαφέρει, εἴπερ καὶ μὴ ποιεῖται δυσχεραίνειν
ἀγαπῶν ἡσυχῇ τὸ κάλλος τῶν λίθων. Δεῖ δὲ
15 μένειν μὲν ἐν οἴκοις σῶμα ἔχοντας κατασκευασ-
θεῖσιν ὑπὸ ψυχῆς ἀδελφῆς ἀγαθῆς πολλὴν δύναμιν
εἰς τὸ δημιουργεῖν ἀπόνως ἐχούσης. Ἢ ἀδελφοὺς
μὲν καὶ τοὺς φαυλοτάτους ἀξιοῦσι προσεννέπειν,

---

[1] προσιόν nunc Henry et Schwyzer: προιόν codd. H-S.

[1] Theiler defends the MSS text (marked as corrupt,
μὴ † ποιεῖται in H-S[1] and [2]) and cites passages (Synesius,

kind of addition come to it and add anything to its body. For where could it come from? The universe includes everything. Nor could one imagine any addition to its soul. But even if one granted to them that there could be an addition, it would not be anything bad.

18. But perhaps they will assert that those arguments of theirs make men fly from the body since they hate it from a distance, but ours hold the soul down to it. This would be like two people living in the same fine house, one of whom reviles the structure and the builder, but stays there none the less, while the other does not revile, but says the builder has built it with the utmost skill, and waits for the time to come in which he will go away, when he will not need a house any longer: the first might think he was wiser and readier to depart because he knows how to say that the walls are built of soulless stones and timber and are far inferior to the true dwelling-place, not knowing that he is only distinguished by not bearing what he must—unless he affirms that he is discontented while having a secret affection for the beauty of the stones.[1] While we have bodies we must stay in our houses, which have been built for us by a good sister soul which has great power to work without any toil or trouble. Or do the Gnostics think it right to call the lowest of men brothers,

---

Dion. 248. 2 and 270. 6 Terzaghi and [Plato] *Theages* 128B5) to show that ποιεῖσθαι can have the same meaning as προσποιεῖσθαι, "pretend." Henry and Schwyzer now agree that the text is sound, but point out that in the passages cited by Theiler ποιεῖσθαι means "affirm" rather than "pretend."

ἥλιον δὲ καὶ τοὺς ἐν τῷ οὐρανῷ ἀπαξιοῦσιν
20 ἀδελφοὺς λέγειν οὐδὲ τὴν κόσμου ψυχὴν στόματι
μαινομένῳ; Φαύλους μὲν οὖν ὄντας οὐ θεμιτὸν
εἰς συγγένειαν συνάπτειν, ἀγαθοὺς δὲ γενομένους
καὶ μὴ σώματα ὄντας, ἀλλὰ ψυχὰς ἐν σώμασι καὶ
οὕτως οἰκεῖν δυναμένους ἐν αὐτοῖς, ὡς ἐγγυτάτω
εἶναι οἰκήσεως ψυχῆς τοῦ παντὸς ἐν σώματι τῷ
25 ὅλῳ. Ἔστι δὲ τοῦτο τὸ μὴ κρούειν, μηδὲ ὑπακούειν τοῖς ἔξωθεν προσπίπτουσιν ἡδέσιν ἢ ὁρωμέ-
νοις, μηδ' εἴ τι σκληρόν, ταράττεσθαι. Ἐκείνη
μὲν οὖν οὐ πλήττεται· οὐ γὰρ ἔχει ὑπὸ τοῦ· ἡμεῖς
δὲ ἐνθάδε ὄντες ἀρετῇ τὰς πληγὰς ἀπωθοίμεθ' ἂν
ἤδη ὑπὸ μεγέθους γνώμης τὰς μὲν ἐλάττους, τὰς
30 δὲ οὐδὲ πληττούσας ὑπὸ ἰσχύος γενομένας.
Ἐγγὺς δὲ γενόμενοι τοῦ ἀπλήκτου μιμοίμεθ' ἂν
τὴν τοῦ σύμπαντος ψυχὴν καὶ τὴν τῶν ἄστρων,
εἰς ἐγγύτητα δὲ ὁμοιότητος ἐλθόντες σπεύδοιμεν
ἂν πρὸς τὸ αὐτὸ καὶ τὰ αὐτὰ ἂν θέᾳ καὶ ἡμῖν εἴη
ἅτε καλῶς καὶ αὐτοῖς παρεσκευασμένοις φύσεσι
35 καὶ ἐπιμελείαις· τοῖς δὲ ἐξ ἀρχῆς ὑπάρχει. Οὐ
δή, εἰ μόνοι λέγοιεν θεωρεῖν δύνασθαι, πλέον ἂν
θεωρεῖν αὐτοῖς γίνοιτο, οὐδ' ὅτι αὐτοῖς φασιν
εἶναι ἐξελθεῖν ἀποθανοῦσι, τοῖς δὲ μή, ἀεὶ τὸν
οὐρανὸν κοσμοῦσιν· ἀπειρίᾳ γὰρ ἂν τοῦ ἔξω ὅ τι
ποτέ ἐστι τοῦτο ἂν λέγοιεν καὶ τοῦ ὃν τρόπον

---

[1] The phrase is taken from Heraclitus's description of the
Sibyl's prophesying (Diels, 22B92), which seems to have

but refuse, in their " raving talk," [1] to call the sun
and the gods in the sky brothers and the soul of the
universe sister? It is not lawful to include the bad in
the bonds of kinship but only those who have become
good and are not bodies but souls in bodies, and able
to live in them in such a way that they are very close
to the dwelling of the soul of the All in the universal
body. This means no clashing with, nor yielding to
the pleasures or sights which hurl themselves upon us
from outside, [2] and not being disturbed by any hard-
ship. The soul of the universe is not troubled; it has
nothing that it can be troubled by. We, while we are
here, can already repel the strokes of fortune by virtue,
and make some of them become less by greatness of
mind and others not even troubles because of our
strength. As we draw near to the completely untroubled state we can imitate the soul of the universe
and of the stars, and, coming to a closeness of re-
semblance to them hasten on to the same goal and
have the same objects of contemplation, being ourselves, too, well prepared for them by nature and
training (but they have their contemplation from the
beginning). Even if the Gnostics say that they alone
can contemplate, that does not make them any more
contemplative, nor are they so because they claim to
be able to go out of the universe when they die while
the stars are not, since they adorn the sky for ever.
They would say this through complete lack of understanding of what " being outside " really means,

been intended to be complimentary. Plotinus, as often,
cares nothing for the context of the phrase he quotes—if,
indeed, he knew it.

[2] Cp. Plato, *Timaeus* 43B7–C1.

40 ψυχὴ παντὸς ἐπιμελεῖται ἡ ὅλη τοῦ ἀψύχου.
Ἔξεστιν οὖν καὶ μὴ φιλοσωματεῖν καὶ καθαροῖς
γίνεσθαι καὶ τοῦ θανάτου καταφρονεῖν καὶ τὰ
ἀμείνω εἰδέναι κἀκεῖνα διώκειν καὶ τοῖς ἄλλοις
τοῖς δυναμένοις διώκειν καὶ διώκουσιν ἀεὶ μὴ
φθονεῖν ὡς οὐ διώκουσι, μηδὲ τὸ αὐτὸ πάσχειν
45 τοῖς οἰομένοις τὰ ἄστρα μὴ θεῖν, ὅτι αὐτοῖς ἡ
αἴσθησις ἑστάναι αὐτὰ λέγει. Διὰ τοῦτο γὰρ καὶ
αὐτοὶ οὐκ οἴονται τὰ ἔξω βλέπειν τὴν τῶν ἄστρων
φύσιν, ὅτι οὐχ ὁρῶσι τὴν ψυχὴν αὐτῶν ἔξωθεν
οὖσαν.

and of how " universal soul cares for all that is soul-less." [1] So we can be without affection for the body and pure, and despise death, and know what is better and pursue it, and not show ill-feeling against others who can and do always pursue it, as if they did not: and not suffer from the same illusion as those who think the stars do not move because their senses tell them they stand still. In the same way the Gnostics, too, do not think that the nature of the stars sees what is outside the material universe, because they do not see that their souls come from outside.

[1] Plato, *Phaedrus* 246B6.

Printed in Great Britain by
Richard Clay (The Chaucer Press), Ltd.
Bungay, Suffolk

THE LOEB CLASSICAL LIBRARY

Latin Authors

AMMIANUS MARECLLINUS. Translated by J. C. Rolfe. 3 Vols.

APULEIUS: THE GOLDEN ASS (METAMORPHOSES). W. Adlington (1566). Revised by S. Gaselee.

ST. AUGUSTINE: CITY OF GOD. 7 Vols. Vol. I. G. E. McCracken. Vol. II. W. M. Green. Vol. IV. P. Levine. Vol. V. E. M. Sanford and W. M. Green. Vol. VI. W. C. Greene.

ST. AUGUSTINE, CONFESSIONS OF. W. Watts (1631). 2 Vols.

ST. AUGUSTINE, SELECT LETTERS. J. H. Baxter.

AUSONIUS. H. G. Evelyn White. 2 Vols.

BEDE. J. E. King. 2 Vols.

BOETHIUS: TRACTS and DE CONSOLATIONE PHILOSOPHIAE. Rev. H. F. Stewart and E. K. Rand.

CAESAR: ALEXANDRIAN, AFRICAN and SPANISH WARS. A. G. Way.

CAESAR: CIVIL WARS. A. G. Peskett.

CAESAR: GALLIC WAR. H. J. Edwards.

CATO: DE RE RUSTICA; VARRO: DE RE RUSTICA. H. B. Ash and W. D. Hooper.

CATULLUS. F. W. Cornish; TIBULLUS. J. B. Postgate; PERVIGILIUM VENERIS. J. W. Mackail.

CELSUS: DE MEDICINA. W. G. Spencer. 3 Vols.

CICERO: BRUTUS, and ORATOR. G. L. Hendrickson and H. M. Hubbell.

[CICERO]: AD HERENNIUM. H. Caplan.

CICERO: DE ORATORE, etc. 2 Vols. Vol. I. DE ORATORE, Books I. and II. E. W. Sutton and H. Rackham. Vol. II. DE ORATORE, Book III. De Fato; Paradoxa Stoicorum; De Partitione Oratoria. H. Rackham.

CICERO: DE FINIBUS. H. Rackham.

CICERO: DE INVENTIONE, etc. H. M. Hubbell.

CICERO: DE NATURA DEORUM and ACADEMICA. H. Rackham.

CICERO: DE OFFICIIS. Walter Miller.

CICERO: DE REPUBLICA and DE LEGIBUS; SOMNIUM SCIPIONIS. Clinton W. Keyes.

CICERO: DE SENECTUTE, DE AMICITIA, DE DIVINATIONE. W. A. Falconer.

CICERO: IN CATILINAM, PRO FLACCO, PRO MURENA, PRO SULLA. Louis E. Lord.

CICERO: LETTERS to ATTICUS. E. O. Winstedt. 3 Vols.

CICERO: LETTERS TO HIS FRIENDS. W. Glynn Williams. 3 Vols.

CICERO: PHILIPPICS. W. C. A. Ker.

CICERO: PRO ARCHIA POST REDITUM, DE DOMO, DE HARUS-PICUM RESPONSIS, PRO PLANCIO. N. H. Watts.

CICERO: PRO CAECINA, PRO LEGE MANILIA, PRO CLUENTIO, PRO RABIRIO. H. Grose Hodge.

CICERO: PRO CAELIO, DE PROVINCIIS CONSULARIBUS, PRO BALBO. R. Gardner.

CICERO: PRO MILONE, IN PISONEM, PRO SCAURO, PRO FONTEIO, PRO RABIRIO POSTUMO, PRO MARCELLO, PRO LIGARIO, PRO REGE DEIOTARO. N. H. Watts.

CICERO: PRO QUINCTIO, PRO ROSCIO AMERINO, PRO ROSCIO COMOEDO, CONTRA RULLUM. J. H. Freese.

CICERO: PRO SESTIO, IN VATINIUM. R. Gardner.

CICERO: TUSCULAN DISPUTATIONS. J. E. King.

CICERO: VERRINE ORATIONS. L. H. G. Greenwood. 2 Vols.

CLAUDIAN. M. Platnauer. 2 Vols.

COLUMELLA: DE RE RUSTICA. DE ARBORIBUS. H. B. Ash, E. S. Forster and E. Heffner. 3 Vols.

CURTIUS, Q.: HISTORY OF ALEXANDER. J. C. Rolfe. 2 Vols.

FLORUS. E. S. Forster; and CORNELIUS NEPOS. J. C. Rolfe.

FRONTINUS: STRATAGEMS and AQUEDUCTS. C. E. Bennett and M. B. McElwain.

FRONTO: CORRESPONDENCE. C. R. Haines. 2 Vols.

GELLIUS, J. C. Rolfe. 3 Vols.

HORACE: ODES AND EPODES. C. E. Bennett.

HORACE: SATIRES, EPISTLES, ARS POETICA. H. R. Fairclough.

JEROME: SELECTED LETTERS. F. A. Wright.

JUVENAL and PERSIUS. G. G. Ramsay.

LIVY. B. O. Foster, F. G. Moore, Evan T. Sage, and A. C. Schlesinger and R. M. Geer (General Index). 14 Vols.

LUCAN. J. D. Duff.

LUCRETIUS. W. H. D. Rouse.

MARTIAL. W. C. A. Ker. 2 Vols.

MINOR LATIN POETS: from PUBLILIUS SYRUS TO RUTILIUS NAMATIANUS, including GRATTIUS, CALPURNIUS SICULUS, NEMESIANUS, AVIANUS, and others with " Aetna " and the " Phoenix." J. Wight Duff and Arnold M. Duff.

OVID: THE ART OF LOVE and OTHER POEMS. J. H. Mozley.

2

OVID: FASTI. Sir James G. Frazer.

OVID: HEROIDES and AMORES. Grant Showerman.

OVID: METAMORPHOSES. F. J. Miller. 2 Vols.

OVID: TRISTIA and EX PONTO. A. L. Wheeler.

PERSIUS. Cf. JUVENAL.

PETRONIUS. M. Heseltine; SENECA; APOCOLOCYNTOSIS. W. H. D. Rouse.

PHAEDRUS AND BABRIUS (Greek). B. E. Perry.

PLAUTUS. Paul Nixon. 5 Vols.

PLINY: LETTERS. Melmoth's Translation revised by W. M. L. Hutchinson. 2 Vols.

PLINY: NATURAL HISTORY.
10 Vols. Vols. I.–V. and IX. H. Rackham. Vols. VI.–VIII. W. H. S. Jones. Vol. X. D. E. Eichholz.

PROPERTIUS. H. E. Butler.

PRUDENTIUS. H. J. Thomson. 2 Vols.

QUINTILIAN. H. E. Butler. 4 Vols.

REMAINS OF OLD LATIN. E. H. Warmington. 4 Vols. Vol. I. (ENNIUS AND CAECILIUS.) Vol. II. (LIVIUS, NAEVIUS, PACUVIUS, ACCIUS.) Vol. III. (LUCILIUS and LAWS OF XII TABLES.) Vol. IV. (ARCHAIC INSCRIPTIONS.)

SALLUST. J. C. Rolfe.

SCRIPTORES HISTORIAE AUGUSTAE. D. Magie. 3 Vols.

SENECA: APOCOLOCYNTOSIS. Cf. PETRONIUS.

SENECA: EPISTULAE MORALES. R. M. Gummere. 3 Vols.

SENECA: MORAL ESSAYS. J. W. Basore. 3 Vols.

SENECA: TRAGEDIES. F. J. Miller. 2 Vols.

SIDONIUS: POEMS and LETTERS. W. B. ANDERSON. 2 Vols.

SILIUS ITALICUS. J. D. Duff. 2 Vols.

STATIUS. J. H. Mozley. 2 Vols.

SUETONIUS. J. C. Rolfe. 2 Vols.

TACITUS: DIALOGUES. Sir Wm. Peterson. AGRICOLA and GERMANIA. Maurice Hutton.

TACITUS: HISTORIES AND ANNALS. C. H. Moore and J. Jackson. 4 Vols.

TERENCE. John Sargeaunt. 2 Vols.

TERTULLIAN: APOLOGIA and DE SPECTACULIS. T. R. Glover. MINUCIUS FELIX. G. H. Rendall.

VALERIUS FLACCUS. J. H. Mozley.

VARRO: DE LINGUA LATINA. R. G. Kent. 2 Vols.

VELLEIUS PATERCULUS and RES GESTAE DIVI AUGUSTI. F. W. Shipley.

VIRGIL. H. R. Fairclough. 2 Vols.

VITRUVIUS: DE ARCHITECTURA. F. Granger. 2 Vols.

Greek Authors

ACHILLES TATIUS. S. Gaselee.

AELIAN: ON THE NATURE OF ANIMALS. A. F. Scholfield. 3 Vols.

AENEAS TACTICUS, ASCLEPIODOTUS and ONASANDER. The Illinois Greek Club.

AESCHINES. C. D. Adams.

AESCHYLUS. H. Weir Smyth. 2 Vols.

ALCIPHRON, AELIAN, PHILOSTRATUS: LETTERS. A. R. Benner and F. H. Fobes.

ANDOCIDES, ANTIPHON, Cf. MINOR ATTIC ORATORS.

APOLLODORUS. Sir James G. Frazer. 2 Vols.

APOLLONIUS RHODIUS. R. C. Seaton.

THE APOSTOLIC FATHERS. Kirsopp Lake. 2 Vols.

APPIAN: ROMAN HISTORY. Horace White. 4 Vols.

ARATUS. Cf. CALLIMACHUS.

ARISTOPHANES. Benjamin Bickley Rogers. 3 Vols. Verse trans.

ARISTOTLE: ART OF RHETORIC. J. H. Freese.

ARISTOTLE: ATHENIAN CONSTITUTION, EUDEMIAN ETHICS, VICES AND VIRTUES. H. Rackham.

ARISTOTLE: GENERATION OF ANIMALS. A. L. Peck.

ARISTOTLE: HISTORIA ANIMALIUM. A. L. Peck. Vol. I.

ARISTOTLE: METAPHYSICS. H. Tredennick. 2 Vols.

ARISTOTLE: METEOROLOGICA. H. D. P. Lee.

ARISTOTLE: MINOR WORKS. W. S. Hett. On Colours, On Things Heard, On Physiognomies, On Plants, On Marvellous Things Heard, Mechanical Problems, On Indivisible Lines, On Situations and Names of Winds, On Melissus, Xenophanes, and Gorgias.

ARISTOTLE: NICOMACHEAN ETHICS. H. Rackham.

ARISTOTLE: OECONOMICA and MAGNA MORALIA. G. C. Armstrong; (with Metaphysics, Vol. II.).

ARISTOTLE: ON THE HEAVENS. W. K. C. Guthrie.

ARISTOTLE: ON THE SOUL. PARVA NATURALIA. ON BREATH. W. S. Hett.

ARISTOTLE: CATEGORIES, ON INTERPRETATION, PRIOR ANALYTICS. H. P. Cooke and H. Tredennick.

ARISTOTLE: POSTERIOR ANALYTICS, TOPICS. H. Tredennick and E. S. Forster.

ARISTOTLE: ON SOPHISTICAL REFUTATIONS.
On Coming to be and Passing Away, On the Cosmos. E. S. Forster and D. J. Furley.

ARISTOTLE: PARTS OF ANIMALS. A. L. Peck; MOTION AND PROGRESSION OF ANIMALS. E. S. Forster.

Aristotle: Physics. Rev. P. Wicksteed and F. M. Cornford. 2 Vols.

Aristotle: Poetics and Longinus. W. Hamilton Fyfe; Demetrius on Style. W. Rhys Roberts.

Aristotle: Politics. H. Rackham.

Aristotle: Problems. W. S. Hett. 2 Vols.

Aristotle: Rhetorica Ad Alexandrum (with Problems. Vol. II.) H. Rackham.

Arrian: History of Alexander and Indica. Rev. E. Iliffe Robson. 2 Vols.

Athenaeus: Deipnosophistae. C. B. Gulick. 7 Vols.

Babrius and Phaedrus (Latin). B. E. Perry.

St. Basil: Letters. R. J. Deferrari. 4 Vols.

Callimachus: Fragments. C. A. Trypanis.

Callimachus, Hymns and Epigrams, and Lycophron. A. W. Mair; Aratus. G. R. Mair.

Clement of Alexandria. Rev. G. W. Butterworth.

Colluthus. Cf. Oppian.

Daphnis and Chloe. Thornley's Translation revised by J. M. Edmonds; and Parthenius. S. Gaselee.

Demosthenes I.: Olynthiacs, Philippics and Minor Orations. I.–XVII. and XX. J. H. Vince.

Demosthenes II.: De Corona and De Falsa Legatione. C. A. Vince and J. H. Vince.

Demosthenes III.: Meidias, Androtion, Aristocrates, Timocrates and Aristogeiton, I. and II. J. H. Vince.

Demosthenes IV.–VI.: Private Orations and In Neaeram. A. T. Murray.

Demosthenes VII.: Funeral Speech, Erotic Essay, Exordia and Letters. N. W. and N. J. DeWitt.

Dio Cassius: Roman History. E. Cary. 9 Vols.

Dio Chrysostom. J. W. Cohoon and H. Lamar Crosby. 5 Vols.

Diodorus Siculus. 12 Vols. Vols. I.–VI. C. H. Oldfather. Vol. VII. C. L. Sherman. Vol. VIII. C. B. Welles. Vols. IX. and X. R. M. Geer. Vol. XI. F. Walton.

Diogenes Laertius. R. D. Hicks. 2 Vols.

Dionysius of Halicarnassus: Roman Antiquities. Spelman's translation revised by E. Cary. 7 Vols.

Epictetus. W. A. Oldfather. 2 Vols.

Euripides. A. S. Way. 4 Vols. Verse trans.

Eusebius: Ecclesiastical History. Kirsopp Lake and J. E. L. Oulton. 2 Vols.

Galen: On the Natural Faculties. A. J. Brock.

The Greek Anthology. W. R. Paton. 5 Vols.

Greek Elegy and Iambus with the Anacreontea. J. M. Edmonds. 2 Vols.

THE GREEK BUCOLIC POETS (THEOCRITUS, BION, MOSCHUS). J. M. Edmonds.

GREEK MATHEMATICAL WORKS. Ivor Thomas. 2 Vols.

HERODES. Cf. THEOPHRASTUS: CHARACTERS.

HERODOTUS. A. D. Godley. 4 Vols.

HESIOD AND THE HOMERIC HYMNS. H. G. Evelyn White.

HIPPOCRATES and the FRAGMENTS OF HERACLEITUS. W. H. S. Jones and E. T. Withington. 4 Vols.

HOMER: ILIAD. A. T. Murray. 2 Vols.

HOMER: ODYSSEY. A. T. Murray. 2 Vols.

ISAEUS. E. W. Forster.

ISOCRATES. George Norlin and LaRue Van Hook. 3 Vols.

ST. JOHN DAMASCENE: BARLAAM AND IOASAPH. Rev. G. R. Woodward and Harold Mattingly.

JOSEPHUS. 9 Vols. Vols. I.–IV.; H. Thackeray. Vol. V.; H. Thackeray and R. Marcus. Vol. VI.–VII.; R. Marcus. Vol. VIII.; R. Marcus and Allen Wikgren. Vol. IX. L. H. Feldman.

JULIAN. Wilmer Cave Wright. 3 Vols.

LUCIAN. 8 Vols. Vols. I.–V. A. M. Harmon. Vol. VI. K. Kilburn. Vol. VII. M. D. Macleod.

LYCOPHRON. Cf. CALLIMACHUS.

LYRA GRAECA. J. M. Edmonds. 3 Vols.

LYSIAS. W. R. M. Lamb.

MANETHO. W. G. Waddell: PTOLEMY: TETRABIBLOS. F. E. Robbins.

MARCUS AURELIUS. C. R. Haines.

MENANDER. F. G. Allinson.

MINOR ATTIC ORATORS (ANTIPHON, ANDOCIDES, LYCURGUS, DEMADES, DINARCHUS, HYPERIDES). K. J. Maidment and J. O. Burtt. 2 Vols.

NONNOS: DIONYSIACA. W. H. D. Rouse. 3 Vols.

OPPIAN, COLLUTHUS, TRYPHIODORUS. A. W. Mair.

PAPYRI. NON-LITERARY SELECTIONS. A. S. Hunt and C. C. Edgar. 2 Vols. LITERARY SELECTIONS (Poetry). D. L. Page.

PARTHENIUS. Cf. DAPHNIS and CHLOE.

PAUSANIAS: DESCRIPTION OF GREECE. W. H. S. Jones. 4 Vols. and Companion Vol. arranged by R. E. Wycherley.

PHILO. 10 Vols. Vols. I.–V.; F. H. Colson and Rev. G. H. Whitaker. Vols. VI.–IX.; F. H. Colson. Vol. X. F. H. Colson and the Rev. J. W. Earp.

PHILO: two supplementary Vols. (*Translation only.*) Ralph Marcus.

PHILOSTRATUS: THE LIFE OF APOLLONIUS OF TYANA. F. C. Conybeare. 2 Vols.

6

Philostratus: Imagines; Callistratus: Descriptions. A. Fairbanks.

Philostratus and Eunapius: Lives of the Sophists. Wilmer Cave Wright.

Pindar. Sir J. E. Sandys.

Plato: Charmides, Alcibiades, Hipparchus, The Lovers, Theages, Minos and Epinomis. W. R. M. Lamb.

Plato: Cratylus, Parmenides, Greater Hippias, Lesser Hippias. H. N. Fowler.

Plato: Euthyphro, Apology, Crito, Phaedo, Phaedrus. H. N. Fowler.

Plato: Laches, Protagoras, Meno, Euthydemus. W. R. M. Lamb.

Plato: Laws. Rev. R. G. Bury. 2 Vols.

Plato: Lysis, Symposium, Gorgias. W. R. M. Lamb.

Plato: Republic. Paul Shorey. 2 Vols.

Plato: Statesman, Philebus. H. N. Fowler; Ion. W. R. M. Lamb.

Plato: Theaetetus and Sophist. H. N. Fowler.

Plato: Timaeus, Critias, Clitopho, Menexenus, Epistulae. Rev. R. G. Bury.

Plotinus: A. H. Armstrong. Vols. I.–III.

Plutarch: Moralia. 15 Vols. Vols. I.–V. F. C. Babbitt. Vol. VI. W. C. Helmbold. Vol. VII. P. H. De Lacy and B. Einarson. Vol. IX. E. L. Minar, Jr., F. H. Sandbach, W. C. Helmbold. Vol. X. H. N. Fowler. Vol. XI. L. Pearson and F. H. Sandbach. Vol. XII. H. Cherniss and W. C. Helmbold.

Plutarch: The Parallel Lives. B. Perrin. 11 Vols.

Polybius. W. R. Paton. 6 Vols.

Procopius: History of the Wars. H. B. Dewing. 7 Vols.

Ptolemy: Tetrabiblos. Cf. Manetho.

Quintus Smyrnaeus. A. S. Way. Verse trans.

Sextus Empiricus. Rev. R. G. Bury. 4 Vols.

Sophocles. F. Storr. 2 Vols. Verse trans.

Strabo: Geography. Horace L. Jones. 8 Vols.

Theophrastus: Characters. J. M. Edmonds. Herodes, etc. A. D. Knox.

Theophrastus: Enquiry into Plants. Sir Arthur Hort, Bart. 2 Vols.

Thucydides. C. F. Smith. 4 Vols.

Tryphiodorus. Cf. Oppian.

Xenophon: Cyropaedia. Walter Miller. 2 Vols.

Xenophon: Hellenica, Anabasis, Apology, and Symposium. C. L. Brownson and O. J. Todd. 3 Vols.

Xenophon: Memorabilia and Oeconomicus. E. C. Marchant.

Xenophon: Scripta Minora. E. C. Marchant.

DESCRIPTIVE PROSPECTUS ON APPLICATION

London   WILLIAM HEINEMANN LTD
Cambridge, Mass.   HARVARD UNIVERSITY PRESS